14.95

D0149885

2010

WEALTH CREATION for SMALL BUSINESS OWNERS

WEALTH
CREATION
for SMALL
BUSINESS
OWNERS

 STRATEGIES FOR FINANCIAL SUCCESS IN ANY ECONOMY

JAMES E. CHEEKS, ESQ.

CCU Library
8787 W. Alameda Ave.
Lakewood, CO 80226

AVON, MASSACHUSETTS

Copyright © 2010 by James E. Cheeks
All rights reserved.
This book, or parts thereof, may not be reproduced in any
form without permission from the publisher; exceptions are
made for brief excerpts used in published reviews.

Published by Adams Business, an imprint of Adams Media,
a division of F+W Media, Inc.
57 Littlefield Street, Avon, MA 02322. U.S.A.
www.adamsmedia.com

ISBN 10: 1-59869-961-X
ISBN 13: 978-1-59869-961-6

Printed in the United States of America.

10 9 8 7 6 5 4 3 2 1

Library of Congress Cataloging-in-Publication Data
is available from the publisher.

This publication is designed to provide accurate and authoritative information with
regard to the subject matter covered. It is sold with the understanding that the publisher is not engaged in rendering legal, accounting, or other professional advice. If
legal advice or other expert assistance is required, the services of a competent professional person should be sought.
        —From a *Declaration of Principles* jointly adopted by a Committee of the
    American Bar Association and a Committee of Publishers and Associations

Many of the designations used by manufacturers and sellers to distinguish their
product are claimed as trademarks. Where those designations appear in this book
and Adams Media was aware of a trademark claim, the designations have been
printed with initial capital letters.

This book is available at quantity discounts for bulk purchases.
For information, please call 1-800-289-0963.

Contents

Introduction

America's business owners have an advantage over the rest of American society when it comes to building personal and family wealth. American business law and its tax systems give entrepreneurs an edge over wage earners and individual investors. You can see this especially:

- In the retirement funds entrepreneurs can build
- In health care
- In ownership of tangible assets
- In life insurance holdings
- In family wealth transfers

But it's also true for ordinary lifestyle items, such as car expenses and personal loans. My aim in *Wealth Creation for Small Business Owners* is to help entrepreneurs exploit the American entrepreneurial edge and build enduring personal and family wealth through the business. I do that through a program of seventy-five wealth creation strategies—strategies built on the transactions and relationships of each entrepreneur's own business. Entrepreneurs who draw on these strategies will:

- Shelter business profits from tax, and invest those profits for future wealth
- Structure daily business transactions and expenses to serve their lifestyle or their estate
- Learn how and by whom business assets should be acquired and held
- Develop techniques for withdrawing business profits, as needed
- Protect personal assets from business creditor claims, in appropriate situations

- Learn how wealth accumulated in the business, and the business itself, can be kept in the family

Consider Stan. He owns a small hi-tech commercial printing business that produces steady income. It's located in office space downtown and he has a couple of full-time employees, and some part-timers when needed. His wife, Helen, helps out and so, from time to time, does his teenage son, Kenny. Stan already has the ingredients he needs to create substantial personal wealth during his lifetime and a sizeable estate for his heirs.

On this modest foundation Stan can build a retirement fund in which he can, over time, accumulate hundreds of thousands of dollars. Taking Helen on as an employee or co-owner can augment the family retirement fund wealth. Added wealth opportunities arise if he hires Kenny as a part-time employee. Stan can build further wealth on his business equipment, business premises, and the type of business entity he operates through.

Will the wealth creation strategies Stan adopts work for every business? No way. No single program fits all. Every entrepreneur's wealth program should work specifically for his own business.

From my practice I've developed a tool to identify those aspects of any entrepreneur's personal and business situation that present wealth opportunities. I call that tool my Wealth Opportunities Audit. As adapted in this book for entrepreneurs' individual use, the audit can identify the wealth opportunities in *your* situation. Keyed to each opportunity is a wealth creation strategy you can adopt and implement.

The Wealth Opportunities Audit is one way to reach the wealth creation strategies and match them to your needs. Some readers will prefer to learn the wealth opportunities inherent in particular business actions or subjects, such as acquiring business real estate, expanding a business, or building a retirement plan. They can use this book as a comprehensive subject-by-subject guide to wealth creation for the small business owner.

What This Book Is *Not*

It's not a book of laws or rules. Sure, if we mean to understand how the American system aids small business wealth creation, we have to know the laws and rules, and talk about them. But they will be laws and rules put to the service of wealth creation—not a treatise or compilation of business or tax law.

There are several wealth-building books and programs. They're motivational, meant to inspire, to improve your personality or attitude, to instill habits of work or self-discipline.

That's not what I do. *Wealth Creation for Small Business Owners* is a practical program for using your business income, expenditures, and relationships effectively to build enduring wealth. Its seventy-five wealth creation strategies are specific, practical, and quantifiable. I hope you will use those that fit your situation in your own wealth program.

A Note to the Reader

Wealth creation is about numbers—dollars, usually. The numbers in case studies and examples in this book are based on conditions and rules in effect when this book went to press in late 2009. Dollar ceilings—for example, ceilings on certain tax-favored business activities or reliefs—are those applicable for 2009. Some ceilings are "indexed for inflation" and vary according to annual changes in the Consumer Price Index. Changes for 2010 are negligible.

For the 2010 ceilings or allowances and for any year-end law changes affecting Wealth Creation Strategies in this book, please see my website: *http://nyretirementplanadvisor.com/WealthCreation.*

—J.E.C.

Building Your Wealth Plan

THE WEALTH OPPORTUNITIES AUDIT

In this chapter you look at specific aspects of your business situation and relationships, using the Wealth Opportunities Audit. Each opportunity is matched by one or more wealth creation strategies fitting that item. With these tools, you can develop your own prioritized plan, using strategies fitting your situation. Wealth creation strategies also include action steps to help implement the strategy. Opportunities are arranged by the following categories:

- Family
- Retirement
- Health
- Business Premises
- Equipment
- Employees (Nonfamily)

- Expansion
- Spending and Enjoying, a Bit
- Retirement Assets and Your Estate
- Succession Planning
- Fourteen Priorities for the Young Business

Select any category and find your situation in the left-hand column. Wealth opportunities arising in that situation appear in the center column. Wealth creation strategies fitting those opportunities are identified in the right-hand column. Go to the numbered strategies in the book to learn what they can do for you and your business.

WEALTH CREATION STRATEGIES

Your Situation	Your Wealth Opportunities	Strategies
Family		
Your spouse is—or could be—employed by the business	The business can invest for your spouse, in the business retirement plan	8
	He or she can invest personal funds in the business retirement plan	7
	You can get personal health care coverage and lifetime care coverage through your spouse	17, 21
	He or she can receive tax-favored fringe benefits	24–27
Your spouse is a co-owner of the business	Generally, your spouse qualifies for all benefits and opportunities available to entrepreneurs	
Your child or children are employees of the business—or could be employees	The business can invest for children employees, in the business retirement plan	8
	Children can invest personal funds in the business retirement plan	7
	Children employees can receive tax-favored fringe benefits	24–27
	Family wealth and business profits can be shared with children employees	51, 65
Children and other family members are or could be business investors or co-owners	Generally, family members as co-owners qualify for all benefits and opportunities available to entrepreneurs	
Retirement		
Children as investors	Business income can pass to them as owners of real property or of equipment leased to the business	38
You're considering building a tax-favored retirement fund	Your plan can be tailored to your situation	1
	The entrepreneur with mid-level to upper-middle level profits may do best adding a 401(k) to the profit-sharing plan	2
	Many mature entrepreneurs do best with a pension plan	3
	Some can build the most plan wealth using two plans	4
	One type of plan, launched now, could be effective for *last* year	5
	For a sideline or just-begun business, there's a starter plan	6
	You can make favored personal investments to increase what business investments have built	7
	To maximize family wealth, put family on the payroll and in the plan	8
	Satellite businesses—another opportunity to increase retirement wealth	39

WEALTH CREATION STRATEGIES

Your Situation	Your Wealth Opportunities	Strategies
Health		
You need to arrange personal and family health care	Provide complete, cost-effective health care through the business	16
	It's sometimes even more cost effective to get coverage through your employee spouse	17
	If your business is incorporated, have your corporation fund your health savings account and your health insurance premium	20
	Cafeteria plans can save health care costs and payroll taxes	19
	Guarantee continued health care after retirement	21, 22
Business Premises		
Your business location is your home	Your home office: a lifestyle showcase	41
	Selling your home office	42
	Moving your home office can be a property swap with tax-free cash	43
	Have your home office (indirectly) bear some of your car expenses	44
You have or are considering business space outside your home	Consider buying more space than your business needs, through the business, and renting out the excess	28
	Maximize depreciation for tax-free cash flow	29, 30
	You or your family can own business space, paying for it with business rents	37, 38
	Deferred exchanges enable a trade up of business real estate	31
	Employee stock ownership plan can help the purchase	32
Equipment		
You're considering a big-ticket equipment purchase	"Expensing" generates tax-free cash flow	33
	The corporate tax system provides modest help for small business corporations' equipment acquisitions	34
	Consider lifestyle equipment and office furnishings	41
	Do exchanges to replace worn or obsolete equipment	35
	Employee stock plan: an equipment acquisition tool for corporations	36

3

WEALTH CREATION STRATEGIES

Your Situation	Your Wealth Opportunities	Strategies
Employees (Nonfamily)		
You must decide about including employees in the business retirement plan	Maximize the entrepreneurs' share of the retirement fund (or minimize business costs) when the business must invest for nonfamily employees	**9, 10, 11, 12, 13, 14, 15**
You must decide about employees in the business health plan	Some employees can be legitimately left out	**18**
	Cafeteria plans can save health care costs and payroll taxes	**19**
	Changing from your current plan to a health savings account can shift costs to employees or have them share costs	**20**
	Employee health care after retirement can be arranged at little or no additional cost	**22**
Expansion		
You're looking to expand your business	Consider a spinoff or satellite business	**39**
	Buy more space than your business needs	**28**
	Lease assets to your business	**37, 38**
Spending and Enjoying, a Bit		
You seek ways your business can enhance personal and family lifestyle	Perks and lifestyle expenses work better when others help pay	**23**
	Some selected benefits are available tax-free and with payroll tax savings	**24**
	Several modest tax-favored perks are available	**25–27**
	Consider lifestyle equipment and office furnishings	**41**
You want to take out some business wealth now	Withdraw capital to diversify your holdings, protect your wealth, or enjoy it	**45**
	Borrowing from the business: a way to cash in business wealth	**46**
	"Frozen" business assets can be converted to usable wealth	**47–49**
	For long-term wealth accumulation, diversify	**50**
	Share assets and future profits with family members	**51**

WEALTH CREATION STRATEGIES

Your Situation	Your Wealth Opportunities	Strategies
Retirement Assets and Your Estate		
You need to plan specifically for retirement assets	Postpone withdrawals for added tax-free plan growth	52
	Minimize required withdrawals	52
	You can work beyond "retirement age"	53, 54
	Invest plan withdrawals in annuities and insurance	57
	In an employee stock ownership plan, corporate entrepreneurs can make tax-deferred stock sales to the plan	59
	Postponing withdrawals won't help in defined benefit plans; do IRA rollover instead	52
	Build a larger fund with a larger surviving spouse annuity	56
	Who you choose as beneficiary determines how long your retirement plan shelter can last	55
	A Roth IRA may be a wealth opportunity for the next generation	58
Succession Planning		
You're planning to pass your business to the next generation	Pass interests and eventual control through periodic gifts of your current business entity	60
	When transferring interests in today's entity is impractical, convert to a new family business entity	61
	Giving business interests to a trust can pass the interests in the future, with continuing income in the interim	62
	Pay stock as compensation to transfer ownership to the next generation	64
	Sell the business to the next generation while retaining control	63
	Sell at today's price to transfer growth free of estate tax	65
	Another sale option helps cash-strapped family buyers while transferring future growth	66
	Installment sale to a trust for a new generation	67
	Use life insurance to hold on to the business until death and still have it pass essentially intact	68
You want to pass the business but provide for family who won't join the business	Allocate non-business wealth to the nonworking heirs	69
	Bequeath or give "inessential" business assets to nonworking heirs	70
	Give nonworking heirs limited control interests	71
	Put limits on what nonworking family members own today	72
	Arrange a buyout of your interest that puts the business in the hands of working family members	73–75

WEALTH CREATION STRATEGIES

Your Situation	Your Wealth Opportunities	Strategies
Fourteen Priorities for the Young Business		
You're considering building a tax-favored retirement fund	Build retirement wealth with a profit-sharing plan	1
	One type of plan, launched now, could be effective for *last* year	5
	Use a starter plan for a sideline or just-begun business	6
	Make favored personal investments to increase what business investments have built	7
	Put family on the payroll and in the plan	8
You need to arrange personal and family health care	Provide complete, cost-effective health care through the business	16
	Get coverage through your employee spouse	17
	Use cafeteria plans to save health care costs and payroll taxes	19
	If your business is incorporated, have your corporation fund your health savings account and your health insurance premium	20
Your business location is your home	Your home office: a lifestyle showcase	41
	Have your home office indirectly bear some of your car expenses	44
You're considering a big equipment purchase	"Expensing" generates tax-free case flow	33
	The corporate tax system provides modest help for small business corporations' equipment acquisitions	34
You need to protect your personal assets	Protect your assets from creditors	Chapter 8

Chapter 2

Your Business Retirement Plan: Taking the Giant Step Toward Enduring Wealth

WEALTH CREATION STRATEGIES 1–8

Dave is an architect well into middle age. Some years he did okay; in some, he just squeaked by. But now the big fees are coming in, and he hopes they offer the chance for real wealth at last.

Dave should set up a defined benefit pension plan and invest in it the maximum he can at his age. The fees he invests, which thereby escape current income tax, could total tens of thousands of dollars a year and grow tax-free until withdrawn at retirement. This chapter shows the wealth creation opportunities of tax-sheltered retirement plans and guides your choices to fit your business income and personal needs.

How Retirement Plans Work

You take a portion of your business profits and set them aside in a special account—usually a trust—for your benefit. You can control the trust if you wish.

- If you've done things properly, the business will never pay tax on those profits.
- The trust invests these amounts, together with future profit set-asides. All investment income and profits are tax-deferred (tax exempt until distributed).
- Amounts in the trust are generally exempt from claims of business creditors, and your share is generally exempt from your personal creditors.

- Eventually, at a time you can control, the original untaxed business profits, augmented by years of investment growth, are distributed to you.

- You will owe tax on these distributions, but you will have more left—usually much more, sometimes vastly more—than if you hadn't used this plan.

These arrangements are confirmed and fortified by U.S. federal and state law. I consider them essential to entrepreneurial wealth creation.

RETIREMENT PLAN AS TAX SHELTER

The retirement plans considered here are the ultimate tax shelter. Any of them gives you these distinct tax benefits.

1. Your business takes a tax deduction for the amount put into the plan (the investment contribution). The business deducts it on the tax return for the year the contribution is made (or in some cases, the year *before* it's made; see Wealth Creation Strategy 5). Deduction today is worth more than deduction tomorrow.

2. You as an individual pay no tax on the investment contribution made for your own benefit, even though you have an absolute right to collect it eventually. You will be taxed only when you collect on your fund at some future date. Tax tomorrow is preferable to tax today.

3. No one has to pay taxes on investment earnings on amounts in the plan trust until you or your heirs take them out. Remember that the business investment contributions go into a trust or insurance company. If it's a trust, you can be trustee and have direct personal control of your investments. The postponement of tax described here, which assumes you use a trust, also applies if you use an insurance company instead.

Build Retirement Wealth with a Profit-sharing Plan

A profit-sharing plan is a good place to start, for many entrepreneurs. Don't attach heavy significance to the term "profit-sharing." There's no need to share your business profits with anyone but yourself, unless you have employees. Even then, you often don't have to share it with them.

With a profit-sharing plan, each year you can put a percentage of your business earnings or salary into a trust account. What you put in is your investment, the amount that, with future investments and future earnings, will become your retirement wealth. The allowable investment escapes current federal and—in almost all cases—state and local tax, so you owe tax only on remaining business earnings. Any investment earnings on what you put in escape current federal, state, and local taxes as well.

Many call profit-sharing plans "retirement plans," though technically they don't have to be, and most aren't. A "retirement" plan is one that pays out only at retirement (or death or disability, or termination of the plan). Most profit-sharing plans let you take out contributions and the earnings thereon *before* you retire. At least two years must elapse between the time a contribution goes in and the time you take it out. The two-year period can be shortened in case of hardship. But hardship means hardship: "present or impending financial ruin, want or privation."

When you start a profit-sharing plan, you can't be sure how much your fund will grow to. Some might find this a problem, though I don't. Profit-sharing plan amounts can't be known in advance for two reasons:

1. With a profit-sharing plan you normally invest a different amount each year. The amounts will vary, even when you contribute the same percentage of earnings, because the amount of earnings varies.
2. Your earnings on your investment also vary each year. This will happen with virtually any investment you make. You might sell or switch any investment once made (often the best move). In any case, each year you have a new amount to invest, and each year's investment climate is different from the year before.

When you retire, you'll be entitled to collect everything that was put in for you, plus everything earned by investing those amounts.

Profit-sharing plans perform best for those a long way from retirement.

Tax Later Is Better Than Tax Now

Postponing the tax on business profits yields greater wealth than by paying tax currently, even after the postponement ends and the tax must then be paid.

CASE STUDY

Peter is forty-one, an associate professor at a state university, with a good salary. Peter is also an entrepreneur, often engaged as consultant and expert witness. His fees in recent years have averaged $75,000 a year. Peter is enrolled in his university's annuity (pension) plan. He's also an active investor, investing much of what's left of his outside earnings after taxes.

A profit-sharing plan works well for Peter's consulting business. He can reasonably expect to build a retirement fund of nearly a million dollars. He can set up a profit-sharing plan into which he puts $15,000 a year of his consulting income. Say he does this each year until he reaches sixty-five (in other words, every year for twenty-four years). Assume he earns 6.75 percent each year on his plan investments.

At age sixty-five, Peter would have a fund totaling $843,420. He could keep it invested thereafter, where it could continue to grow at a tax-free 6.75 percent a year.

Compare Investing Outside a Plan

The earlier in the year you invest, the greater investments grow. However, for the convenience of this example, assume investment contributions go in at year's end, and start earning thereafter.

Peter's $15,000 a year totaled $360,000. The rest, $483,420, is investment earnings.

Now let's see what would happen if Peter had invested without such a retirement plan.

Assume the $15,000 a year is invested outside his retirement plan. First of all, it would not really be $15,000. Outside a plan the $15,000 is taxable. In the 33 percent tax bracket, $15,000 becomes $10,050. So he has $10,050 to invest each year, not $15,000.

So Peter invests $10,050 each year, on which he gets a 6.75 percent return? No. Outside the plan, he must pay tax on his investment income. So his after-tax rate of return, in the 33 percent bracket, is 4.5 percent, not 6.75 percent.

After twenty-four years, Peter's nest egg outside a plan would total $418,976 (at 4.5 percent). So are we comparing a $843,420 nest egg inside the plan with $418,976 outside it? Not exactly. It won't have escaped your notice that the fund outside the plan is fully tax-paid, while tax will still be owed when money is withdrawn from the plan.

So let's go another step and assume Peter wants to withdraw 10 percent of his nest egg in the twenty-fifth year. Outside the plan, he gets $41,898 tax-free. Withdrawing from the plan, it's $84,342 less tax. We can't know tax rates twenty-five years hence, but using the 33 percent rate assumed for the preceding twenty-four years, he has $56,509 left after taxes, or 35 percent more than outside the plan. If a lower tax rate applies in year twenty-five—as could happen in retirement years, because of lower brackets for lower total income, or state retirement income tax relief—Peter would have still more after-tax income. And Peter has much more wealth invested for future years in the plan than outside it.

THE KEOGH PLAN LAW

A retirement plan always involves two people: an employer and an employee. A retirement plan is a plan for employees. However, under a special law for retirement plans (the "Keogh plan" law), self-employed persons are considered employees, just as traditional employees and corporate stockholder-employees are. The self-employed person is also the employer. (If the self-employed person is a partner, the partnership is the employer.)

There is also always a third party to a retirement plan. That party is either a trustee or an insurance company. You can make yourself your own trustee.

Entrepreneurs with a long earnings and investment horizon can build major retirement wealth through a profit-sharing plan. But it's not necessarily the path to the largest possible accumulation. For that, you can choose from several additional options: 401(k) plans; defined benefit plans; and a combination of plans. Some of these options can be augmented by further investments from your personal funds from outside the business.

You can choose the option that suits your circumstances. But each option costs you something by way of deferred profits. For example, your business over the years can put $400,000 in a plan to build a retirement fund for you of $950,000. If you later decide, say, to have it build to $1,500,000, you should expect it to cost the business a good bit more than $400,000.

For some investors, this comparison understates their investment return outside the plan. Some of their investments could be in assets that generate long-term capital gains, taxed at favored rates. Lower total tax means a greater investment return.

So now let's assume that half of each year's investment income outside the plan is long-term capital gains from mutual fund capital gains distributions and from sales of assets. That (depending on the assumed capital gains rate) produces an after-tax return of about 5 percent (rather than 4.5 percent), and a total fund after twenty-four years of $447,245 (rather than $418,976). But that's still much less than with the plan.

These comparisons show the entrepreneur both *investing more* and *earning more* on those investments inside than on those outside the plan. Investing more because he's using untaxed current business earnings, and earning more because of the tax postponement for plan investment earnings. These factors produce greater wealth even after taxes are paid on money withdrawn from the plan.

More wealth from more tax postponement

Peter had $843,420 before paying any tax on it. If he buys an annuity with this money, he won't have to pay any tax until he starts collecting the annuity. So he can spend the full amount on the annuity. If the annuity is based on a 6 percent interest rate, $843,420 will buy Peter an annuity of $71,691 a year for life from age sixty-five.

Use a 401(k)
"Elective Deferral"

A 401(k) plan is a profit-sharing plan with an added feature called an "elective deferral." That feature lets most entrepreneurs build a larger fund than with any other plan. 401(k)s, which today work splendidly for entrepreneurs, are best known as retirement savings plans for *employees*: 401(k)s give employees the option to take all of their salary in cash or have the employer put part of it (the "elective deferral") into a retirement plan. The deferred amount, and investment earnings thereon, are tax-free until the employee takes it out.

To encourage employees to save for retirement, employers sometimes put in additional amounts to match those an employee chooses to defer. Matching might be in a ratio such as fifty cents for every dollar the employee defers.

For example, an employee earning $60,000 might have the option to defer, say, 10 percent of her salary. If she chose to defer that much, her company would pay her $54,000 and put $6,000 as an elective deferral into the retirement plan for her. If the company also matched deferred amounts at fifty cents on the dollar, it would put an additional $3,000 into the plan for the employee, who would then have $9,000 in the plan and would pay income tax on $54,000. The company could also make other, non-matching, investment contributions on the employee's behalf, called "discretionary contributions." These, in fact, are regular profit-sharing contributions.

As business owner, you can set up a 401(k) in which you are both "employer" and "employee," as you are in other retirement plans.

The elective deferral amount, plus any "employer" matching and discretionary contributions you make, count as profit-sharing investment contributions on your behalf.

There's a dollar limit on the elective deferral, and there are the contribution and deduction ceilings that apply to regular profit-sharing plans (see "Deduction, Contribution, and Benefit Ceilings" later in this chapter).

CASE STUDY

Sandra, who is self-employed, wants to maximize deductible contributions to her 401(k). She has earnings of $81,000. She can put in at least $32,700, that is, $16,500 of elective deferral and $16,200 as employer contribution.

Entrepreneurs and others age fifty or over can make a further deductible contribution as employee. This is the catch-up contribution described in Wealth Creation Strategy 7.

When you are the only person in your plan, there's no reason to provide for separate matching contributions. Your plan will have more flexibility, at no cost to your deduction, if all your employer contributions are discretionary.

Elective deferrals are technically *employer* contributions, as discretionary and matching contributions are. This is what lets employers—including self-employed persons as employers—deduct elective deferrals. Understandably, most employees think that deferrals out of *their* pay are *employee* contributions. The law says otherwise.

What makes 401(k) plans richer?

The dollar ceiling on business contributions for any individual is the same for regular profit-sharing plans as for 401(k) profit-sharing plans. Yet we say 401(k)s usually allow richer plans. This is because the elective deferral features allow a larger proportion of pay or earnings to go into the plan than with profit sharing alone (except at the top pay or earnings levels, above $245,000). Here's what I mean:

- When self-employment income is $140,000, $28,000 can go in the regular profit-sharing plan, but $44,500 ($28,000 plus $16,500) can go in a 401(k) profit-sharing plan.

- When self-employment earnings are more than $245,000, no more than $49,000 can go in either plan.

At age fifty or over, catch-up contributions can go in a 401(k) plan but not a regular profit-sharing plan. Catch-up contributions aren't subject to business contribution ceilings.

401(k) withdrawals

As you'll recall, money can be withdrawn from a profit-sharing plan after it has been in the plan at least two years—assuming the plan is written to allow this. This is also the rule for withdrawal of matching and discretionary employer contributions to a 401(k). But elective deferral amounts can be withdrawn only in narrower circumstances: death, disability, severance from service, retirement, reaching age fifty-nine and a half, termination of the plan, or (where the plan is written to permit this) participant "hardship."

Elective deferral complications

You can be in more than one elective deferral plan—in two businesses, say, or a business and a 403(b) annuity plan (offered by a tax-exempt organization or university). But the dollar ceiling amount is the ceiling for *all* your elective deferral funds combined. This is why Peter wouldn't benefit from adding a 401(k) elective deferral feature: he's already maxed out in his university 403(b) annuity.

The elective deferral feature and its consequences make 401(k)s technically harder to start up, which means they can cost more to start. For firms with employees, it's well worth the cost; see Wealth Creation Strategy 11.

The Richest Plan When You're Approaching Retirement

A defined-benefit pension plan is more complicated than other Keogh plans—more complicated because it is potentially the richest plan for older entrepreneurs. You'll see why I say "older" shortly.

Remember, in a profit-sharing plan you choose the amount (percentage) of compensation or business earnings you want put in the plan. A defined benefit plan is different.

With a defined-benefit plan, you select the amount of pension you want at retirement. Then you work back to figure the amount you'd need to put in to buy such an annuity on the basis of your life expectancy.

The richest plan you're allowed to have will pay you each year about as much as you made in any good year from your business. Specifically, you can collect each year what your pay averaged in the three consecutive years in which pay was the highest. If your business is a corporation, pay is your salary, bonuses, etc.; in other business types, it's self-employment net earnings.

In private industry a pension that's equal to your salary is unbelievably generous. With entrepreneurs, charity can begin at home. A pension equal to your pay (the average pay in your best three consecutive years, that is) is entirely up to you.

You could set some lower pension if you want to—say, 60 percent of your average high three years. But for the largest possible retirement fund, you should go after the highest pension you're allowed.

To reach the fund you've set for yourself, your business will make an investment contribution each year, or most years, and take a tax deduction for it, reducing business taxable income to that extent. You'll get only the fund the business pays for. You may have a fund of $800,000 in mind. But if what you put in, plus what you make investing it, adds up to only $560,000, then $560,000 is what you get.

CASE STUDY

Alan's sole proprietorship generates an average $150,000 in profit a year. Alan is fifty and plans to retire at sixty-two with a retirement fund large enough to pay him $120,000 a year—that is, 80 percent of his average annual business earnings. On our assumptions (an annuity at 6 percent and a 23.5-year life expectancy), the fund he needs is $1,491,240. Assuming that his plan investment contributions earn a 6.5 percent rate of return, Alan, starting today, couldn't reach his goal with a profit-sharing 401(k) plan. He can put in $52,000 a year: $30,000 of profit-sharing contributions, $16,500 of elective deferral, and $5,500 of catch-up contributions (more on these in Wealth Creation Strategy 7). At 6.5 percent, this gets him to $903,240—a handsome figure, but not his dream.

He *can* reach his dream with a defined benefit plan, which would allow annual investment contributions of $88,396.

Retirement Age Leverage to Build Your Fund

First, decide on the amount of pension you want when you retire, remembering *you have to pay for it*—with tax-deductible investment contributions and tax-deferred investment earnings. Second, decide when you want to retire. You must decide both before you can know how big an investment fund you'll need.

Let's say you want a pension of $120,000 a year for life. If you retire "early," you'll collect your pension for a longer period. That means you'll collect more and will need a larger fund. That's only part of the story. When you select your plan's retirement age, you're setting the period of time over which you will put money into your plan. The closer you are now to that retirement age, the more you'll have to put in each year.

Assuming the same amount of pension, the earlier you retire, the more you collect. And the earlier you plan to retire, the less time you have now to fund that larger amount. So with an early retirement age, you build a larger fund faster.

For example, suppose your pension is to be $72,000 a year. If you have a twenty-one-year life expectancy when you retire at age sixty-five, you'll collect $1,512,000 if you live to be eighty-six. If you retire at sixty with a 25.2-year expectancy, you'll collect $1,800,000 by age eighty-five.

Of course, an annuity to pay $72,000 a year over 25.2 years costs more than one paying $72,000 a year over a twenty-one-year expectancy—say, $913,176 for 25.2 years compared to $847,008 for 21 years (assuming a 6 percent interest rate). And you have a shorter time to build to that larger fund. At age forty-eight you'd have twelve years to accumulate $913,176, compared to seventeen years to accumulate $847,008. It costs $28,719 a year to build $847,008 in seventeen years at 6 percent. It costs $52,570 a year to build $913,176 in twelve years, again at 6 percent. In each case, costs are tax-deductible.

The earlier your retirement age, the more your business puts in each year and the more you'll have in your retirement fund when you reach that age. So you maximize your defined benefit fund if you adopt a relatively young retirement age.

 ACTION POINT ✓ Pick the earliest age at which someone in your line of work might reasonably decide to retire. You should aim to make your contributions fully tax-deductible. That means you shouldn't shoot for a fund so large that your annual investment contributions average more than your business income.

Using Interest Rate Forecasts to Build Your Fund

You will have noticed my repeated reference to interest rates or rates of return: that an investment of so much will buy a pension of so many dollars. I really mean any kind of profit on investment, be it interest, dividends, rents, or realized or unrealized capital gains.

Interest (rate of return) is crucial to two elements of building the defined benefit plan:

1. Your professional advisor (an actuary) will have projected what it will cost to buy the annuity you want at retirement age.

2. The projected interest rate is used to figure how much you must put in (invest) each year, between now and retirement age, to get to that annuity amount.

You may not want an annuity. That's okay. You don't have to buy one. But the annuity is part of the planning, and you'll need the concept until you discard it (at retirement age).

Say you've decided on an annuity of $72,000 a year for life, from your retirement sixteen years from now. You—or, more likely, your actuary—will project what such an annuity would cost for your life expectancy then (assume it's twenty years). Say that's $860,428.

When you buy it, sixteen years hence, you're in effect investing that $860,428. You'll receive $72,000 each year, but everything you don't receive is invested to build toward future $72,000 installments. Look at it this way:

Under a standard annuity you'll receive a total $1,440,000 if you live your twenty-year life expectancy (more if you live longer, less if shorter). But you paid only $860,428. The $579,572 difference is the interest return on your $860,428 investment—here at an assumed rate of 5.5 percent.

The other element is what you must put in (invest) each of the sixteen years before retirement age to accumulate to the annuity purchase cost (here $860,428). The actuary calculates that too, using official rates based generally on bond yields (with some option to use different rates).

For example, you would put in $33,515 in each of sixteen years to get to $860,428, using a projected rate of 6 percent. (Rates will vary over the period of time to retirement.)

You're Not Locked In

In a defined benefit plan, you—or your advisor—will be expected to:

- Pick the pension amount you'll pay for out of future earnings
- Choose the age you expect to retire
- Project how much you'll make investing the money you put in
- Project what the pension will cost when you retire

How can you be sure of any of this when you set up your plan? You can't be sure. No one expects certainty, and no one punishes mistakes.

You and your advisor can change whatever doesn't work out as you planned.

You aim for a pension based on the income you make and, to a degree, the income you *expect* to make. You can change the pension amount if things work out differently. You forecast a certain rate of return on investments. But in fact, what you earn varies from year to year. So you change your forecasts and what you do about them to fit your actual experience. You choose a retirement age. It's no big deal if you later decide to retire at an older or younger age.

What matters to most people is how changes in assumptions change the amount they pay into the plan each year. You can put in more if your income rises, or you retire sooner, or your investment earnings are less than you figured. You usually will reduce your contributions if the reverse happens. But in any case, you have some latitude in what you must put in from year to year for any given pension.

If you choose a pension plan, you have a commitment to make regular contributions to it. But it's not quite like a duty to pay rent or taxes: your contributions can fluctuate. Your duty to contribute will end once your pension is "fully funded"—meaning the fund already has as much as will be needed at retirement, or with expected future investment earnings will reach that amount. You'll still be allowed to contribute (and deduct) a limited amount more, as a "cushion."

If your pension is fully funded, you can start a second, different plan, such as a profit-sharing plan, and make further wealth-building investment contributions to this new plan.

How Joint-and-Survivor Annuities Increase the Fund

Joint-and-survivor annuities provide a pension for the entrepreneur and then another pension after his death, to his spouse. These two pensions cost more than one paying the same amount, and they are worth more. If you include a joint and survivor annuity with your spouse in your planning, you can build a still larger fund. See Chapter 11.

Can You Inflation-Proof Your Retirement Fund?

A defined-benefit plan can deliver more protection than other plans can, thanks to the feature that lets you increase your retirement pension as your income rises. If your average earned income in your three best self-employment years is $100,000, you can have a $100,000 pension. If the

"DEFINED BENEFIT" VERSUS "DEFINED CONTRIBUTION"

With a defined benefit plan, you're building toward a specific ("defined") retirement benefit. With a defined contribution plan, the amount put in is normally a specified ("defined") percentage of compensation or business earnings, and what you get at retirement or other withdrawal is what this fund has grown to. All plans considered in this chapter, except the defined benefit plan discussed here and under "Insured 412(i) Defined Benefit Plans," later in this chapter, are defined contribution plans. Businesses with nonfamily employees are much more likely these days to offer defined contribution plans.

average rises to $150,000, you can have a $150,000 pension. Pension experts and U.S. government officials consider that this power to increase the pension amount fosters retirement security and provides a measure of protection against inflation. But it doesn't matter *why* your income has risen. You can have the larger pension whether your income went up because of inflation or because your business is more prosperous.

And nowhere is it written that your business income has to rise just because inflation is at hand. You might have reduced your activity as you neared retirement. You wouldn't have to reduce your pension amount because your income dropped. But the pension you collect, calculated in pre-inflation dollars, will be worth less when collected in inflationary times.

But assume the usual case: your income rises and you want a correspondingly larger pension. The larger pension will cost more. To pay for it, your business will have to pay in more of its earnings (though not necessarily a greater proportion of earnings) than before.

ACTION POINT

Inflation protection after you retire will come more from your investment policy than from the type of plan you choose. Many advisors think the following investments do well in inflationary times: common stocks generally (and of course particular stocks), variable annuities based on stock investments, and inflation-adjusted U.S. Treasury bonds. Arrangements with those who will run the business after you leave can help, too; see Chapter 12.

Other Qualified Plans

Money purchase pension plans

These days you should consider such plans only when you have non-family employees; see Chapter 3.

Stock bonus plans

These are, effectively, corporate profit-sharing plans that invest heavily in employer stock and can pay out their benefits in employer stock. Start-up corporations often use such plans to recruit employees, offering stock when they are unable to offer high cash pay. That can help the business. It's not practical to build small business entrepreneurs' plan wealth through such plans.

Employee Stock Ownership Plans (ESOPs)

These are stock bonus plans that are allowed to borrow to buy stock of the sponsoring corporation. They may invest heavily in employer stock and pay out their benefits in employer stock.

Such plans are often used to benefit the corporate entrepreneur. But the benefit is primarily through using the plan funds to finance the purchase of business assets or purchase of a retiring entrepreneur's stock and not primarily through the entrepreneur's participation in the retirement fund.

WHAT'S A "QUALIFIED PLAN"?

It's any plan that *qualifies* for the full tax, labor, and debtor-creditor benefits I describe in this chapter. Specifically, profit-sharing plans, including 401(k)s, defined benefit pension plans, money purchase plans, stock bonus plans, and ESOPs, are qualified plans. This is contrasted with IRA-based plans: SEPs and SIMPLEs, explored later. Qualified plans have existed for generations; IRA-based plans, created more recently, are simpler, with many but not all the characteristics of qualified plans.

When the Richest Plan
Is Two Plans

You can't use two or more of the same types of plan—two defined contribution plans, for example—to up the ceiling on the amount you're allowed to invest (much less the amount you're allowed to deduct). Two or more of the same type of plan are combined when figuring allowable investment contributions and deductions.

Defined benefit and defined contribution are different types of plans, but there are still limits. In general, the most the business can invest and deduct when there's both a defined benefit plan and a defined contribution plan is the amount needed (as determined by the actuary you use) to fund the defined benefit plan, or 25 percent of payroll (salary or self-employment earnings), if that's greater.

But there's a way to deduct much more: If your defined contribution plan is a profit-sharing 401(k), the business can deduct 6 percent of your compensation or earnings, plus the 401(k) elective deferral amount up to the annual ceiling, plus the amount needed for the defined benefit.

CASE STUDY

Steven, who will earn $140,000 this year in self-employment, has a defined benefit plan that will pay him $100,000 a year at retirement. Assume the annual cost of funding this amount is $50,000.

By adding a profit-sharing 401(k), he can make a 401(k) elective deferral of an additional $16,500, plus six percent of $140,000 ($8,400), thus contributing and deducting a total of $74,900.

The business is legally allowed to put in more than the deductible amount, but the nondeductible portion is subject to a 10 percent excise tax. Excess contributions to defined benefit plans generally avoid this tax.

So much for running two or more plans simultaneously. The limits I mentioned are *annual* limits and so don't prevent you from funding one plan to the max for a number of years, then freezing that plan to start and fully fund a second, different plan, with different contribution or benefit ceilings.

I gave one example earlier, in Wealth Creation Strategy 2: a fully funded defined benefit plan that you could freeze and then start up another plan, say, a profit-sharing plan.

Or you could run a profit-sharing 401(k) into your early fifties, accumulating a big sum, then freezing that plan and starting a defined benefit plan.

A plan that's "frozen" takes in no new investment contributions but otherwise continues to perform according to its terms. It continues to invest and reinvest, and makes distributions to participants, on their retirement or otherwise, as plan terms require.

Simplified Employee Pension (SEP)

A simplified employee pension (sometimes called a SEP-IRA) is not technically a qualified plan but is much like a qualified profit-sharing plan. With a SEP, the idea is that the employee sets up her own retirement plan—an IRA—to which the employer contributes.

This concept can extend to entrepreneurs who, as with qualified plans, are both employer and employee. As an employee, you would set up an IRA for yourself. Then, in your capacity as employer, you have the business make a tax-deductible investment contribution to the IRA of up to the ceiling for profit-sharing plans. (The usual IRA contribution ceiling—$5,000—doesn't apply to contributions as employer to a SEP-IRA. Should you want to make an IRA contribution as well, do so through a separate IRA.)

As the name proclaims, a SEP is a simplified plan. Little is required in the way of formal reporting to government agencies, and plan investments are handled as with any other IRA. It's not, in the usual sense, a pension, where withdrawal is generally postponed to retirement age. There's no legal barrier to withdrawing amounts from your SEP whenever you please. There can be a tax cost, though: Besides regular income tax, there's a 10 percent penalty tax (as with profit-sharing and other qualified plans) on early withdrawals (generally, withdrawals before age fifty-nine and a half).

Use a SEP to Bypass a Deadline

Simplicity is the SEP's chief attraction, but it has another: It offers a one-time opportunity to cure a failure to set up your qualified plan by the deadline. For example, suppose you want the business to make an investment contribution for this year. To do that, your business must set up your qualified plan by December 31 of this year. The business then has through April 15 of next year (or October 15 of next year if there's an extension to file the tax return) to make a deductible contribution, but the plan must be in existence during this year. The business may not have time to set it up before this December 31. Worse, it's now the next year, you're working on last year's tax return, and you realize how much you'd save if the business could make a tax-deductible contribution for last year.

SEP rules, using IRA principles, come to the rescue here. IRAs can be set up *this* year, for the *preceding* year, as late as the due date, including extensions, for the preceding year's tax return. The deductible SEP contribution for *last* year can be made from January 1 through to April 15 of *this* year—or October 15 of this year, if there's a valid return filing extension. So if you missed the December 31 deadline for setting up the qualified plan, you have several additional months to salvage a qualified-plan-like benefit: Have the business set up the SEP and put up to the ceiling amount into your SEP-IRA. This would be in addition to any contribution to a separate IRA you want to make.

Putting, say $45,000 for last year into a SEP in this year's up to nine-and-a-half months window (before the October 15 extension expires)

27

can save, say, $15,000 (say, 33 percent of $45,000) in federal tax due for last year, plus, usually, state tax savings. The entire $45,000 can be working, tax-free, toward your retirement wealth.

Can you have a SEP and a qualified plan?

Yes. If you have a qualified plan of any kind and a SEP as well, the SEP is treated as a profit-sharing plan. The limits on contributions and deductions that apply when a profit-sharing plan is present apply if a SEP is involved.

I recommend a SEP to salvage a deductible investment contribution for a year in which you have substantial business earnings but no qualified plan. SEP contributions you make one year don't commit you to make SEP contributions in future years. You're free to choose in later years the type of plan—or plans—that suit you best, and set up and arrange investment contributions to that (or those).

A Plan for Modest
(Even Very Modest)
Business Income

SIMPLE is a retirement plan specifically designed for small business. SIMPLE is the acronym for "savings incentive match plans for employees." You can have one whether or not you have employees.

SIMPLEs contemplate investment contributions in two steps: first by the employee out of salary, and then by the employer, as a "matching" contribution (which can be less than the employee contribution). In a corporation, the entrepreneur or other employee contributes out of salary and the corporation makes a matching contribution. When SIMPLEs are used by self-employed persons who don't have employees, the self-employed person is contributing both as employee and employer, with both contributions made from self-employment earnings.

How much you can put in and deduct. With a SIMPLE, you can put in and deduct some or all of your self-employed business earnings (or pay, if the business is a corporation). The limit on this "elective deferral," $11,500, rises with the cost of living.

If your earnings exceed that limit, you can make a modest further deductible contribution—specifically, your matching contribution as employer. Your employer contribution would be 3 percent of your salary or self-employment earnings, up to a maximum of the elective deferral limit for the year.

SIMPLEs are an easy way to shelter profits from a sideline or starter business—for entrepreneurs who also have a main business, and employees or homemakers with a sideline.

Why SIMPLEs

A start on the journey toward retirement plan wealth is to get the thousands and tens of thousands from a sideline business as early as you can.

Thus, $10,000 a year at 5.5 percent gets to $97,216 in eight years. If your business takes off then, or at any other time, you can switch to a richer plan—for example, to a profit-sharing 401(k) which would let you put in $36,500 ($42,000 if age fifty or over) on self-employment earnings of $100,000.

Note these special characteristics of SIMPLEs:

1. Catch-up. Persons aged fifty or over can make a further deductible contribution as employee.
2. Ease of withdrawal. There's no legal barrier to withdrawing amounts from your SIMPLE whenever you please. There can be a tax cost, though: Besides regular income tax, the 10 percent penalty tax on early withdrawal (generally, withdrawal before age fifty-nine and a half) rises to 25 percent on withdrawals in the first two years the SIMPLE is in existence.
3. Ceiling. There's a limit on the amount you can put in a SIMPLE as an elective deferral, if you also have one in another business, as in a 401(k), or as an employee: The total amount can't be more than the amount for elective deferrals: 16,500, or $22,000 if catch-up contributions are made by someone age fifty or over.

WEALTH CREATION STRATEGY 7	Invest Personal Funds in the Plan for Further Wealth Increases

Besides investment contributions by the business, you as an individual "employee" may make your own personal investments through the plan out of your individual income or assets. Remember, every owner working in the business can be an "employee" to the plan.

Why Invest as Employee?

Through your added investment contributions as employee you build an even larger fund for yourself personally, enriched with additional benefits.

There's no tax on what these contributions earn while in the plan, and there's limited tax relief when money is withdrawn by you or your heirs. *Catch-up* contributions (see below) are deductible when made. And unlike with employer investment contributions, your plan can let you take your employee investment contributions out when you feel like it.

CASE STUDY

Assume John is able to invest $5,000 a year in addition to his contributions as an employer. He could put this amount directly into fixed-income securities. Or he could invest the same amount in the same securities, using his employee contributions. Assume in either case that John invests $5,000 a year over fifteen years ($75,000 in all) at six percent and that his tax rate over that period is 33 percent.

Fifteen years hence he'd have $103,890 if he invested directly, but $116,380 if he invested through his plan. The tax he will owe on his investment earnings will depend on when and how much he withdraws, in the year he withdraws. But as we saw in Wealth Creation Strategy 1, his after-tax investment return will still outpace direct investment.

Plans employees contribute to are called contributory plans. Contributions may be either mandatory—the employee *must* contribute if she wants to participate in the plan—or voluntary. A mandatory arrangement may be desirable if you have employees. In this chapter, all employee contributions are voluntary.

Deductible "catch-up" contributions

People age fifty or older can make modest deductible plan contributions as employees in addition to any deductible contributions as employer or nondeductible contributions as employee. In business settings, these catch-up contributions are allowed only for contributions to 401(k)s, SIMPLEs, and SARSEPs (a type of SEP formed before 1997). The maximum deduction is generally $5,500 (however many plans you may be in), rising with the cost of living. The amount is $2,500 each year for SIMPLEs.

Catch-up contributions are exempt from the ceilings I consider below. So when the maximum deductible employer contribution ($49,000) is made to a 401(k), a further $5,500 contribution as employee is allowed and is deductible.

Creditor protection

A participant's money in a retirement plan is effectively protected against claims of the participant's creditors.

Creditor protections apply whether the funds arise from employer or employee contributions. They don't apply to money the participant put in defraud of existing creditor claims. Other limitations:

- The funds aren't protected against federal tax liens. (Well, you expected that.)
- Plan funds once distributed to the participant lose full protection, but are granted limited state law protection.

Deduction, Contribution, and Benefit Ceilings

The legal limit on how much can be put aside for any individual depends on the kind of plan you have:

Profit-sharing plan ceilings

Percentage ceiling. A business can deduct contributions for each employee (including owner–employees of self-employed businesses) up to 25 percent of "pay," which is salary and other compensation for employees and self-employment net earnings for others.

For *self-employed* participants, that 25 percent is figured in a way that has confused thousands: it's a percentage of self-employment net earnings *after reduction for* the deductible contribution. The formula to get that number looks like this: X (earnings after contribution) equals earnings before contribution minus 25 percent of X. Suppose earnings before contributions are $125,000. From junior high school algebra, this becomes 1.25 percent of X equals $125,000, which makes X equal $100,000. 25 percent of X is $25,000.

Why these convolutions for self-employeds, you may ask, when it's a straight 25 percent of pay for corporate entrepreneurs and other employees? Tax theorists answer that the economics for corporations is really the same: That employers take profit-sharing contributions into account when they set salary. So a corporation with $125,000 to spend on its entrepreneur's pay and profit-sharing contribution would pay him or her a salary of $100,000 plus a $25,000 profit sharing contribution.

Not persuaded by this approach? That's okay with me. The *rule* is inescapable: the percentage is applied to straight pay for employees and to earnings after the reduction for the contribution where it's for self-employeds. In my examples I'll get to the percentage ceiling by contributing *20 percent* of earnings, an IRS-approved shortcut with the same dollar result: 20 percent of $125,000 (earnings) is the same as 25 percent of $100,000 (self-employment net earnings under the formula).

Dollar ceiling. Profit-sharing investment contributions for any participant can't exceed a specified dollar amount—$49,000—adjusted annually for inflation. So a profit-sharing investment contribution for a corporate entrepreneur with $300,000 in salary and bonuses tops out at $49,000, not $75,000.

Contribution ceiling. The business is allowed to contribute beyond the percentage ceilings, up to 100 percent of the participant's pay or earnings. Such contributions when invested earn and compound tax-free. But there's an "excess contribution" penalty (an excise tax on the amount in excess), intended to offset the tax-free compounding benefit. This means don't contribute more than can be deducted.

401(k) plans

These are profit-sharing plans with an elective deferral feature. The elective deferral is technically a contribution by—and deducted by—the business.

With or without a 401(k), you can't put in more than the profit-sharing dollar ceiling.

ELECTIVE DEFERRAL CEILING

This lets contributions exceed the profit-sharing percentage ceiling, though not the profit-sharing dollar ceiling or the contribution ceiling. Elective deferral investment contributions for any participant can't exceed a specified dollar amount—$16,500 adjusted annually for inflation.

EXAMPLE

Susan earns $60,000 this year in her sideline business, a sole proprietorship. She could put $28,500 into her 401(k): $12,000 as a profit-sharing contribution and $16,500 as an elective deferral.

Further limits apply where your business has employees besides yourself and your spouse; see Chapter 3.

Defined benefit plans

Pension professionals speak of "benefit limits" and "funding limits" (meaning contribution limits) for defined benefit plans.

BENEFIT LIMITS

In figuring average pay or earnings on which benefits are based, you can't count amounts in any year in excess of $245,000 (adjusted annually for inflation). So if you earned $180,000, $270,000, and $220,000 in three consecutive years, your average is $215,000 ($180,000 plus $245,000 plus $220,000, divided by three), not $223,333.

If you're in the business for less than ten years, your pension can't be more than your high three years, divided by ten (years), times the number of years of service. (For example, an allowable $80,000 pension based on your high three years is reduced to $64,000 if you're in business only eight years.) Your annual pension can't exceed a specified dollar amount— $195,000—adjusted annually for inflation. (The limit is further reduced, under a formula, for retirement occurring before age sixty-two.)

If your business has employees besides yourself and your spouse, there may be further limits.

FUNDING (CONTRIBUTION) LIMITS

There's no percentage or dollar limit on how much a business can put in for participants' pensions. The business puts in what's necessary to build the projected benefit.

And how much is that? It depends on how close the participant is to retirement, how much the plan has in it from past contributions, and investment earnings, life expectancy factors, and expected future investment earnings, as determined by a pension actuary. The IRS almost always accepts the actuary's judgment, but has the right to substitute its own.

Defined benefit plans expect the business to contribute the amount required for the planned benefit, in lean years as well as fat. Contributions may vary from year to year. Employers often seek to prepay in fat years for obligations expected in the future. Such prepayments put more money to work tax-free. Such a practice, in theory subject to "excess contribution" rules, is now effectively allowed.

Money purchase pension plan
Same ceilings as profit-sharing plans.

SEPs
Same ceilings as profit-sharing plans.

Employee contributions
Catch-up contributions for any participant can't exceed a specified dollar amount, adjusted annually for inflation. A catch-up contribution

isn't counted in the dollar or percentage ceilings of whatever plan you have adopted.

Other voluntary or mandatory contributions. The plan will make these a percentage of compensation, maybe with a limit such as 10 percent of compensation, for voluntary contributions. The annual ceiling for such contributions is the percentage ceiling amount mentioned above for profit-sharing plans, minus contributions by the business and the participant's share of forfeitures by other employees.

Plan Investments

Most retirement plans leave investment decision-making for the entire plan fund up to the plan trustee, or the trustee's nominee. This decision maker can be you, if you have made yourself the plan's trustee—which is not unusual. Some defined contribution plans—more and more plans after the Enron scandal—let the individual plan participant make investment decisions for her own account, especially with 401(k) plans. In any case, the business has some oversight responsibility for investment decisions (when decisions are made by the trustee or other nominee) or for investment options available to participants (when the individual participant picks the investments).

This is my basic retirement investment philosophy:

1. Make investments you feel comfortable with. You can be as active as you please, moving in and out of whatever you like. Or you can invest for the long-term. You can be in stocks, bonds, mutual funds, money market funds, real estate mortgages, or anything else. The only legal limitation is that your qualified plan can't invest in collectibles: paintings, antiques, postage stamps, and the like. Small loss, this. There's no place for collectibles in a tax-exempt portfolio. SEPs and SIMPLEs—IRA-based plans—can't invest in these either, and also can't invest in life insurance.
2. Always keep in mind just how important it will be to you to have this money available at retirement. If you're like most retirement plan investors, safety and steady appreciation will be your goal.
3. Forget about tax-exempt bonds and tax shelters. Qualified and IRA-based plans are completely exempt from tax. All income is tax-free, and no one gets any benefit from tax losses.

Diversifying your portfolio

Investment advisors always urge investors to diversify their investments. Investors, they say, should own a variety of common stocks
(equities), a variety of bonds or other interest-paying debt instruments
(securities), including international holdings, and maybe other investments (gold, real estate) as well. Diversifying your investments will give
you income, growth of capital, and safety.

Advisors suggest that you make your more secure and conservative
investments in your plan and your more aggressive and growth-ori-
ented investments personally.

Life Insurance and Qualified Plans

Insured qualified plans are retirement plans whose funds consist primarily of annuity contracts. Your plan buys annuities for you, year by year,
while you're still working. They are called deferred annuities because
you start to collect them in the future.

Trusteed plans, on the other hand, are ones in which the entrepreneur
controls his own investments, though insured plans may use trustees
too. The qualified plan rules and opportunities we've considered earlier
apply to insured plans as well. You can have insured defined-benefit
plans, insured money-purchase plans, and insured profit-sharing plans.

The entrepreneur may want to include "death benefits" (the pension industry's way of saying "life insurance") in her plan. Such a policy
typically provides $1,000 of life insurance for every $10 of monthly
annuity payment.

Instead of investing in an annuity, you can invest through the insurance company's "immediate participation guarantee contract." Here
you invest your money with the insurance company, generally until
retirement. You share in the company's investment results (minus something off the top as its profit). So your investment return is not insured,
or guaranteed. But the company guarantees the rate or price at which
the annuity can be purchased.

You can also consider variable annuities. Monthly payouts are
fixed in typical annuities. With variable annuities, payouts, well, vary,
depending on the performance of the portfolio of securities in which
annuity premiums are invested. Usually the investor chooses a portfolio
of common stocks as an inflation hedge.

Insured 412(i) defined benefit plans

You may hear some advisors call the "412(i) insured defined benefit plan" the plan that allows the largest tax-deductible contribution. True enough, but not the whole story.

The 412(i) name derives from a section of the tax code—as does 401(k). A 412(i) plan, like other defined benefit plans, reflects the employer's commitment (yours, if you're an owner) to pay the employee (you again) a predetermined pension amount, like an annuity, at or after retirement. The 412(i) plan allows you to put the annuity feature together with life insurance. With the life insurance feature, a participant who dies before retirement can leave a substantial asset (the insurance proceeds) to her heirs if the annuity wasn't fully funded at death. Such an arrangement is more costly than a typical defined benefit plan would be.

With a 412(i) defined benefit plan, your contributions are invested only in guaranteed insurance products: annuities and, if you want, life insurance policies. You contribute a level premium amount each year. With a 412(i) plan, your projected rate of return would be the insurance company's guaranteed rate.

The actual return may be higher than the guaranteed rate. If so, the excess is used to reduce future contributions.

So with 412(i)s, deductions tend to be higher in earlier years, diminishing in later years as earnings in excess of the guaranteed rate build up. Put another way, 412(i)s can be preferable to other defined benefit plans for those who want to maximize deductions now and for the next few years. Actuarial reporting to the government is not required for a 412(i) plan.

You can add guaranteed life insurance coverage to this plan. A form often chosen allows life insurance coverage equal to 100 times the monthly annuity. The premium cost of such a policy will vary widely.

Employers deduct the cost of the annuity, whether the employer is self-employed or incorporated. Self-employed owners may not deduct the cost of life insurance allocable to themselves. Corporations may deduct the cost of life insurance but employees are taxed on the current term insurance value of their coverage.

Insurance product return rates tend to be lower than rates prudent investors could get on their own. On the other hand, the insurance rate of return is guaranteed.

The ideal candidate for a 412(i) is within fifteen years of retirement, with a large steady income. For such a person, 412(i)s can deliver the highest deductible contribution. Some vendors sell the size of the deduction rather than the value of the investment. Paying more for a retirement benefit than it's worth to you is a bad deal, even if what you overpay is deductible.

If the insurance is needed in your case, check that cash values build adequately in the early years. Where they don't, you can lose a lot if you have to cancel prematurely.

Does life insurance belong in your plan?

That depends on whether you need insurance. An insurance agent would have you look at it this way: Your plan is building a nest egg for retirement. If you should die before you retire, your plan may not have reached the financial goal you set for it. Of course, you won't need a retirement nest egg if you don't live to retire. But suppose your plan was to help support family members when you stopped working. You might then want to consider a life insurance arrangement to cover any shortfall in plan wealth that might be caused by your premature death.

Plans Covering Family Members Add to Family Wealth

Retirement plans, the best wealth machines I know of for the small business owner, can be adapted easily to help build wealth for family members, too, if they work in the business.

Every family member working in the business has the chance to build a personal fortune using plan investment contributions from the business. Your business can be used to enrich these family members, as well as yourself. Part of their pay can go for their own tax-sheltered fund.

The likeliest candidate is the entrepreneur's spouse. Investment contributions on his or her behalf will be based on pay (salary, bonus, commissions, etc.) if he or she is an employee (including a stockholder employee), or on self-employment net earnings if a working partner or LLC member.

Adding your spouse to your retirement plan

Here are the economics of including your spouse when you're a sole proprietor. Adding your spouse as your employee generally won't hurt your income tax picture, assuming you file a joint return. Your business income is reduced by what your spouse is paid, but his or her income is increased by the same amount, generally with no effect on total taxable income. The tax grief comes via the Social Security tax on the pay of a spouse who was previously unemployed. This is an extra tax, one that, unlike the income tax on a joint return, always reduces family after-tax income.

But your spouse as employee can participate in the business retirement plan. Depending on the plan you have and how much your spouse is paid, the benefit from that added tax-sheltered retirement investment can far outweigh the Social Security tax burden.

You can see this best with a 401(k) profit-sharing plan. Say you pay your spouse $30,000. He or she could put a tax-free (tax-deferred) $16,500 of that pay into a 401(k)—plus a further tax-free $5,500 "catch-up" contribution if age fifty or over. You as employer could contribute a further $7,500 (25 percent of $30,000) to the plan on your spouse's behalf. So for a spouse earning $30,000, $24,000 can go tax-sheltered into the 401(k). There's an overall tax saving here, which I'll get into, but the important thing is how much more you have working for family retirement and estate building with your spouse in your plan.

The tax picture is based on these facts (I assume a joint return):

Family business income has gone down by $39,795, for the spouse's pay ($30,000), your Social Security tax on that pay ($2,295), and your $7,500 profit-sharing contribution for your spouse. The family's wage income—before considering the spouse's 401(k) contribution—goes up $30,000.

TAXES

Social Security. The family now bears extra Social Security tax of $4,590—that is, your business share of that tax (just mentioned) plus the spouse's equal share as employee.

Self-employment tax. The reduction in business income reduces this tax—say, by $1,154.

Income tax. Family income tax goes down, reflecting the $24,000 added to the plan for the spouse (and the income tax effect of the Social Security and self-employment taxes).

Overall, a couple in the 33 percent bracket has $5,051 in total tax savings, after Social Security tax increases are offset by income tax and self-employment tax savings. But the bigger story is the tax-sheltered $24,000 you now have working for family retirement and estate building.

YOUR OWN 401(K) CONTRIBUTIONS

The business income you shift to your spouse or other family members in this way, through salary and profit-sharing contributions, can reduce the amount you can put in for yourself—since that's based on your net business earnings. For sole proprietors contributing at the maximum rate, this would happen when pay to your spouse brings net business earnings below $162,500.

The calculations would be different if the business were a corporation (no self-employment tax would apply), or where hiring your spouse would affect profits of co-owners.

Where spouse and *kids are in the plan*

Here we'll assume that you and your family members are in the same plan. Consider this case study involving a profit-sharing 401(k):

CASE STUDY

Dave is a construction general contractor operating a single member LLC. Dave's wife, Cindy, and their son, Jim, work in the firm. Dave's net profits this year, before paying Cindy and Jim, are $300,000. Cindy's pay is $50,000, Jim's is $70,000, and all three individuals, and the family business, put the maximum into the firm's profit-sharing 401(k). If Dave and Cindy are age fifty or over, the family together has invested $118,000 tax-free for their retirement. Dave's taxable business income is now $101,000, Cindy's is $28,000, and Jim's is $53,500. Cindy and Jim will owe Social Security taxes on their pay and elective deferrals at a rate of 7.65 percent—as will the LLC. Dave owes self-employment tax on his net earnings. (We ignored the LLC's Social Security tax in computing its profits.)

ACTION POINT

Employ family members the right way. The family member employee must be a genuine employee, meaning he should have real work to do, with something in place showing that you as owner or co-owner know the work is being done. The employee's services, whatever they are, should be worth what the business pays, including what it pays into the retirement plan. If the family member is an adult, do an employment contract that states his duties, pay, and expected weekly or monthly hours of work.

How Retirement Plans Work
for Business Partnerships

Each working member of a partnership, or LLC treated as a partnership, is considered self-employed. All such members can participate in a single partnership plan. Or, within limits, each partner can have her own plan. Or, some partners can be together in one or more partnership plans and not participate in others.

The plans available can be any plan allowed to a sole proprietor, except that very large partnerships can't have SIMPLEs.

The partnership is always the sponsor of all plans in the partnership. Yes, this is saying that the partnership is the sponsor of a plan designed to fit one partner's needs, which excludes all others. This can present sticky problems, especially when there are non-partner employees, but it can be done. For example, a law partnership might have one plan for staff employees (paralegals, secretaries, bookkeepers, and the like), no plan for the lawyer associates (lawyer employees, who are expected to become partners or leave the firm), and individual plans for each lawyer partner. The plan for staff employees should be "comparable" to the partners' plans, and exclusion of lawyer associates should pass the tests for allowing certain employees to be excluded (called, with no gender or racial overtones, "discrimination tests").

Contributions to all plans are made by the partnership. Contributions for partners are based on "net earnings from self-employment," which include the partner's share of partnership earnings and, if applicable, "guaranteed payments," in the nature of salary. Contributions for a particular partner reduce that partner's share of partnership profits. Deductions for that contribution are taken on the partner's return. Contribution and deduction ceilings are based on the partner's self-employment income ("net earnings from self-employment"). For those ceilings, see "Deduction, Contribution, and Benefit Ceilings" earlier in this chapter.

Silent partners

Only co-owners who work in the business can participate in the plan. If they are merely investors—nonworking limited partners, for example—they can't participate because they won't have self-employment earnings or compensation for personal services.

Corporate elections

Partnerships and LLCs may choose ("elect") tax treatment as corporations. Individual owners of single-member LLCs may elect to be treated as corporations (otherwise they are treated as sole proprietors).

Members of partnerships or LLCs that elect status as corporations are treated as corporate stockholders and employees, and not as self-employed. Elections to be treated as corporations apply for federal tax purposes and don't determine how the entity in question is treated under state business or tax law.

KEOGH PLANS AND CORPORATE PLANS

A Keogh plan is a qualified plan of an unincorporated business. The Keogh program was created to allow owners of unincorporated businesses the same tax-favored retirement opportunities hitherto allowed owners of corporations.

A small amount of discrimination against self-employed plans remains, however, caused by Social Security rules. For employees, including corporate owner-employees, there's no Social Security tax on the retirement plan investment contribution. But a self-employed owner-employee's retirement plan contribution for his or her own account bears Social Security (self-employment) tax. This tax burden is partly offset by an income tax deduction for half the self-employment tax, including the self-employment tax falling on the retirement contribution. But that income tax deduction slightly reduces self-employment net earnings, and hence the amount the self-employed owner-employee can put in toward his own account.

The result of these convolutions is that for corporate-owner employees and self-employed owner-employees in the same circumstances, the corporate guy tends to pay slightly less total personal tax (counting income and Social Security taxes) and is allowed a slightly greater retirement plan investment contribution. The self-employed guy thereby qualifies for a slightly larger Social Security benefit. And then there are *business* taxes, federal and state, which might fall more heavily on the corporate guy.

A corporate employer with employees may set up a retirement plan that invests in its own stock, and distributes that stock to employees as a benefit. These may be *stock bonus plans* or *employee stock ownership plans* (ESOPs). There's nothing comparable for unincorporated business.

Your plan in hard times

Hard times are tough on plan contributions, and on plan investments. When profits fall, must the business continue contributions to the plan? Generally not, but some plans nominally require contributions in all economic weathers. Mostly, these are pension plans and safe-harbor 401(k)s.

If yours is a pension plan, you should ask the IRS for a contribution waiver, because of business hardship. IRS charges a fee for the waiver, and you'll need to make up the shortfall in installments over future years.

If yours is a safe-harbor 401(k) (these are for businesses with employees), you should amend the plan to reduce or suspend the employer contribution during the business hardship. No future makeup is required; the full contribution can be restored when the hardship lifts.

Other options:

- Amend the plan, to reduce future benefits. Do this especially for pension plans if you think your vision of retirement wealth was over-ambitious or that your business downturn will continue. Usually, such amendments are meant to become effective for benefits earned in future years, but it's not impossible, for example, with 401(k)s, to have the amendment apply to later periods in the current year.
- Terminate your plan, paying off all benefit claims earned to date. You'll still be free to start a more affordable plan—such as a profit-sharing or SEP plan—which requires no commitment to periodic contributions.

Investment asset values fall in hard times, raising the risk that you won't have all you planned to retire on. Defined benefit plans can make up for reduced investment returns by means of larger (tax-deductible) contributions in later years. Those with enough time and earnings before retirement can still reach their retirement fund target—though at greater-than-expected cost. This won't work for some in defined benefit plans, or for those in other plans. Entrepreneurs in these groups may want to postpone retirement. If you're in a pension or other plan with a fixed retirement date, you can amend the plan to postpone the date.

Plan loans

Your plan can be written to let you borrow from your retirement fund. The loan limit is $50,000, or half your account if that's less. If you're married, you'll usually need your spouse's consent to the loan. The loan must be repaid within five years (longer if it's to buy a principal residence). The loan will bear interest (at relatively low rates). Your debt is an investment asset of your account and the interest you pay goes to increase the account.

Loans are repaid with after-tax dollars—no tax deduction for the principal (of course) *or* the interest. Like all true loans, it's tax-free—though amounts not repaid when due are taxable distributions.

Borrowing against your retirement fund is no way to build wealth, of course. But it's worth considering for needed funds when your only other option is to take a taxable distribution.

Plan Duties and Obligations

If, like most owner-employees, you have chosen to act as your plan's trustee, you have the duty to make plan investments for the good of plan participants. You have this duty even if you have no employees and are your plan's only participant.

"Imprudent" investments can be another problem if you're the only participant in a defined benefit plan. Trustees should act as "prudent" investors of plan funds. It's rare for the IRS to second-guess plan investments, even those that turn out badly, but it's sometimes done. What most bothers the IRS are investments that seem intended to do something other than increase the plan fund: that are meant to help a customer, supplier, friend, or relative of the owner, for example.

Trustees generally, including qualified plan trustees, have a duty to diversify investments. Failure to diversify is a sign of imprudence. So putting a large proportion of plan money in a dubious investment invites trouble from the IRS. Along with diversifying, it's a good idea to approach your plan investment task by acting as if you were investing for participants other than yourself.

In defined contribution qualified plans (money purchase plans, and 401(k) or other profit-sharing plans), the prudent investor rules don't apply if you're the only one in the plan. There, investment decisions controlled by you the participant are exempt from the investment rules.

ACTION POINT ✓

You need a written retirement plan, which pension professionals call a plan document, and a written trust agreement.

Both of these are fairly complex legal instruments. In the plan document, you as employer set forth in detail what you will provide. Then you specify the conditions that employees, including you as employee, must meet in order to belong to this plan and benefit from it. You say when and what you will collect. You lay out any options you will have, such as the option to contribute as an employee.

In the trust agreement you as employer set forth what the trustee should do about trust investments and payments to employees. You may of course decide to be trustee. No matter; you still need a written agreement giving yourself directions.

Certain housekeeping details connected with the plan must be handled by the plan administrator—often you. That too calls for something in writing. To do all this, you'll either adopt a master plan or have a pension professional draw up a tailor-made plan.

A master plan reduces the start-up costs and simplifies your side of the paperwork. With a tailor-made plan, you will have to pay up front for the advice of a pension professional. Besides that, you must pay for having the necessary legal documents drawn up and getting the plan approved by the IRS. With a master plan, no charge is made for advice; you get no advice. Nor are you charged for preparing documents; the documents are already prepared. In a master plan, one basic set of plan documents is reproduced for use by all businesses adopting that plan.

The prudent investor rules also don't apply to IRAs, including SEP IRAs and SIMPLE IRAs. But loans from an IRA to its owner are barred.

About master plans

Master plans are offered by professional associations and trade associations, by law firms and pension firms, and by financial institutions of all types: banks, insurance companies, mutual funds, and securities dealers. In master plan terminology, the firm or institution that offers the plan is the plan sponsor. If an entrepreneur approves of a master plan's terms and conditions, her business will adopt the plan as employer, and make business contributions to an account with that plan sponsor.

An employee covered by the plan is called a participant. An entrepreneur is a participant in her capacity as employee. The trustee will usually be someone the sponsor selects.

Prototype plans are a kind of master plan in which the employer names the trustee, and so can control the investments. You, the business owner, may name yourself trustee. *Plan sponsor charges* for handling your account are relatively minor nowadays.

About a tailor-made plan

- You can directly control all plan investments.
- You can have a plan that gives you exactly what you want.

Consider tailor-made especially:
- For those who select defined-benefit plans, to get the full range of options for building plan wealth. The tax-deductible cost of a tailor-made plan is often quickly recovered out of the higher tax-deductible contributions you are allowed and the higher tax-sheltered earnings.
- When employees (in addition to entrepreneur and spouse) are involved.

IRS OKAY

Every master plan will have an IRS okay or will be in the process of getting one. If you have a tailor-made plan, the pension professional you engage to prepare it will advise you to have it approved by the IRS, and may handle the approval process. Approval is a practical necessity, not a legal requirement. You need IRS approval because you have so much at stake. You will be investing many thousands of dollars because of the many tax advantages and creditor protections. If you're in danger of losing those advantages and protections because of some defect in your plan, you should know that right away.

After examining the plan (the IRS charges for this) and making sure it meets legal requirements, the IRS will give you a written commitment that its revenue agents will treat the plan as qualified. The IRS will do this for existing plans. More important, the IRS will do it for a plan before it goes into effect. The commitment binds the IRS if you live up to the terms of your plan.

SETTING UP IRA-BASED PLANS

Simplified employee pension (SEP) IRAs are offered by the same financial institutions that offer IRAs, master plans, and SIMPLEs. Setting up a SEP for your business is much like setting up a profit-sharing master plan, though with fewer choices. You'll be given a plan document and an adoption agreement, and maybe guidance on operating the SEP. And you'll be establishing an IRA for yourself as participant.

Strategy Review

Your goal in this chapter is to defer taxes on business profits, and use these profits in a tax-sheltered investment program to build a six- or seven-figure fund for your retirement and an estate for your heirs. Here are your leading opportunities:

1. When you're decades from retirement, consider a profit-sharing plan allowing periodic investment contributions, free of income taxes, based on your salary or business earnings.
2. Adding a 401(k) elective deferral feature to a profit-sharing plan allows investment contributions that are a larger proportion of your salary or business earnings. This especially favors those with middle and upper-middle incomes who want to maximize retirement wealth through larger current contributions.
3. When retirement is nearer—twenty years or less—a defined benefit plan lets you invest greater tax-deferred profits to build the largest retirement fund possible for your situation.

Other plans can be made to fit specific needs:

4. A simplified employee pension (SEP) offers about the same wealth-building as a profit-sharing plan, with the added limited opportunity to shelter business profits for the year *before* it's adopted.
5. A SIMPLE plan can suit a sideline or starter business.
6. Two plans for the same business can build wealth still further—in the right circumstances. Adding a 401(k)'s elective deferral to a defined benefit plan is one way. Another is to freeze one well-funded plan and start another.

7. Qualified plans and SIMPLE plans can be enriched by participants' additional tax-sheltered investments of personal funds. This can be coupled with personal tax savings, in the case of personal contributions to 401(k)s and SIMPLEs, at or after age fifty.

8. Family member employees or co-owners may participate with the entrepreneur in the plan, building sizable funds of their own.

Chapter 3

Can You Afford Plan Investments for Employees?

WEALTH CREATION STRATEGIES 9–15

The answer is: "401(k)." Okay, now what's the question? It's: "How can I make retirement plan investments for myself without having to make them for my employees?"

In theory, and sometimes in practice, plan investments for employees can come entirely out of what the employee already earns, at no additional cost to the employer beyond the cost of running the plan.

This works fine for some employers. Others with larger incomes or larger ambitions may want to invest more for themselves than 401(k)s allow, even when the business must invest something on behalf of some employees.

This chapter considers how to shelter business profits through business retirement plans when the business has non-owner employees. The qualified retirement plan—and its IRA-based junior partner—are woefully underused wealth-building tools. U.S. government statistics show that of those sole proprietors who *could* use it, only one in thirteen *does*.

Ignorance or inattention explains much of this omission. But some entrepreneurs believe they have a good—or at least plausible—reason to pass up such a plan:

The cost to the business. They've heard—accurately—that if a business has a retirement plan, it may have to include employees in the plan in addition to the working owner. These entrepreneurs figure the business can't afford what it would cost to cover employees—so they forego a plan from which they themselves could richly benefit.

That problem won't stump us. This chapter will show you ways to build your own retirement fund as high as possible, while saving plenty in plan costs for employees.

This may seem a tall order when your plan, by law, can't "discriminate" in your favor. In retirement plans, discrimination means illegally favoring the business owner over his employees. However, there are a number of things your plan can legally do for you that might *seem like* discrimination. To see what I mean, consider these questions:

Q. *Who makes the most money from the business?*
A. The boss, the owner-employee, usually. But it's not prohibited discrimination to award greater plan benefits and plan investment contributions to those who already make more than rank-and-file employees.

Q. *Who's in the business the longest?*
A. The boss, of course (unless he bought it or inherited it from someone else). But giving greater benefits to those in the business longer—benefits based on "length of service"—isn't discrimination.

Q. *And who in the business is least likely to quit before retirement?*
A. The boss, naturally (except when she sells the business). But plan provisions turning funds forfeited by departing participants over to those who stay on aren't discrimination.

Plan provisions that do all these things, even in combination, are okay ways to build an entrepreneur's retirement assets at little business outlay for other employees.

Save Costs by Leaving Some Employees Out

A business is allowed to leave some of its employees out of its plan. Naturally, you have no plan costs for employees you don't cover. You can always exclude the following:

- Employees younger than twenty-one.
- Employees who work for the business part-time. Plans normally define full-time as 1,000 hours a year or more, so part-time is less than 1,000. If your business is a sideline for you, you would define full-time to include yourself—say, 500 hours or more a year—and part-time as less than that.
- Employees who have worked for the business less than one year. Or employees who have worked for you less than two years if they are fully vested in all the business contributes for them upon two years' service.

If your plan is a simplified employee pension (SEP), the business can exclude those who have worked for it less than three years. Entrepreneurs whose businesses have high turnover might therefore favor SEPs. Employees can also be excluded for specific reasons, based on:

1. Union membership—on the theory that the union has bargained for the benefits its members need (which of course could include your business's contributions to a separate multi-employer plan for union members).

2. The location they work in, or the kind of work they do. Remember the law firm mentioned in Chapter 2, which excluded lawyer associates. Some businesses exclude their commission sales reps.

There are rules requiring that a minimum percentage of employees be included—and rules defining who is an employee.

You can't get around the rules by breaking up your business into separate units, granting coverage to yourself and maybe a chosen few others in one unit and excluding those (or providing no plan for those) in other units. All the units you (or your family) control are combined in testing whether the required minimum percentage of employees gets coverage.

Some readers may be troubled by this chapter's theme: How to get *disproportionately* more for yourself than your employees get. Well, the whole book is about getting more.

You don't have to do what this chapter advises. Your plan can be written to give you only proportionately more, or even less, than your employees. Maybe your employees will reward your generosity with more productive labor, which produces greater profits. Maybe your reward will come in other ways, or in another place.

Just remember that it *is* generosity.

ACTION POINT ✓

One limits the number of employees by the way the plan defines categories of employees covered or excluded. This should be worked out with a pension professional.

Opportunities to avoid putting in for employees—though not exactly *excluding* them—arise in 401(k) plans (see Wealth Creation Strategy 11) and in plans where the business contributes for an employee only if the employee contributes for himself or herself (see Wealth Creation Strategy 15).

Independent contractors and other special workers

Should your business use independent contractors instead of employees? I can't answer this for you. Some entrepreneurs think the independent contractor route is cheaper, and it often is. But you are responsible to your customers for the quality of what your business puts out. You'll usually have more control of quality if you can control the worker's work. Consider how important such control is in your case: that control is what makes a worker an employee rather than an independent contractor.

Key legal and economic reasons favoring independent contractors over employees:

- "Employer" duties to provide workers compensation and work environment and safety measures, and the like, don't apply to independent contractors.
- Compensation to independent contractors doesn't incur employer payroll taxes, such as Social Security, unemployment tax, and federal and state wage withholding, or the cost of reporting on these to government agencies. Employers save these costs and burdens.
- Independent contractors can't be included in benefit plans for employees, thereby saving employee costs for such programs.

Independent contractors' fees may of course be higher than employees' salaries, maybe partly to cover the independent contractor's cost of providing herself the benefits foregone because she's not an employee.

This is no place for the pros and cons of what twenty-first-century business management calls alternative employment arrangements—staffing through independent contractors, professional employer organizations (PEOs), employee leasing organizations, or staffing referral agencies. The issues there go far beyond retirement plan costs and savings. But if someone who does work for your business is not an *employee* of a business you own, the business doesn't have to, and in fact is not allowed to, include her in the business's retirement plan.

Key Plan Features When You Have Employees

Plans that would work just great for you if you had no employees may need modification, or replacement, to avoid burdensome costs when you have employees.

If you already have a plan with employee participants, review the strategies that follow for ways to modify the plan—prospectively—to reduce business costs or increase your share.

Defined benefit plans

The defined benefit plan suits entrepreneurs close to retirement because the business can put aside large amounts of tax-deferred profits for their retirement. But a small business with more than four employees generally can't have a defined benefit plan unless it covers at least 40 percent of its employees (counting partners as employees). That need not always mean large outlays for employees included in the plan.

<table>
<tr><td>WEALTH
CREATION
STRATEGY

10</td><td>

Using Age or Service to Augment the Entrepreneur's Share

</td></tr>
</table>

The following example, for a defined benefit plan, exploits two factors favoring the owner: age (closeness to retirement), and owner earnings.

> ### EXAMPLE
>
> Say the plan allows retirement at 80 percent of pay at age sixty-five. The business owner, age fifty-three, makes $200,000 salary, and her five employees, age thirty, make $40,000 each. This year's cost for the owner's pension is $116,420 and for all five employees combined it's $17,625. Collectively, owner and employees make the same amount, but the business puts in almost seven times more for the owner.

Length of service is another tool. Designing the plan to reward long service usually benefits the owner most, as the longest-serving employee. With a plan that credits 3 percent of compensation per year of service, the business buys the entrepreneur a pension at the owner's full pay (over thirty-three and a half years). When an employee leaves after eight years, the business pays for a pension of no more than 24 percent of the employee's pay—but often much less, because of the vesting/forfeiture rules discussed in Wealth Creation Strategy 13.

You can ratchet up the owner's edge by crediting *past* service.

CASE STUDY

Phil ran his business solo for seventeen years, but last year he took on four employees. This year his business set up a pension plan that awards 3 percent of pay for every year of service—so that a participant would get a pension at full pay after thirty-three and a half years. And the plan awards credit for past service. Phil is credited this year with 52 percent of his pension, based on past earnings; employees are credited with 3 percent each, of last year's pay. So a huge proportion of the tax-deductible business contribution goes for Phil—though contributions and deductions for amounts for past service are spread over future as well as current years.

Age and Service in Other Plans

The cost of including the prescribed percentage of participants in a defined benefit plan could be prohibitive.

But the age and service feature for augmenting the entrepreneur's share also applies for profit-sharing and money purchase plans.

Age-weighted profit-sharing plans

Here the age/service feature is an "age-weighted profit-sharing plan." It allocates the business's profit-sharing contribution among employees based on age or age category—with allocation percentages increasing by age. Though older employees are favored, no specific retirement benefit is targeted and no actuarial projection is needed.

The plan can base benefits on compensation and length of service rather than compensation and age (closeness to retirement), or on all three—compensation, age, and length of service. (So can defined benefit plans.)

Money purchase pension plans

Here the age/service feature is called a "target-benefit plan." The owner determines the retirement benefit: for example, 25 percent of the average of the participant's final five years' earnings. The actuary consulted for the plan will compute what the contributions and rate of return on investment must be to pay for the targeted pension. Though this is much like a defined benefit plan, no annual recalculations are made to reflect differences between assumed and actual investment returns, and no further actuarial reports are required.

A business owner might adopt a target-benefit plan if the persons to be benefited earn about the same amount but are of widely differing ages: an owner aged fifty-seven and an employee aged thirty-one, for example. A target-benefit plan to fund a particular benefit level at age sixty-five might cost a tax-deductible 20 percent of earnings for the owner (with only eight years remaining before retirement) but 1.34 percent of earnings (with 34 years to go) for the employee, even if their earnings are the same.

Target benefit plans can base benefits on compensation and either age or length of service, or on all three—compensation, age, and length of service.

Profit sharing as incentive

Business owners can use profit sharing as a reward for employees. Contributions can be varied or suspended to fit current business needs. For example, you might promise to put an additional 10 percent of salary into a plan for your employees if business profit exceeded $500,000, but nothing if it was less than that.

This course of action is designed to enrich your *business*, not your plan. A richer business may be what really matters, but it also helps your plan indirectly. The larger your business earnings—after any contributions for employees, of course—the more you can contribute for yourself.

Business profit-sharing investment/contributions for entrepreneurs and other participants are typically a percentage of the participant's compensation (pay or earnings). They are additional compensation, not instead of (not a reduction of) compensation. Profit-sharing contributions based on compensation favor the entrepreneur when he is the highest paid, in salary or business earnings.

11 Cut Plan Costs with a 401(k)

I considered 401(k) plans in Chapter 2 (Wealth Creation Strategies 2 and 3). I return to them here because of their cost-cutting uses when you have employees.

Look at 401(k) as a salary-reduction plan. When one of these is installed, employees get to choose: continue to take all of their salary in cash; or divert some of it, as elective deferrals, into the 401(k).

The owner is the real winner with a pure 401(k) plan. The owner can defer part of her pay or earnings, tax-free, into the retirement investment fund, without any additional business cost for employees. If the employee takes it all in cash, the owner is exactly where she was before. If the employee instead defers collecting some by diverting it to the 401(k), he, like the owner, pays less tax now, and has the untaxed funds working toward retirement. The business escapes income tax on amounts so invested, which are officially profit-sharing contributions even though only elective deferrals are involved.

But there aren't many pure 401(k)s around. Owners generally aren't allowed to have 401(k)s for themselves unless some employees defer, and can't have *rich* 401(k)s unless employees defer "enough."

Employees may not choose to defer, or to defer enough, without encouragement. There are many ways, described below, to get employees to defer. Some ways add costs for the business, but may allow greater proportional increases in what the entrepreneur can set aside for himself or herself, and for other top level employees or co-owners, such as the entrepreneur's family.

These are:

Automatic enrollment. Employees can be automatically enrolled in the company 401(k)—when the plan begins, when they are hired, or after some trial period. The business can specify the elective deferral amount or percentage of pay, and the type of investment these funds go into. But employees must have the right to refuse to participate, or to select a different amount or percentage and to opt out later even if they go along at first.

Participant-directed investments. Whether or not employees are automatically enrolled, they may be more inclined to defer—or defer more—if they can decide where their money is to be invested. The plan can offer a wide range, a narrow range, or a virtually unfettered choice of investment (from within the wide spectrum allowed to profit-sharing plans).

Investment guidance. Deferral may be encouraged if the business offers or arranges investment education for participants generally, or specific guidance tailored to the individual participant.

Businesses have some responsibility and potential liability—which I won't get into here—for investment options offered and investment instruction given.

Loans from the plan. Amounts electively deferred can be withdrawn (before retirement) only under specified conditions. This rule, which may discourage deferrals, can be countered by allowing employees to borrow against their accounts, see Chapter 2.

Catch-up contributions. 401(k) plans may allow employees to make such (tax-deductible) contributions to create a larger retirement fund. Catch-ups are allowed only when the participant has electively deferred the maximum under the plan. So allowing catch-ups tends to cause larger elective deferrals.

Matching contributions. This and automatic enrollment are the most effective devices to encourage elective deferral. For every, say, $3 or $5 an employee diverts into the 401(k), the business will add $1 more. Any such matching contribution is a profit-sharing contribution, which adds to business cost.

When some employees don't defer "enough"

The law requires that tests be made to assure the 401(k) plan is fair to rank-and-file employees. One test—tests, actually—checks for discrimination in favor of the owners and any others who are highly paid, a group we'll call "the bosses." Generally, a plan discriminates when the bosses' elective deferrals are a higher proportion of their pay than the proportion for others in the plan—whom we'll call "the workers." But a higher proportion for bosses is still allowed if it's not too high.

A bunch of rules define what's too high, when the tests are run, and how you determine who belongs in which test population. If deferral ratios flunk the tests, the business can return the excess deferral (the part that flunks the test) to the bosses. Using another option—which trashes the aim of a no-*employer*-cost retirement plan—the business makes contributions for the worker population, raising their deferral ratio so the plan can pass a deferral test. If offered as matching contributions, they may stimulate still more employee deferral.

If the imbalance for bosses isn't cured, the business must pay a penalty excise tax on the bosses' "excess" deferrals.

But there's an answer, sort of, to the administrative burdens and headaches of running the tests: Make a certain level of employer contributions into the 401(k) for the workers and you can skip the bosses/workers comparison tests, so that any disproportion between bosses and workers is okay. The amount required: at least 3 percent of pay for each worker in the plan (you can contribute at the same rate, a lower rate, or zero, for bosses). If business contributions are set up to match employee deferrals, a different formula is used—more complex, naturally. You may hear this called a "safe harbor 401(k)." Here the business makes a commitment to match at a certain level. If no worker elective deferrals are made, the business has no cost for them, but the plan is still okay under "safe harbor" rules. Like other retirement plans, a 401(k) must also cover the required minimum number of employees.

401(k) and . . .

401(k)s are often the first plan adopted by a business with employees. As the business grows or the entrepreneur ages, he might seek out a richer plan, one offering greater retirement wealth, with greater invest-ment contributions. Some do this by fleshing out the profit-sharing part of the 401(k), with sizable business profit-sharing contributions for the entrepreneur (and maybe less sizable contributions for employees). Another favorite is the defined benefit plan with the 401(k).

401(k) "discretionary" contributions

These are regular contributions by the business to the profit-sharing part (as opposed to the elective deferral part) of the 401(k) plan. They are typically made as a uniform percentage of compensation, but can be arranged to further favor entrepreneurs through the devices described in this chapter for profit-sharing plans: age-based contributions; vest-ing/forfeiture; integration with Social Security; and mandatory contri-butions. Put it this way: A profit-sharing plan can have all the devices for disproportionate contributions favoring the entrepreneur, plus a 401(k) plan.

Consider a
Roth 401(k) Option

A Roth 401(k) is a regular 401(k), as in Wealth Creation Strategy 11, with an option that favors high-income individuals.

In the regular 401(k), participants make tax-free elective deferrals of pay or earnings into a tax-exempt investment account. That is, pay or earnings, currently taxable if taken in cash, go into the 401(k) account without tax. Future distributions from the tax-exempt investment account (maybe decades later) are taxable.

The Roth 401(k) is that same regular 401(k) with the additional option to have all or part of the elective deferral go into a Roth account. Amounts going into a Roth aren't tax-free; the participant owes current tax on that amount. Later investment earnings while retained in the Roth account are tax-free, as in the regular 401(k), and future distributions from the Roth are tax-exempt, if requirements are satisfied.

It's a case of tax occurring at the point of elective deferral, Roth 401(k), or tax occurring at the point of distribution, regular 401(k). To identify which distributions will be tax-free, regular and Roth 401(k) accounts must be kept separate.

A Roth 401(k) is not a separate type of plan—it's a rider, an option, on a 401(k). The business decides whether to make it available. A single dollar amount ceiling ($16,500) applies to the total 401(k) deferral. The participant decides how much, if any, of his elective deferral goes into the Roth 401(k) portion—assuming the business plan has adopted the Roth option.

WHY ENTREPRENEURS LIKE ROTH 401(K)S

The Roth principle (taxable going in, tax-exempt coming out) tends to favor the well-to-do entrepreneur or executive.

- Adding a Roth feature has no downside, except for more book-keeping. So long as employee rank-and-file participation in the 401(k) as a whole is adequate, it doesn't matter whether or not they put money in the Roth part.
- Roth 401(k)s effectively override current Roth IRA limits. As I say in Chapter 11, Roth IRAs build slowly because of dollar contribution limits on how much can be put in each year—and because of participant income limits that preclude top earners from contributing. Roth 401(k)s can grow much larger—to real wealth—because participant income limits are removed and 401(k) elective deferrals can be three times Roth IRA contributions.
- Voluntary 401(k) catch-up contributions at age fifty or over enjoy comparable advantages. The allowable contribution (ceiling amount $5,500) can go into the regular or the Roth part—taxable going in the Roth, and tax-free forever after, as with Roth elective deferrals. Allowable catch-up contributions into the Roth 401(k) are more than five times the allowable catch-up to a Roth IRA.
- Roth IRA owners can postpone IRA withdrawals as long as they please—a wealth-building advantage for retirement plan owners (see Chapter 11). Roth 401(k) owners can do the same by rolling their Roth 401(k) money into their Roth IRAs.

Employer matches of employee elective deferrals are profit-sharing contributions, tax-free to the participant, paid into the regular 401(k) fund, and taxable when withdrawn.

Money purchase pension plans

As with profit-sharing plans, business investment contributions for entrepreneurs and other participants are typically a percentage of the participant's compensation (pay or earnings). Unlike profit-sharing plans, the business is committed to making periodic investment contributions—they're an obligation of the business. With a money purchase plan, you don't target a specific retirement pension. Instead, you make periodic investment contributions and invest and reinvest what they earn. You don't know when you start out what your fund will grow to or how much "retirement" it will buy when you come to withdraw your funds.

Distributions to participants are generally postponed to retirement.

Money purchase plans can provide business contributions for entrepreneurs that are more than proportional to their pay, through the devices of: target benefit features; vesting/forfeiture; integration with Social Security; and mandatory contributions.

Simplified Employee Pensions (SEPs)

Business investment contributions for entrepreneurs and other SEP participants are a percentage of the participant's compensation (pay or earnings). They are additional compensation, but not currently taxable.

SEP contributions based on compensation favor the entrepreneur when she is the most highly paid in salary or business earnings. SEP contributions can be arranged to favor entrepreneurs still more, through the device of integration with Social Security.

Use Late Vesting to Cut Business Costs or Increase Your Share

Your plan can require participants to be in the plan for some specified minimum period before they become absolutely entitled to its benefits; that is, before the benefits become vested. If employment ends before that period is up, the participant forfeits money. This period for vesting is in addition to any waiting period before the employee is included in the plan (becomes a participant). Benefits can be made to vest a certain percentage each year.

Vested amounts are amounts participants can take with them when they leave, or collect when they reach retirement age, whether or not they work for you at that time. Amounts that are forfeited stay in the plan when the participant leaves.

Employers tend to believe that their most valued employees are those who stay with them the longest. Hence delayed vesting, which encourages employees to stay. But there's also a financial reason to postpone the time when employees' shares of the retirement fund vest. Postponement increases the possibility that departing employees will forfeit all or part of their shares. Forfeited amounts can generally be used to reduce future plan contributions. Money purchase and profit-sharing plans have the added option to share out what departing employees forfeit among those who remain, including owner participants, thereby increasing the owner's share of the total fund.

Vesting and forfeiture expectations get figured into calculations of how much pension or profit sharing the business can afford. With delayed vesting and high turnover, a plan that includes employees may

not cost much more than a plan for the owner alone. Not that you necessarily want a high turnover. An employee's departure may hurt your
business more than it helps your share of the plan. You're the best judge
of that. But if you want to keep an employee, it helps to have her in a
plan, one with delayed vesting.

Except in rare cases, you have only two options in a retirement
plan:

1. Everything must vest by the end of the participant's third year of
   service. That means that if you wish you can postpone any vesting
   to the end of that third year.
2. Vest 20 percent after two years of service and 20 percent at the end
   of each succeeding year's service, so that it's all fully vested at the end
   of six years' service.

Sometimes the first option postpones the greater dollar amount;
sometimes the second option does. It depends on your employee mix.
(The plan may adopt any faster method.)

Exactly what and how much vests depends on the type of plan you
have. In money purchase and profit-sharing plans, what vests is the
amount in the employee's account at that time—that is, the contributions and investment earnings up to that point.

Though vesting/forfeiture rules must apply to all participants, owner-
participants risk little or nothing: they'll be the last to leave.

Delayed vesting doesn't apply for employer contributions to SEPs;
for elective deferral amounts in 401(k) plans; or for amounts employees
put in out of their own pocket. Such amounts vest immediately.

ACTION POINT ✓ If your plan is a defined contribution plan, specify how forfeited money is to be allocated among the remaining participants' accounts. Allocating based on how much one has already ("To him that hath shall yet more be given") is technically legal but rarely allowed in practice. The accepted allocation that usually benefits owners the most is one based on the formula for allocating employer contributions (generally, "compensation" as defined in the plan).

Use Integration with Social Security to Cut Costs

Integration with Social Security is a complex device used to keep down business contributions for lower-paid employees. (A more formal term for integration is "permitted disparity.") The concept, much oversimplified, is this: The old age (OASDI) part of Social Security is our basic retirement system. That system contemplates paying you a pension benefit based on, though not exactly proportional to, your wages over the years. Say that for most people it's something like $1 a year of pension for every $3 of wages that you and your employer paid Social Security tax on for an average year. If you (and your employer) paid a Social Security tax on wages around $40,000, you would get a Social Security pension around $13,700.

When wages are more than the old age benefits and tax wage base ($106,800) employee and employer pay no old age Social Security tax on the excess, and you as employee get no Social Security benefits for that excess. (The principle is the same for self-employed individuals, who are both employee and employer.) It's here that the integration concept comes in. To see how it works, consider this. . . .

CASE STUDY

Walker, a dentist who owns his own business, decides he will give himself and his employees a defined benefit pension of 30 percent of pay, but he will count what Social Security provides as part of the pension. He feels entitled to count the Social Security portion since he paid toward that portion when he paid the employer's share of Social Security taxes. He will make up through his business contributions whatever is necessary to provide a retirement benefit of 30 percent of pay, counting Social Security as part of that benefit.

Consider how this might work for Walker and his two aides, Janet and Regina. Walker makes $200,000, Janet makes $50,000, and Regina makes $40,000. Social Security will pay Janet $15,900 a year, Regina $13,700 a year, and Walker $26,800 a year. But Walker's plan entitles him to a pension of $60,000—that is, 30 percent of $200,000—but including the $26,800 of Social Security. So he can put enough into his plan to buy himself an additional $33,200 pension a year.

What about Janet and Regina? Walker need not put anything in for them. He owes them a 30 percent pension counting Social Security. They've got that without any help from plan contributions, through Social Security alone.

Our explanation greatly overstates what happens. In fact, Walker would have to put in something for Janet and Regina. The rules are complex, but the potential benefits are worth exploring with a pension professional, if you have employees.

Integration can also be used in defined contribution plans, such as money purchase or profit-sharing plans.

For example: The boss is paid $230,000; her employee gets $40,000. The business's money purchase plan contributes 10 percent of pay reduced by the amount the business pays for the old age portion of Social Security (6.2 percent up to $106,800). On this principle, the business would put in $1,520 for the employee and $16,378 for the boss. But this overstates. Under current rules the boss would need to put in more for her employee—but still with substantial potential savings.

Have Employees Put In for Their Retirement

Your plan can provide for employee contributions. Mostly, these are after-tax contributions, not excludable or deductible from taxable income, though allowable catch-up contributions (see below) can be deducted or excluded. Wealth Creation Strategy 7 in Chapter 2 covers the benefits employee contributions offer employees—including you as employee. They can also save costs for the business:

Employee contributions are often part of 401(k)s, but can be attached to other plans. Or, they may stand alone, often called "thrift plans."

Employee contributions may be either mandatory (the employee must contribute if he wants to participate in the plan) or voluntary.

How Mandatory Employee Contributions Cut Costs

Mandatory contribution plans, like voluntary plans, can in theory operate on participant contributions alone. Employees ought to be attracted, some might think, by the tax-free investment growth feature (like nondeductible IRAs, though not subject to IRA contribution limits). But in reality the mandatory plan is a cost-cutting device for businesses with employees. They're used to reduce what the business would otherwise put in, not completely replace business contributions. The business puts in only for employees who put in for themselves. For example, if you have six employees but only four of them contribute on their own behalf, you don't have to contribute for the others. You may put in one business dollar per employee dollar, or two for one, or one for two, and so on.

The Good and Bad of Employee Contributions

Making an employee contribute a lot in order to be included is a way to keep down the number of employees you must make contributions for. But there are limits on your power to keep employees out of your plan through this device. Bosses tend to have more disposable income than their rank-and-file employees do. So they tend to make heavier after-tax contributions than the rank-and-file. That's okay with the tax law if the boss's contributions aren't "too disproportionate." Tests should be run periodically to check the proportion going in for the bosses as compared to the workers, the rank-and-file employees. Cutbacks for the bosses should be made if they're getting what the law considers "too much." The tests and rules, much like those for 401(k)s, are complex, and should be discussed with a pension professional.

Voluntary contribution plans are also tested under these rules for whether the bosses have too much—with limits (cutbacks of bosses' participation) when the tests are flunked. Businesses encourage participation by telling employees of the joys of tax-free investment, by making contribution easy (through payroll deduction), and sometimes by making some ratio of matching contribution—an additional business cost.

EXAMPLE

Your business could have this mandatory plan: Anyone who puts up 5 percent of salary or business earnings gets another 10 percent ($2 for $1) from the business. Then you could add a voluntary feature, which you match on a dollar-for-dollar basis, up to 3 percent of pay or earnings. Such a plan (assuming adequate employee participation) would let you as owner-employee put in a tax-deductible 13 percent of your salary or earnings for yourself, plus the nondeductible 8 percent you contribute in your capacity as employee. You would have to put in a further tax-deductible 13 percent of salary for any employee who paid in a nondeductible 8 percent of salary out of her own pocket.

For flexibility and employee incentive, the mandatory part could be a money purchase pension plan and the voluntary part a profit-sharing plan. You as employer could choose to match the employee's voluntary contribution (and yours) at a ratio based on the profits you consider employee efforts produced for the business. Here, too, there are limits to be discussed with a pension professional.

Employer matching contributions. These, like employee contributions, can't "too disproportionately" favor the bosses. Here, too, the test for what's "too disproportionate" is like that for 401(k) elective deferrals. One way employers avoid violating this test is to offer matching contributions only for lower-paid employees.

Catch-up contributions. These can be part of 401(k)s. They are deductible up to a dollar ceiling ($5,500), but are allowed only after the participant has made the maximum allowable elective deferral. They count in testing whether bosses are getting too much of the 401(k) as compared to the workers. A pension professional might suggest reducing that risk by preventing catch-up contributions from the bosses.

Different Plans for Different Folks—in the Same Business

A business can have two plans for the same employee populations. When this happens, it's almost always because one of the plans (maybe both) is funded largely by employee elective deferrals or employee contributions.

A business is also allowed to have one plan for part of the work force (say you alone, or you with other execs) and a different plan for the rest. Different plans for different classes of employees are allowed if the employer can show that the benefits are comparable among the plans (or, when one of the plans is a qualifying defined benefit plan, the allocation of contributions is comparable). These are called "new comparability" plans. Pension professionals say, and I agree, that two-plan arrangements that favor the owner can qualify, if they (the professionals) design them.

Other plans you may hear about

SIMPLE Plans. These are useful for sole owner-employees of starter or sideline businesses. They are also used for small businesses with employees, but in that context they do little for the entrepreneur's personal wealth creation.

SIMPLE 401(k)s. SIMPLE 401(k)s don't do much. I prefer "safe harbor 401(k)s," which allow greater elective deferrals.

ESOP (employee stock ownership plans). ESOPs have their advocates. Some promote ESOPs as a way to get employee participation in, and commitment to, the business. I prefer using them to build business capital (see Chapter 6) and their estate-building value as a market for the entrepreneur's stock.

Putting a floor under employee benefits

The following two general rules limit how much plan contributions or benefits can go for the bosses as compared to rank-and-file employees:

1. You can't count *all* that pay. All plans in this chapter base what entrepreneurs and other participants get, at least in part, on what they receive as pay: salary or business earnings. Other factors can count too, like age or length of service, but pay is essential.

   Rules for computing percentages of pay—such as 20 percent of compensation—are tweaked by law to limit skimping on benefits to rank-and-file employees when bosses draw very high pay. For example, suppose the boss earns $1,000,000 while his four covered employees average $30,000 each. By setting a money purchase plan contribution rate of 4.9 percent of pay, he could get the maximum deductible contribution allowed for himself—$49,000—while contributing only $5,880 for the four employees combined ($1,470) each.

   The law limits this "inequity" by limiting the amount of pay or earnings "taken into account" in figuring percentages of compensation. That limit (a ceiling of $245,000) means that with a plan rate of contribution of 4.9 percent, the boss would get a contribution of no more than $12,005—4.9 percent of $245,000, the limit of the amount taken into account—despite his actual $1,000,000 of earnings.

   This "taken into account" rule is to encourage higher contribution rates. Now, for the boss to get the full $49,000 deductible contribution allowed, a 20 percent rate is needed. This will give the employees a total $24,000 ($6,000 each).

   The same principle applies with defined benefit plans. Here, benefits are typically based on earnings during the period when earnings are highest. But only earnings up to the "taken into account" ceiling are considered.

   Remember, though, the other factors that can reduce what the business needs to put in for covered employees: age, length of service, vesting, Social Security integration, 401(k) features, employee contributions.

2. Where you have a top-heavy plan. A plan is "top heavy" if more than 60 percent of plan assets (or accrued benefits, if it's a defined benefit plan) are held for "key employees." Key employees are owner-employees, their employee family members, and other execs, if any.

   A top-heavy plan must have certain features to stay qualified. It must provide for faster vesting than under the usual rules in Wealth Creation Strategy 13 and provide minimum contributions or benefits for "non-key" employees for that year. (401(k) safe harbor plans, under Wealth Creation Strategy 11, are exempt from top-heavy rules.)

   Top-heaviness is checked each year, and minimum contributions or benefits generally are required only for years the plan is top heavy. Top-heaviness isn't considered a big problem today.

PLAN DUTIES WHEN YOU HAVE EMPLOYEES

You may face extra plan costs when you have employees. And you will have further duties.

With a defined benefit plan, you as business owner make yourself responsible for the plan's investment success. You can hand off investment decisions to outside experts. But if plan assets fail to meet the pension commitment you have made to employees, you (meaning your business) must make up the shortfall.

Mostly, this makeup is done through additional pension plan contributions. The plan may also need plan termination insurance to protect employees against loss of their vested benefits because the business fails to put in enough funds. Insurance is provided by a government agency, the Pension Benefit Guarantee Corporation. The business pays the premiums, which are deductible.

> **ACTION POINT** ✓
> Some employers reduce their exposure to liability by letting employees choose from a range of investment options. They may even offer employees more or less complete freedom of choice through "self-directed" programs. Programs offering employee choice are more complicated to administer.

As plan administrator, you have reporting duties to the IRS, the U.S. Department of Labor, and the employees themselves. Also, the plan operation will usually need grievance and review procedures so employees will feel they are being fairly treated.

In defined benefit plans, investment risk is on the business owner. Some employees, especially older employees, like it that way.

In money purchase and profit-sharing plans, including 401(k)s, the employee bears the investment risk. Sometimes the plan trustee—which could be you—directs how money in each employee's account is invested. Trustees aren't answerable for unsuccessful investments but can be penalized for imprudent investment. Depending on circumstances, the trustee's exposure for imprudent investment can be reduced by using an outside investment advisor—who thereby becomes answerable for imprudent investments.

Strategy Review

This chapter described features your plan can adopt that:

1. Exclude certain employee categories in all cases, and other employee categories depending on circumstances.
2. Allow "disproportionately" higher amounts for entrepreneurs that reward their longer service or their age.
3. Postpone when employees own (vest in) contributions from the business, so that amounts departing employees forfeit go to reduce business costs or increase the entrepreneur's share.
4. "Integrate" plan benefits—reducing what the business commits to provide by counting what Social Security costs or promises.
5. Use 401(k) elective deferrals to sometimes fully shift to employees the cost of providing their own retirement funds; more often, deferrals are used to share costs between business and employee.
6. Add a Roth 401(k) option to a regular 401(k) plan. This lets high-income entrepreneurs choose Roth treatment if they wish.
7. Mandate that employees put in money of their own to get business contributions. This tends first to reduce workforce participation and second to share plan costs between the business and those who participate. Consider this feature for a selected, informed workforce.

Complete Family Health Protection, Forever

WEALTH CREATION STRATEGIES 16–22

NOTE TO THE READER

Health care for the small business owner will be revolutionized—in a few years. The health care reform that's being considered by Congress as this book goes to press is scheduled to become effective mostly in 2013. You'll want to be ready for that. But the Wealth Creation Strategies in this chapter will generally continue to be valid at least until then.

For a summary of the new health care system when enacted, please see my website: *http://nyretirementplanadvisor.com/WealthCreation.*

—J.E.C.

Adequate but affordable health coverage is essential to personal and family well-being. Sure, some businesses provide that already. But well-crafted business health programs can go beyond that to become instruments of true family wealth protection and enhancement. You can achieve this through, for example, disability, post-retirement and long-term care coverage, and through health savings accounts.

Where should we begin? By designing for complete health care coverage, for you and your family? Or by planning for the lowest cost coverage likely to meet your needs?

If you thought I was asking you to choose, you guessed wrong. I'm going to come close to providing both. How's this for a start: If the health care you wish for will be costly—as it all seems to be—why not get someone to share the cost? Who could you get to do that? Well, everyone—that is, all taxpayers.

Your fellow taxpayers share the most when all your health care comes through a business plan.

It's not news to you that you can take a limited personal tax deduction for health care expenses—to the extent that those expenses exceed 7.5 percent of your adjusted gross income. So the larger your income, the less likely you will be allowed a personal deduction—except, that is, for catastrophic expenses, which you would be better off covering with insurance.

Have Your Business Buy
All Your Health Care

The aim is to shift your medical expenses to your business. Properly arranged, your business's outlays for your and your family's health care are business deductions—reducing to that extent the business profits you must pay tax on. And the health insurance dollars you and your family receive as individuals—or the value of health care coverage or care you receive in kind—are tax-free to you. Also, if your business is incorporated, both you and your business avoid Social Security taxes on your health care costs. Each of you owes Social Security tax on your wages, but business payments for your health care aren't wages.

CASE STUDY

Fred expects that his corporation will earn $95,000 this year, and he expects to spend $15,000 on family health insurance. See how he comes out buying the insurance personally, and buying it through the corporation:

Personally

Fred's salary ($95,000 less Social Security tax).........	$88,249
Corporation's Social Security tax on Fred's salary.......	$6,781
Fred's Social Security tax...........................	$6,781
Fred's health insurance payment....................	$15,000
Fred's personal deduction for the insurance...........	$8,381*
Fred's income tax.................................	$12,342*
Left after health insurance and all taxes..............	$54,006

Through Corporation

Corporation's insurance payment $15,000

Fred's salary $74,315

Corporation's Social Security tax on Fred's salary $5,685

Fred's Social Security tax $5,685

Fred's income tax . . . .$10,954★

Left after health insurance and all taxes $57,676

Corporation payment saves Social Security tax for both and income tax for Fred. Savings here total $3,670, effectively cutting the health insurance cost 24 percent ($3,670 of $15,000).

★*This technically depends on a variety of income and deduction items. This calculation considers only the facts stated in this example.*

ACTION POINT ✓

You'll need a health care **Plan** for **Employees**. Not that this is hard or complicated. *A plan* is a commitment to do something specific for persons covered by the plan: provide insurance for sickness or injury, or arrange for delivery of medical care, or reimbursement for medical expenses—or all or a mix of these. Decide, and put it in writing with your business records before expenses are incurred.

The plan must be for employees. You can be included as an employee if your business is incorporated. It doesn't have to be for all employees (more about that later) and there can be different plans for different employees. Make sure all employees covered know about their coverage. You can be the only employee covered. But don't make it just for owner-employees when there are other employees, not covered, who meet any coverage conditions you set.

Your plan should say generally what benefits you want to offer and who (what category of employee, if not all employees) should get what benefits.

You don't need a plan for employees if you're the only one in an unincorporated business, nor is it necessary in such a case to get the insurance in a business name.

Covering Your Family

The business can cover health care costs of an employee and the employee's family—spouse and dependents. If your business isn't incorporated, you're an owner or co-owner but not an employee; the business can cover your health care as a self-employed person, plus that of your spouse and dependents.

Employ Your Spouse in Your Unincorporated Business

You owe self-employment tax on what you pay for your health insurance, in an unincorporated business. But you avoid that tax if you employ your spouse and your spouse gets family health coverage as employee. Here's an oversimplified example:

> ### EXAMPLE
>
> Ellen's business earnings are $90,000 before $14,000 of family health insurance to be covered by the business. She hires her husband, Ed, part-time, who takes his $14,000 pay entirely as family health care coverage.

Ellen escapes income tax on the $14,000 whether she or Ed buys the coverage. But she escapes self-employed tax too, where *Ed* obtains the coverage, which saves 15.3 percent of $14,000, or $2,142.

Group Health Insurance

Insurance is supposed to spread the risk of loss over a pool of individual participants. If you're healthy and the insurer knows that, its risk is less and it can reduce your premiums accordingly. But if you're the only one in the risk pool, the risk isn't spread and the insurer generally charges more, even for someone healthy. To minimize your insurance costs, for most care you should be in a group.

ACTION POINT ✓

Make sure the spouse is hired the right way. Your spouse must be a genuine employee, meaning he or she should have real work to do, with something in writing to show that you as owner or co-owner know the work is being done.

You don't have to pay cash wages. It's okay for this purpose if the spouse's "pay" is no more than the health care coverage. But the services, whatever they are, should be worth what the business pays for the health care. And observe the formalities: Do an employment contract that states the spouse's duties and expected weekly or monthly hours of work. It will help if your health plan is a Flexible Spending Account with a salary reduction agreement allocating the spouse's pay to the account.

Which group? If your business has employees, the business may be the group. You can be in the group even if you, a self-employed person, aren't an employee. But even here, maybe your business should be part of a larger group, especially if it has only a few employees.

Insurers will always be interested in your group's size, industry, geographic location, and the ages of its members. The smaller the group, the higher the insurer's risk. With five or fewer members, insurers may want to review the health of those to be covered, using that information in setting premium costs. Professional employer organizations (PEOs) arrange lower premium costs than might otherwise apply by combining small employer groups into one buying unit.

All states have programs designed to make health insurance available to small business (defined as fifty or fewer employees). And for groups of two to fifty, federal law won't let insurers deny insurance based on members' current health or previous health claims.

That's the good news. But states also make insurers cover certain specified health conditions. This means insurers must cover things you'd rather not pay for, and insurers will pass on to you in the premium the costs of such coverage. A few states regulate how much insurers may charge small business.

Most states, though not all, allow premium costs to take some account of the age and health of the covered pool—so you can pay less if your group is healthy. Most states don't allow group rates for a group of one, even for a corporation; a few states do. State and federal laws assuring that small businesses have access to insurance also tend to require insurers to renew policies once granted (though with no guarantee against higher premiums on renewals).

Insurers offer different plans for different markets. Coverage you get through your professional or trade association may be "better" (broader coverage, lower premium, lower deductible) than what you would get from the same insurer in its "small business" offering.

In some states, health purchasing alliances help small businesses get health insurance. State plans may offer health care cheaper than PEOs.

Cost Savings When You Have Employees

I can't tell you what health benefits your work force should get, or what you should pay for, or toward, these costs. Nor do I assume that your business won't suffer if you deny benefits or cut them back. You know best about that.

What I *can* do is show you where and how to save on costs for employees—should you want to do that—while providing full coverage for yourself, at costs the government shares or subsidizes through business tax deduction. These will be your tools:

- Using insured plans
- Excluding some employees from coverage
- Using a Health Savings Account
- Sharing costs with employees through a cafeteria plan

Save Costs by Excluding Employees

Your business plan "for employees" need not include all, or even most, employees. You can generally exclude employees with less than three years' service, employees under age twenty-five, union employees (usually), part-time employees, and seasonal employees. You can exclude others if there's a rational basis for it. For example, depending on circumstances, you might be able to exclude some based on their duties or work location. Of course, you shouldn't exclude employees for failing to meet tests you yourself don't meet.

How about providing greater benefits for key employees or owner-employees? This can be okay, justified by their greater responsibilities. And it's clearly okay when your non-management work force has health care benefits under a union contract (collective bargaining agreement). You and other management employees can have a much more generous plan. This could be a reason to initiate collective bargaining agreements with employees.

Large corporations commonly, and legally, deny health benefits to categories of employees. If employee coverage will be a major cost factor for you, consider getting advice from a tax or employment law professional.

Health insurance for bosses only

It's okay with federal tax law and most state insurance laws to have an insured plan for bosses only. Premiums the business pays reduce business taxes. Insurance payouts to reimburse the boss's medical expenses aren't taxed. And, if the business is incorporated, neither business nor boss owes Social Security tax on the premiums.

Cost of coverage may be high, though—a higher cost per person covered than if a group, such as the whole work force, is covered. Depending on the situation, the economics of insurance costs may push you toward group coverage—or a Health Savings Account.

For *long-term care coverage*, a boss's-only plan may be an especially good choice. Such coverage will be priced for you individually based on your age and health. If you're in good health, your individual rate will be lower than a group rate.

Use Cafeteria Plan
to Cut Costs

Under a cafeteria plan, employees are offered a chance to take part of their pay in tax-free benefits. The employer decides how much of one's pay goes in the cafeteria plan. The employee can choose to allocate that portion to one or more of the tax-free benefits, or take some or all of it in (taxable) cash. You can see where this is going: Health benefits the employee gets through the cafeteria plan are paid for by the employee, out of salary. This truth comes home to cafeteria plan participants when they are asked to sign a "salary reduction agreement" authorizing a designated part of salary to be paid for the chosen benefit.

Tax-free treatment means the employee is sharing his health care cost with other taxpayers.

CASE STUDY

Employee Janet, a single mother, gets paid $60,000 a year. But her employer says 10 percent of that can be allocated to the company cafeteria plan. The plan offers a choice of benefits—say, high-deductible medical insurance, dental insurance, and child care services, up to 10 percent of pay ($6,000 in Janet's case)—or employees can take in cash any portion not allocated to benefits. Janet allocates $6,000 to high-deductible insurance and dental insurance, which is about how she would have spent that $6,000 if received in cash.

> Disregarding other possible income and deduction items, Janet's cafeteria plan saved her $1,125 (at head-of-household rates), cutting the effective cost of the high-deductible and dental insurance from $6,000 to $4,875.
>
> Janet now has health care at no extra cost to the employer, apart from administrative costs to set up and run the cafeteria plan.

Okay, now let's reduce or eliminate even that employer cost.

Wages you pay in cash are subject to Social Security tax on you and your employees. Wages diverted to tax-free health benefits (or other tax-free benefits) escape Social Security tax.

This will be welcome news for your employees, should you introduce such a plan; for Janet, it's worth a further $459 of Social Security tax, on top of the $1,125 income tax saving, cutting her true cost further.

But it's also a saving for you. In fact, you may encounter advisors or promoters who encourage your business to install a cafeteria plan just so you can get this addition to your wealth.

For example, if you have five Janets on your payroll making around $60,000 each, a 10 percent cafeteria plan, used fully for health or other tax-free benefits, saves each employee $459 and you a total $2,295. And such a saving would go to help defray the administrative costs of a cafeteria plan.

You can automatically enroll your employees in your cafeteria plan—when the plan begins, when they are hired, or after some trial period. Employees must have the right to refuse to participate and to opt out later even if they go along at first. But unless they refuse, or until they opt out, you've saved Social Security tax on the cafeteria amount.

How *You* Fit in a Cafeteria Plan

You can't fit at all, if your business is unincorporated or an S corporation. You may, of course, still want, and profit from, a cafeteria plan for your employees that cuts payroll costs, as shown above.

If your business is a C corporation, you face two sets of rules—on health care and on cafeteria plans—and several options.

First, your business must meet the health care rules outlined in Wealth Creation Strategy 18, before it can share your health care costs with other taxpayers. But the cafeteria plan makes that easier to do. Since employees who take cafeteria plan tax-free benefits reduce your payroll tax costs, you have no motive to exclude employees. On the other hand, cafeteria plan rules can punish your "over participation" in cafeteria plan benefits.

For example, suppose your cafeteria plan allocates 10 percent of pay to the plan and you're paid $240,000. You could allocate, say, $16,000 to medical care and $8,000 to child care, four times Janet's $6,000 health care allocation. Like hers, your allocation is tax-free (you pay tax on $216,000). But you can lose the tax exemption if your share of cafeteria plan benefits is more than 25 percent of the total cafeteria plan benefits for you and all your employees. For a way around this over participation obstacle, see "Cafeteria Plan—One Part of Your Program" shortly.

C corporations are taxable corporations. S corporations generally aren't subject to federal income tax; their income and deductions pass through to be taxed directly to stockholders. In the health care context, S corporation stockholders usually can't get tax benefits designed for employees, and are bound by rules governing unincorporated owners.

"Use it or lose it!"

In the health care context this cry comes from cafeteria plan participants as the year ends. They have allocated a certain part of this year's pay to health care (allocation is made before the year begins and usually can't be changed). What's still unused for health care at year's end is forfeited.

It's not your problem. You as entrepreneur aren't in the cafeteria plan anyway, unless your business is a C corporation. In any case, funds "lost" by cafeteria plan participants are forfeited to the business—*your* business. You could allow participants a limited carryover of unused balances, or could otherwise spend the total of unused balances for participant medical care in some equitable manner. But you're not obliged to; you could just take it all back. Your relationship with your employees can determine what you do.

Cafeteria plan—one part of your program

A cafeteria plan can bring health benefits to all or much of your work force, including you as a C corporation employee. But cafeteria plan benefits are often just part of a larger program, which can be designed specifically for you. Thus, you could have a cafeteria plan that allocates up to 5 percent of pay to the employee's choice of health care expense (or cash). You as owner can have the business buy high-deductible insurance and long-term care insurance for you alone, outside the plan, and you could use your 5 percent of pay in the cafeteria plan to pay health care expenses up to the deductible. The company's overall plan is company-paid insurance (for you only) and cafeteria plan-paid health care at each employee's choice, which at your choice is reimbursement of outlays not covered by your insurance.

Consider what this program delivers:

- The 5 percent of pay your employees spend on health care comes at no extra cost to you (apart from the cost of running the cafeteria plan), and reduces business Social Security tax,
- Your high-deductible insurance and long-term care insurance are deductible by the business at no income or Social Security cost to you, and
- The 5 percent of your own pay that goes for your medical expenses (up to the deductible) also reduces business income tax at no income tax to you and reduces your own, and business, Social Security tax.

Cafeteria Plans, Flexible Spending, and Health Reimbursement Arrangements

Cafeteria plans and flexible spending plans, terms often used interchangeably, are technically different. A cafeteria plan is a choice among tax-free and taxable benefits; one or more of each must be offered. In the health care context, a cafeteria plan can offer health insurance or medical expense reimbursement, or both.

A flexible spending account, on the other hand, can reimburse medical expenses but can't pay or reimburse health or long-term care insurance premiums or long-term care costs. It can be a choice only among tax-free benefits, or can be a tax-free component of a cafeteria plan.

A plan offering only nontaxable benefits is an extra cost to the employer, something layered on top of existing payroll. (Cafeteria plans can be an extra cost, too—for example, where they offer matching contributions.)

Health reimbursement arrangements, as the name tells you, are usually used to reimburse out-of-pocket medical expenses not covered by insurance. It's a company expense on top of, not instead of, cash pay. Install one if you want a generous plan for employees. Health reimbursement accounts need pose no "use it or lose" risk for employees. It's okay to let them carry over unused health reimbursement account balances for future medical expenses.

Health Savings Accounts

If you're well off and rarely sick, have financial planners got a health plan for you! It's the health savings account, the HSA, up to 100 percent of the deductible.

Well, business planners like HSAs, too. HSAs make a good fit for employers who want tax-favored health care benefits for themselves in a program that avoids the cost of covering their employees. With an HSA, you invest dollars in an account roughly like a deductible IRA. Your HSA investment deduction effectively reduces your taxable business profits by reducing income generally, including those profits. You can have an HSA personally, without making it a business plan. But you can also make it part of a business plan, for more benefits.

What's good about HSAs?

High-deductible insurance—usually essential to qualify for an HSA— *can* save on overall health care costs. A shift from high-premium/ low deductible—where you may be now—to low-premium/high deductible may in itself save money (lower total of premiums and expenses) for those who are healthy. Of course, this saving is available with or without an HSA.

Health care expenses, otherwise nondeductible (except to the extent they exceed 7.5 percent of income), become fully tax-deductible when paid with HSA funds.

Tax sheltered. HSA funds that aren't withdrawn are a tax-sheltered retirement fund.

Here's an example of HSA success, worked up by an HSA proponent:

> **EXAMPLE**
>
> Assume a three-member family with a $500 per person deduct-ible health insurance policy, costing $650 per month. The family has $1,200 of total family medical expenses that are not covered by health insurance. The traditional health insurance policy has a $1,500 maximum out-of-pocket risk (the $500 deductibles of each of three persons). The family then switches to an HSA-qualified insurance plan with a $5,000 family deductible, costing $325 per month. The family puts the premium savings into a HSA account. The result is a net saving of more than $2,000 for the year.

But even HSA proponents recognize that some people won't ben-efit from switching to HSAs: Those with low insurance premiums and low deductibles, especially when insurance is paid or subsidized by an employer.

HSAs are a tax shelter, and a unique one. There's a tax deduction for amounts you invest in the account, plus tax-free buildup for invested funds, and then maybe tax-free treatment for withdrawals, depending on how you spend them. That means tax breaks at every stage: contri-bution, investment earnings, and withdrawal. Nothing else quite offers that. To qualify for an HSA, you must not be enrolled in Medicare and you must have a high-deductible health insurance plan. You can have this through your work, as employee or self-employed—but you can have it individually, whether or not you work. It's high deductible if the deductible for self-only coverage is $1,150 or more, or $2,300 or more for family coverage. You may want a *higher* deductible, to maximize your tax shelter.

Why *high* deductible? Proponents say high deductible is an incentive to keep medical expenses low, and not "overuse" medical care, since your expenses up to the deductible are on you. High deductibles push total medical expenses down, or so the theory goes. (There are limits on what *other* health-related insurance or other coverage you can have and still be eligible for HSA, and on your use of HSA funds to pay health insurance premiums.)

Once your high deductible is in place, you can put investment funds in the HSA. With family coverage, the investment limit is $5,950. The dollar limit increases each year with inflation. With single coverage it's $3,000. The ceilings increase for those fifty-five or over (or whose spouses are covered and age fifty-five or over), by $1,000. Your contributions go into a trust, are invested, and investment earnings are tax-free until withdrawn. *You* control the investments and can pick any investments you please, except collectibles and life insurance.

Amounts you withdraw for medical bills are tax-free, up to the amount of the bills. The HSA in effect gives you a 100 percent deduction for medical bills paid from your (deductible) HSA contributions.

If you don't withdraw, your money continues to build, tax-free. If you withdraw more than that year's medical bills, you owe tax and may be subject to a tax penalty. The penalty—10 percent of the ordinary income amount—doesn't apply for withdrawals in the case of disability, death, or after reaching Medicare eligibility (age sixty-five). No further HSA contribution is allowed if you enroll in Medicare, but the HSA can continue to grow through investment earnings, reduced by any withdrawals you make.

The less you spend on medical bills during the year, the more you'll have at year-end in your HSA.

Fund Health Savings Account Through Your Business

There are two situations in which a Health Savings Account through the business can grow your wealth:

- If you're incorporated
- If you're already providing health care to employees

HSA if You're Incorporated

Acting on the aim to shift as much medical cost as possible to the business, here's what to do:

1. Have the business pay your high-deductible premiums. The business deducts the cost and employees owe no tax on it, assuming the insurance is part of a plan for employees. In a corporation, you qualify as an employee.
2. Have the business put the maximum allowed into your HSA ($5,950), if it's a family high-deductible policy; $6,950 if you're age fifty-five or over.

"So with premiums and HSA contributions that's around $10,000 of business profits going tax-free to benefit me and my family," you might say. "So far, so good. But I'll still have some out-of-pocket medical bills, up to the deductible. Can the business pay these, too?"

No, but it's okay for the business to cover:

- Expenses of a specific illness, or a fixed daily amount of hospitalization, if done through insurance
- Expenses of accidents, disability, dental care, vision care, preventive care, or long-term care—any or all of these, through insurance or direct reimbursement

Other expense items you can pay through tax-free withdrawal from your HSA. All benefits just described come free of Social Security tax as well as income tax, if you, or you and your family, are the only ones in your business. It's more complicated if you have employees. It's okay to exclude some employees from your plan. But some things you get aren't tax-exempt if your plan benefits you unduly as compared to "eligible" (that is, not otherwise excluded) rank-and-file employees. Here's how that works for HSAs:

- High-deductible premiums. It's okay if rank-and-file employees get no coverage, or less coverage than you.
- HSA contributions. If the business puts in for you, eligible employees must get comparable amounts. "Comparable" means the same amount, or the same percentage of the deductible, for the same type of coverage (family or single).
- Other company-paid medical expenses. For insurance premiums, it's okay to exclude rank-and-file employees or cover them for less. For other expenses, eligible employees should qualify for the same benefits as you, or for benefits subject to the same conditions as apply to you.

Stockholder-employees of S corporations get the same results as those in taxable corporations for company-paid insurance premiums and HSA contributions. Though these items are taxable income, S corporation stockholders get offsetting deductions, and no self-employment tax or Social Security tax is due from stockholder or corporation.

But company-paid medical expense *reimbursements* are taxable income (and subject to Social Security tax); the stockholder employee generally gets no medical deduction (except where expenses exceed the 7.5 percent deduction floor).

If You Now Provide Health Care to Employees, Switch to HSA

HSAs are about reducing health care costs, including costs you may incur as employer. Your business can reduce its costs if it switches to an HSA-based plan. In the right setting, you will no longer decide what or how much health care your employees get, and need no longer monitor or police their health care claims.

ACTION POINT ✓ Encourage employees to set up their own HSAs, with (high-deductible) insurance that protects them against heavy or catastrophic expense. Depending on the plan you currently offer and other factors, such as employees' health, this can be a win-win for both you and your employees.

CASE STUDY

Sam pays premiums averaging $750 per month per employee for family health care, with a relatively low per-person deductible. A high-deductible plan would cost $400 monthly per employee for family coverage.

Switching to the high-deductible plan effectively reduces employee pay. Employees can be expected to complain, or worse. Sam can overcome such objections by integrating HSAs into the switch. He urges employees to set up HSAs for themselves and offers HSA contributions of $200 a month (the encouragement I mentioned above) to every employee who does so. Sam can deduct these contributions, which are tax-free, to employees with HSAs, and employees can deduct their own HSA contribution/investments (up to the deductible limit minus Sam's contribution).

Each employee thereby can have a mini-tax shelter and medical expense reimbursement fund. Assuming every employee with family care goes along, Sam's business has cut costs by $150 per employee per month.

Some individuals won't benefit from switching to high-deductibles and HSAs. What works for your business will depend on your work force. But it's perfectly legal to offer HSAs and high-deductibles as a health care option that employees can choose as an alternative to your current plan.

Protect Earnings with a Disability Plan

Disability insurance isn't specifically for health care. It's to replace income lost because of long-term disability. Your disability generally means that your individual business activity stops. You can, of course, continue as business owner, but what in your business goes on if you're out of action?

The cost of disability insurance, to you or your business, depends on these factors:

- Your age and state of health—cost is higher if older or unhealthy
- How much the insurance is to pay on disability—cost is higher to replace higher income
- What "disability" means under your policy: unable to do *this* job or unable to do *any* job? Social Security subsidizes part of the benefit where you're unable to do *any* job.

Your business can share the cost of your disability insurance—meaning it's tax-deductible by the business, if it's a C corporation. The insurance can be for you alone, if you wish; you need not cover other employees. All the same, be sure it's written as a plan for employees that defines who is (or isn't) covered.

The law says that if the business deducts the insurance premiums, the disabled recipient must pay taxes on the insurance distributions. You can see this as a choice between relief now and burden later, or the reverse. Relief now means the business pays, reducing its taxable profit, at no out-of-pocket cost or tax cost to you. Burden later means you pay tax (if you become disabled) on disability insurance distributions received.

The alternative to this is burden now. *You* pay the premium out of pocket, after tax (disability insurance is not a deductible medical expense), but insurance distributions received are tax-free.

Consider a Disability Plan to Protect the Business

We've just considered disability insurance to replace your individual earnings. You might instead, or in addition, want insurance designed to keep the business going. Here your business entity is the beneficiary. It collects insurance proceeds if you become disabled, and uses them to pay whoever replaces you, or to buy out your interest. This is a form of keyman—okay, key*person*—insurance, and is expensive. The business can't deduct the premiums, but distributions are tax-free. An alternative is to make your chosen successor the insurance beneficiary. "Overhead expense disability insurance" reimburses the periodic costs of running your business—rents, utilities, employees' salaries, and the like—while you're disabled. This type of insurance contemplates relatively short-term disability, and does not cover lost profits or your salary.

ACTION POINT

My philosophy, here and elsewhere, is: get relief now. Set the disability payout level high enough to keep you comfortably, after taxes, should disability happen, and have the business pay the premium.

You can have your business pay premiums for your employees. Or, your plan can let employees buy disability insurance at their expense, with no cost to your business. This can even be done through a cafeteria plan—which will save Social Security taxes for them and for your business, on salary diverted to pay disability premiums. Disability insurance proceeds obtained through a cafeteria plan are treated as paid by the business, and so are taxable to employee recipients.

If your business is unincorporated or an S corporation, you can't deduct disability premiums; they don't qualify as health insurance. In this case, the *law* makes the choice: burden now and relief later.

Consider Business-Funded Long-Term Care Insurance

Consider it as *wealth protection*, that is. It wasn't so long ago that the government resisted including long-term care in tax-favored health plans. After all, the argument went, help in "activities of daily living," like eating, bathing, dressing, and so on, were custodial, not medical, care.

Pressure from an aging population, and its children, changed that position. Now, business-paid premiums for "qualified long-term care insurance" can be deducted from taxable business profits, as health insurance premiums are. Long-term care insurance payouts typically are a specified amount per day (say, $160), reflecting that they are for daily living rather than medical treatment, and for a specified period (say, three years). Payments are generally tax-free to the recipient up to $280 a day. Most states offer further tax relief.

As insurance bought through the business, it can be just for you, or you and co-owners, without the need to cover rank-and-file employees. For small business, likely long-term care plans would be (a) individual (owner only), or (b) individual plans with a group discount (which might cover owners, co-owners, and selected managers), or (c) group plans for a larger employee population, where the insurer asks questions about individual and family health, to screen out high risks. People in good health get better deals in individual than ingroup plans. Cafeteria plans could offer group long-term care as an option, at minimal cost to the employer.

Long-term care, often approached as a plan to ease the frailties of age, may also be needed in youth or middle life, because of a disabling illness or injury. It's an extremely complicated insurance product, with many different benefit options. Choice is made more difficult still because one is deciding today about services maybe to be delivered decades hence.

A generous plan would cover 120 percent of the daily cost of nursing home care in your area; would cover 100 percent of home care (reflecting that home care can be more costly than nursing home care); would be a commitment for the insured's life, with zero "elimination" (that is, payable from the first day care is needed); and would have automatic inflation protection compounded at 5 percent. All this is costly.

Is long-term care coverage for you?

Many weigh the value of long-term care coverage against its cost and the likelihood of needing it, and say no. But you may give a different answer if you can reduce its effective cost by having your business pay for it.

The usual long-term care promotion goes like this:

"Suppose some day you'll need to go into a nursing home. Think what it will cost you each year in any place decent. [The promoter here obligingly suggests a six-figure, or high five-figure, dollar amount.] And think what such a sum each year would do to your assets. So why not cover that cost, or most of it, through long-term care insurance? Remember, the younger you buy it, the less it costs."

I'm not really trying to refute this argument. Sure, it can be less per year but more over all because you're carrying it many more years. (Premiums can increase over time for an insurer's policyholders, based on claims made against that insurer.) On the other hand, even in your younger years you're covered for long-term care needs that might arise from a disability or illness.

So does long-term care insurance pay off? There's no definitive answer. But the effective cost-sharing through the business will encourage some otherwise undecided owners to get long-term care coverage.

Health Care for Life

We've done pretty well up to now in getting your business to cover your health care and that of your family—your spouse and dependents. Now for a bigger challenge: Health care when you're no longer working in your business. Maybe the business goes on, but it's no longer yours—that's one kind of challenge. Or maybe there's no business at all—a different problem.

Getting health care for you is the paramount concern, but we wealth-builders also want arrangements by which other taxpayers share the full cost of quality care you and your family receive.

WEALTH CREATION STRATEGY 21

Get a Lifetime Care Contract from Your Business

A C corporation owner can be fully covered under the corporation's health plan as a retired employee. But where someone else will be running the business, you'll want a guarantee that health coverage will continue for your lifetime.

Make a contractual severance agreement with your corporation when you retire (or earlier) that will include a binding promise of family health care for your lifetime. Normally such agreements promise continuation of the coverage you had while working. But it can be specifically tailored to what you want.

Your contract should guarantee the prescribed benefit whether the corporation changes its health plan for continuing employees, changes ownership, or liquidates. Put this matter in the hands of your lawyer.

The cost of this health care passes from you to your business successors (though the anticipated cost may reduce what you can get from selling your interest, or the share of profits you will receive after you retire). The ongoing corporation would be allowed tax deductions for the cost of care provided retired employees. (Tax deduction for retiree care would not necessarily be allowed a successor company buying your corporation.) You as a retired employee get the same tax-exemption on coverage that you got while working.

Retired entrepreneurs will be subject to tax on benefits they receive under uninsured plans that favor them disproportionately. Many really want the coverage and won't object to the taxation: Tax on one's health care costs less than paying for the care.

Health *insurance* can disproportionately favor the entrepreneur without tax problems. But the insurance company may balk. Some companies won't insure unless substantially all retirees are covered and the corporation pays a large part of the premiums.

Companies often set up health reimbursement accounts just for retirees to reimburse out-of-pocket expenses not covered by Medicare or other insurance. Note that arrangements that unduly favor retired key employees over other retired employees can bar tax-exemption for the favored few.

For owners of unincorporated businesses or S corporations

The ongoing business may be a partnership, an LLC, or an S corporation, in which you may or may not have a continuing ownership interest. Or it may be a single owner LLC or sole proprietorship owned by someone else.

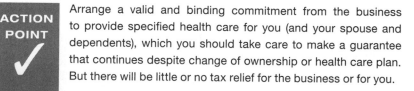

ACTION POINT ✓

Arrange a valid and binding commitment from the business to provide specified health care for you (and your spouse and dependents), which you should take care to make a guarantee that continues despite change of ownership or health care plan. But there will be little or no tax relief for the business or for you.

The business gets no deduction. You're not working for it and you're not a retired employee (even in an S corporation). The cost of your health care will usually be considered a nondeductible capital expenditure—part of the cost of acquiring part or all of your interest in the business—or a nondeductible distribution of profits.

And, as for you, even if you're still a co-owner, you can't deduct the full value of any health insurance the business provides. You no longer have earnings from self-employment against which to take such a deduction. And health care or reimbursement the business provides is taxable. The best the tax law can offer is a deduction for whatever expenses exceed 7.5 percent of your adjusted gross income.

Coverage via an Employee Spouse

If you got coverage through an employee spouse who is still employed, your coverage could continue that way. If he or she retires, such coverage could continue through him or her as a retired employee, deductible by the business and exempt to him or her, under the conditions above. Here too, you'd want a contract guaranteeing his or her coverage. (It's also important that he or she continues to be your spouse.)

Really Want to Use Your HSA for Health Care?

HSA promoters say the HSA is designed to serve you well in retirement. If you're in Medicare, you can't put new money into the HSA. But promoters expect that your previous unused contributions, plus tax-deferred investment earnings thereon, will yield a healthy sum for coping with health needs in retirement. If you're in Medicare, you can withdraw money tax-free to pay Medicare health and drug insurance (though Medigap insurance payments aren't tax-free), and pay expenses not covered by insurance.

But wait.

We didn't offer all this advice, for your business or former business to cover your retirement health care, to then watch you dip into your personal HSA wealth, if this can be avoided.

ACTION POINT ✓ Go forward with any available arrangement to have a business pay your health care in retirement. The arrangement can pay Medicare insurance, and any other insurance including Medigap, and medical expenses not covered by insurance. HSAs are available for retirement health care if you're unable to make such an arrangement.

You can treat you HSA more or less like an IRA, except (unlike IRAs) there's no duty to take periodic withdrawals after age seventy-and-a-half. You can draw on the HSA as needed in retirement. There's no tax penalty on withdrawals after age sixty-five, but withdrawals are taxable except to the extent used for health care. Amounts not withdrawn continue to grow tax-free.

The HSA tax shelter continues for your spouse at your death, if he or he is your designated HSA beneficiary. Otherwise, HSA status ends at your death and your beneficiary takes the balance as taxable income.

Unlike some retiree programs considered in this section, employers can't keep employees from tapping HSA accounts *before* retirement. And the HSA rules and benefits apply whether you're retired or still working.

Have Your Pension Fund Pay for Retirement Health Care

Part of your business pension plan can be put aside to pay for your health care in retirement, and that of your spouse and dependents (who of course need not themselves be retired). If you have eligible employees, the same benefit must normally extend to *their* health care in retirement, and care of their spouses and dependents. This is for pension plans only—it's not fully available for profit-sharing plans and not available at all for the other retirement plans covered in chapters 2 and 3.

Pension plans must be primarily for retirement benefits, but it's okay to add a health care plan that's "incidental" to retirement. This rule allows up to 25 percent of what a business puts into the plan to go for retiree health. As a generalization, the richer you make your retirement plan, the richer you can make the health care part. However, business contributions must be reasonable for the benefits provided.

The health part of a pension plan is for retirees only; your pension plan can't reimburse even incidental *pre-retirement* health insurance or expenses. As with the retirement plan part, the health plan can't unduly favor you over rank-and-file employees. The health part must be a health plan for employees (which in this case can include self-employed persons covered by the retirement part). It must be clear what benefits are provided, with a rule for determining how much will be paid. Thus it might say that it pays for medical expenses below a defined Medicare deductible.

Funds in the health care account are paid out for designated medical care only. They can't be taken out for any other reason, such as retirement needs, nor can they be transferred to the retirement part.

A pension plan may provide for the health care part from the start, or add the health part later by plan amendment—say as retirement nears. Through this arrangement, the business escapes tax on business profits put into the health account, investment earnings grow tax-free, and participants owe no tax on proceeds used for health insurance or expense reimbursement. This is close to what HSAs do.

Overfunded pension plans can also transfer excess funds to the health account, with similar results.

Profit-sharing plans

These can also be used for retiree health care, with fewer benefits. The leading options are: a retirement account, funded with employer contributions, and a retiree health account, funded by after-tax employee contributions that grow tax-free. Later withdrawals to pay for health care are also tax-free. Employees get tax-free treatment for investment earnings used to pay future medical care, at no cost to you or the business.

VEBAs

Voluntary employee beneficiary associations (VEBAs) are mechanisms for pre-funding future employee benefits. Employer-funded VEBAs in which the entrepreneur participates can produce results like those for pension retiree health care, if some complicated requirements are met.

Business Gone, Health Care Goes On

What would it take to relieve your worries that your health care could be lost when your business goes? For one thing, the knowledge that the money will be there when the health need arises. For the other, the certainty that your absolute right to the money will survive the business. To achieve that result, use a prefunded trust for continued care:

1. Have your business prefund its health care commitment, putting up the necessary money before you leave the business. You should have an amount adequate for lifetime health insurance, with a deductible, plus an amount adequate to cover each year's deductible. A health care actuary, hired at the business's expense, could determine how much to set aside for that.

2. Have the money go into a trust administered by an independent trustee. The trustee is bound to look after your interests, the trust

survives whatever becomes of the business, and the trust ordinarily is immune from claims of business creditors.

What program can accomplish all that? I've covered these: HSAs and pension retiree health care.

Also, Medicare Part A (hospitalization) goes on after your business ends. Medicare Part B goes on if premiums are paid, usually out of Social Security receipts. Other medical expenses, such as co-pays, deductibles, prescription drug insurance (Medicare Part D), and other items, could be paid out of retirement income, investment income, or savings.

Strategy Review

Your goal in this chapter is to protect and, if possible, enhance wealth through a complete, cost-effective health plan. Options are many in this increasingly complex area:

1. The most cost-effective option for virtually all health care programs is to buy health care through the business.
2. Health costs can be effectively reduced in unincorporated businesses or S corporations where coverage is obtained through the owner's employee spouse.
3. To get the full benefit of business-paid coverage, nonfamily employees must sometimes be included in the business plan.
4. Some employees can be excluded from coverage, under objective standards. Health insurance can be provided to owners only.
5. Through a cafeteria plan, the employee can pay for health benefits out of salary, at little cost to the employer. This can also cut company payroll costs.
6. You can lock in health care coverage to continue long after you stop working, and throughout your lifetime. Your options, which can survive even after your business is ended, include:

   - A binding agreement for continued health care from the business or successor owners
   - Health saving accounts
   - Pension-funded health care for retirees

5

Giving Back— to Yourself

WEALTH CREATION STRATEGIES 23–27

Lifestyle and individual wealth can benefit when personal or family expenses are *legitimately* covered through the business. This will not be a tale of company jets, chauffeured limousines, and skyboxes. Instead, I will look realistically at opportunities and possible risks when the small business covers specific items for the entrepreneur or family members in the business.

Business Perks—What They Really Cost

You can have what Jack Welch and Dennis Koslovski got, but you can't have it for free. The largesse these corporate execs enjoyed came from what would otherwise have gone into the pockets of tens of thousands of stockholders. Yours will come mostly out of your own pocket, or the pockets of your co-owners or successors, in the form of diminished business profits.

A perk costs you again if you must pay taxes on it. But there are still cases, and we'll describe them, when a perk can pay off economically if it is something important for you to have, and especially if it's something you'd buy with your own money anyway.

Virtually all the perks I describe here are deductible by the business, reducing taxable business profits. The federal income tax deduction recovers up to 35 percent of the cost of the item, depending on the business's tax rate. This would mean, for example, that a $10,000 perk could cost the business $6,500.

Maybe the perk you get is worth 65 percent of its cost; maybe it isn't. But there's also a cost to you personally, if the perk is fully or partially taxable (some are tax-exempt). And if the perk is paid as compensation for services, it will also be subject to Social Security taxes.

Thus, a $10,000 perk could cost the business up to $6,500—actual cost less taxes saved—and cost you the tax you must pay (maybe up to $3,500) on a fully taxable perk, as well as Social Security tax if it's compensation.

State and local taxes, where applicable, are relevant here too. A perk that a business can deduct for federal tax purposes is almost always deductible for state taxes. So if the state's effective business tax rate is 6 percent (net of any federal deduction for the state tax), the $10,000 perk costs the business $5,900 after federal and state taxes. Your receipt of the perk may or may not be fully taxable for state tax purposes; any state tax on you would increase your tax cost.

Some perk arrangements require the perk recipient to reimburse the business for personal use of the perk. Reimbursement shifts the entire cost of the personal portion to the recipient, and not just the tax cost.

The business could reimburse the entrepreneur's tax—sometimes called "grossing up." My thoughts on that follow shortly.

Perks often aren't worth it. But in some cases they are. . . .

When Perks Work

In some cases, perks can build wealth or enhance your lifestyle at minimal cost.

For instance, some of the perks the business deducts are exempt from Social Security taxes, for the business and the recipient. Think of certain cafeteria plan benefits, charitable gifts, group-term life insurance, certain low-interest loans, paid parking, relocation, and travel-related items. And then there are the biggest ticket items—thousands and tens of thousands a year—for retirement (tax-deferred), health care (tax-free), and health savings accounts (tax-free or tax-deferred). I've already discussed these in chapters 2 through 4.

Businesses usually deduct the costs of perks for federal tax purposes, but the cost is taxable income to the entrepreneur. Business-paid perks get modest encouragement in some cases, when state and local tax laws differ from the feds.

For example:

- When the state or locality taxes business income but not personal income (Alaska, Florida). A business deduction reduces business taxes owed the state, with no personal (individual) state tax.
- When the state gives you relief for things the feds tax more heavily (life insurance, for example). A business deduction reduces business taxes owed the state, with no corresponding individual state tax.
- When the state or locality taxes partnerships, LLCs, or S corporations. The business deduction reduces tax owed the state with no corresponding increase in individual state tax.
- When the state or locality tax rate on business income is higher than the rate on the corresponding amount of individual income. The business deduction saves more state/local tax than the individual rate costs.

A downside: In the few states that allow deduction for federal income tax, the state tax goes up (somewhat) when federal tax goes down, because of a deductible perk (or other deduction).

Get Co-owners to Share the Cost of What You Get

Sometimes co-owners have the right to object to the perk, but effective objection is less likely in family settings. A valued perk for you alone is worth more when paid for out of profits you'd otherwise have to share with others.

Think what's possible when entrepreneurs retire—especially when they pass all or most of their ownership interests to the next generation. Here's where the entrepreneur can have a big perk payday, with relatively little concern for what his bounty costs the business.

ACTION POINT Perks for one co-owner become a matter of negotiation if other co-owners have a right to object. Working entrepreneurs are of course entitled to reasonable compensation for their work; in some cases, there's a tax requirement that they receive not less than reasonable pay. Since perks usually are compensation, consider using the tax requirement as justification for particular perks.

Who Gets Perks

Almost all tax-favored perks are for employees only. Owner-employees in C corporations are employees, as are owner-employees of LLCs electing tax status as C corporations. Sole proprietors aren't employees. S corporation owner-employees, partners, and LLC members usually aren't employees when it comes to perks but can be allowed some perks.

Certain perks can go to S corporation owner-employees or partners as compensation for services—paid in kind rather than in cash. What's paid as compensation affects how profits are split, since profits are determined after deduction for business expenses, which include compensation. So the more one S corporation stockholder or partner gets as compensation, the less they and their co-owners get as profits. A perk might even be preferable to cash, when co-owners would more readily agree to the perk—such as a company car—than to more cash.

An entrepreneur who uses perks to increase her share of business receipts pays higher taxes, of course, but on higher income.

EXAMPLE

Phil is the managing member of Phil's Jewelry, LLC. He owns 70 percent of the business; his two daughters, who don't work in the business, own 15 percent each.

The business nets $240,000 before Phil's compensation. Phil takes $160,000 compensation in cash. The business has $80,000 of profit, split $56,000 to Phil and $12,000 to each daughter. Phil's total take is $216,000.

But say the business provides Phil with club memberships costing $10,000. Now Phil's compensation is $170,000, and business profits are $70,000, split 70 percent to Phil and 15 percent to each daughter. Now Phil's total take is $219,000. His tax is higher this way but he *has* more too—at his daughters' expense.

Perks for family members

You may make your choice of perks available to family members working in the business. It can be easier for them to qualify for tax breaks than it is for you, since they can be employees—which you as owner can't be, unless the business is a corporation.

But their situation is more like yours when you and they are co-owners of the business.

Who Can't Get Perks

Most perks are off limits to sole proprietors. Perks that are limited to employees are out because sole proprietors aren't employees. Other business perks are effectively precluded because the business can't deduct them unless they're treated as compensation to the recipient. Sole proprietors get only business profits, not compensation. For sole proprietors, getting a perk from the business is no different from paying for it personally, out of one's own pocket.

The member of a single member LLC is a sole proprietor unless the business elects status as a corporation. Limited partners who don't work in the business won't qualify for employee perks.

There are a few exceptions to this:

- Sole proprietors qualify for retirement plans (where, uniquely, they can be employees) and some health care benefits.
- Entrepreneurs' business clients sometimes offer them benefits of the kind I list as perks.

Use a Cafeteria Plan for Specified Benefits

I've mentioned the idea before—the employee pays for a benefit out of what would otherwise be taxable pay. The employee likes this because she gets a benefit she wants at a reduced overall tax bill.

The leading example of this arrangement is the cafeteria plan, sometimes called a flexible benefit plan. Cafeteria plans let the employee choose to take a portion of her pay either as a tax-free benefit (say, health care) or a taxable benefit—cash, of course, but sometimes something else.

How does a cafeteria plan help you, the business owner? Two ways: You—if you can qualify as an employee—can get the same benefit at the lowered tax cost. And your business—whether or not you're an employee—gains increased profits through reduced business taxes.

If the employee chooses a tax-free benefit, there's no income or Social Security tax on the benefit. This saves the business the Social Security tax it would have had to pay on the cash the employee chooses to forgo in favor of the benefit—that's up to 7.65 percent of every tax-free benefit.

EXAMPLE

Your work force opts to take, say, $150,000 of what would otherwise be taxable pay in the form of tax-free benefits offered by your cafeteria plan. This can save your business up to $11,475 (7.65 percent of $150,000), less the tax value of an $11,475 deduction.

Any employer, regardless of business type, can decide to offer a cafeteria plan, and can choose what benefits to make available. Leading tax-free cafeteria plan benefits are:

- Health care, in various forms or plan types
- Disability (income replacement) insurance
- Dependent care programs
- Adoption assistance programs
- Group-term life insurance

The business deducts the cost of the benefit provided through the plan. It bears the after-tax cost of the benefit, rather than the after-tax cost of the pay foregone to get the benefit. Though it saves the Social Security tax, there's an administrative cost to running the plan, which somewhat reduces the saving.

How you can benefit personally

Only employees or former employees can participate in a cafeteria plan—meaning that you, the entrepreneur, can benefit only if your business is a C corporation.

You can set up the plan to include the tax-free benefits you prefer. You personally can get those benefits free of income and Social Security tax. However, you can lose this tax break if you, or you and other "key employees," get more than 25 percent of the total cafeteria benefit. Also, you lose the tax break if the particular benefit is skewed too much in your favor—for example, a dependent care allowance that pays you three times what a rank-and-file employee gets.

Charities, Clubs, and Credit Cards

Business-Paid Charitable Contributions on Your Behalf

I'm not saying that contributions to charity will make you richer in dollar terms. But when you intend to contribute to charity in any case, contributing through the business can be best, in dollar terms, depending on the form of your business. Here's how it works for various types of business entity:

C corporations. Assume you make a $10,000 cash contribution through your C corporation. The company gets a deduction that saves, say, $3,500 in income taxes, at no tax cost to you. This is a better tax result than if you contributed and deducted funds you took out of the corporation as compensation (which incurs Social Security taxes) or as a dividend (losing the corporate deduction).

Partnerships. Partnerships can make charitable contributions but can't take charitable deductions. Instead, your proportionate share of the partnership contribution is deductible by you personally on your return. Here there's usually no benefit from having the partnership contribute, and no reason for a contribution perk.

Or a charitable contribution on your behalf could be made as additional compensation for your services to the partnership. This causes smaller profits all around, but more overall for you (as in the previous example under "Who Gets Perks")—and here the increase in compensation is deductible (by you, of course) as a charitable contribution.

Partnership documents describing the entrepreneur's compensation (technically called a "guaranteed payment") should state that the payment to charity is made as part of the entrepreneur's compensation.

S corporations. S corporation stockholders have the same options as partners, except that when a distribution is a dividend (because the S corporation was once a C corporation), the corporation gets no deduction.

Club Memberships

Country clubs, social clubs, athletic clubs, luncheon and dining clubs, even airline clubs, all signal a wealthy lifestyle. You and your business have alternative ways to handle these memberships.

1. Assuming you establish the portion of business use, you're tax-exempt on that portion, but the business can't deduct that portion. The portion allocable to personal use is deductible by the business and is taxable compensation (pay) to you.
2. The business treats the entire membership cost as pay, and you're taxable on it all, but can separately deduct the business portion.

For entrepreneurs in corporations, any amount you're taxed on is subject to tax withholding, including Social Security tax. The first option is better for you as an individual; the second is better for the business.

You establish the business portion by keeping adequate records, generally of business and personal club use. To use the first option, the entrepreneur would provide those records to the business.

Business payment of dues for the entrepreneur's membership in a professional association are a tax-exempt perk, deductible by the business.

Company Car

By company car, I mean a car owned or leased by your business that you use for personal and business driving. For some entrepreneurs, the company car is a convenience the business pays for. For others, the car they choose is a showcase for their lifestyle—a way to display personal and business success. When a company car is used partly for personal purposes, tax authorities insist that the user be made to pay, in some way, for such use.

In a sole proprietorship, the entrepreneur directly bears the cost of personal use. If taxes are reported correctly, the business can't deduct the cost of the entrepreneur's personal use. This is true whether the business owns or leases the car.

In corporations and partnerships, the business can pay the cost of personal (as well as business) use, but treat the cost of the entrepreneur's personal use as part of the entrepreneur's pay. The business bears the net cost (after its deduction); the entrepreneur bears only the tax cost of personal use. This is true whether the business owns or leases the car. Failure to establish the portion used for business makes the value of all use of the car compensation. (The entrepreneur can then deduct the value of business use—as is the case with sole proprietors.)

EXAMPLE

Sue is sole owner of her C corporation, which pays $8,000 a year to lease the car Sue uses for business and personal purposes. If Sue used it 60 percent for business, she has $3,200 of compensation income from the personal use. Her federal income tax cost on this is $960 (assuming a 30 percent tax rate), plus Social Security taxes on her and the corporation.

If Sue had been a sole proprietor, she would have borne $6,560 of the $8,000 cost. That's the cost after income tax of the business portion ($3,360) and all of the personal portion ($3,200). She would also owe self-employment tax on the $3,200.

Tax rules effectively limit business deduction for higher-priced cars ("luxury" cars), whether owned or leased by the business. The business deducts less than it spends on the car, making the entrepreneur's company car more costly than other perks of equivalent value.

Establish the proportion of business use by providing the business with records that separately state your business and personal mileage. From these records the business can determine the personal portion of car use value to be treated as compensation.

Company Credit Card

For most employees, someone in Accounting scrutinizes the charges on their company credit cards for compliance with company expense ceilings to see that no personal item is charged, or to ensure that the employee promptly reimburses the company for personal charges.

Then there are the cards the owner or top execs use. At this level, it's mostly an honor system, especially for the owner's charges. And for this crowd, the IRS has a flat rule: If the user isn't required to prove within the company that charges were for business expenses, all company payments on the card are compensation. They are subject to income tax and (for employees including entrepreneurs in corporations) Social Security tax.

The law treats everything the business pays as compensation (for partners, guaranteed payments or distributions) except to the extent you reimburse the business for a cost. When you reimburse, *you* bear the full cost of the amount being reimbursed. If you don't reimburse, you just bear the *tax* cost of the item; the business pays the rest. Your tax cost is the income tax on the compensation, and the Social Security tax if the business is a corporation. Tax should be withheld on the amount treated as compensation for employees, including entrepreneurs in corporations.

If the business is a partnership, you have income and self-employment tax, though self-employment tax is not necessarily an extra cost.

The entrepreneur can deduct the properly substantiated business portion on his own tax return (eliminating taxes on that portion).

Life Insurance

Life insurance as an entrepreneur's perk is usually group-term insurance or split-dollar insurance (less popular today than formerly).

As usual with perks, the business bears the actual cost of the perk, less the tax value of its deduction when it treats the perk as compensation, and *you* may bear the tax cost of the perk.

26   Group-Term Life Insurance

Group-term insurance provides insurance for a group of employees—here, employees of your business. The insurance pays a death benefit if the covered employee dies while it's in force. It has no cash value: It can't be cashed in or borrowed against. It may, however, be convertible to a permanent policy, which can build up cash value.

If your group is nine employees or fewer, every insurable full-time employee must be covered, and the insurance coverage must be a uniform percentage of pay, or within coverage brackets prescribed by the insurance company. (An example of uniform percentage would be a $150,000-a-year entrepreneur getting $300,000 of coverage and a $30,000-a-year employee getting $60,000 of coverage.) For larger employee groups, additional employees can be excluded from coverage, subject to certain "fairness" rules. In no case can persons other than employees, or former employees, be covered—which means, for entrepreneurs, that their business must be a C corporation. (S corporation entrepreneurs can participate in the group plan, but get no tax relief.)

If your plan is in compliance the first $50,000 of your coverage is tax-free and the cost of coverage in excess of $50,000 is figured under favorable rules. These rules generally tax you on less than what the business pays in premiums, but the business deducts its actual cost.

Of course, if the business is providing insurance for a group of employees, it's running up costs to cover others besides you. So wouldn't it be nice if these others paid their own costs?

Sure, and you can have them do it, if they want coverage. Include it in a cafeteria plan, to which they can divert part of their pay for group-term premiums. They pay the actual cost of the insurance, but are taxable on less than that, under favorable rules for costs of coverage—an inducement for them to sign up.

Low-Interest Loans

Using loans as a way to cash in your business capital is covered in depth in Wealth Creation Strategy 62. Here we're into more modest borrowings—something you might take out short-term, maybe between major paydays, during temporary cash crunches, or for a big vacation.

The interest charged on the loan is income to the lender (the business) but is not deductible by the borrower (unless the loan is for a deductible purpose, such as investment).

The low-interest loan can be one of the completely tax-free perks. You may if you wish offer it to family members working in the business, but have no obligation to offer it to other employees. It's even cost-free—no interest need be charged—when the loan is less than $10,000.

When interest is charged, you'll be hit with the (usually nondeductible) interest cost. What to do about that?

The lender business could increase the borrower's pay, to reimburse the borrower's interest cost. The lender gets a compensation deduction for this, which offsets its income from the borrower's interest payment. The borrower's net cost of the loan is the tax on the increased pay.

If you do this sort of transaction, insist on a written record of the loan, something that appears on the books of the business, with a planned repayment date—and provable repayment. Interest should be charged, at least at the relatively low U.S. Treasury Applicable Federal Rate, see Chapter 10. But you can skip the interest (or charge less) if the outstanding loan balance is less than $10,000.

We need these formalities so the tax authorities won't treat the loan amount itself as taxable pay or, in the case of a C corporation lender, as a dividend.

Paid Parking

When your business pays the cost of your commute, it's a taxable perk. But reimbursing the cost of parking at the end of your journey to work can be a tax-free perk, though a modest one.

You'd expect it to be tax-free if the business owned or leased premises with space for parking that you could use for free—and you'd be right. But the business could instead reimburse you with tax-free cash to cover your parking fees paid to outsiders, up to a specified ceiling amount—which is $230 a month, $2,760 a year.

And you can offer a parking arrangement to employees, for business savings, whether or not you participate. Employees could be given the option to divert up to, say, $2,500 a year of pay to a parking subsidy, van pool, or transit pass (such programs are called transportation reimbursement incentives). For each employee who signs up, the business saves up to $191.25 (7.65 percent of $2,500), less any cost of administering the plan.

What you as employee divert to pay parking reduces your taxable pay (and Social Security tax), though spent on a personal expense. You could, if you wish, restore your full income by increasing your pay by $2,500. You have the same income as before, plus the tax-free parking, a personal expense.

Reimbursed parking near your *residence* is compensation, not a perk.

Personal Financial and Tax Counseling

Usually, these are taxable perks when paid by the business. That is, the amount the business pays is compensation, subject to income and Social Security taxes.

There's a minor exception for retirement planning services paid for by a business with a qualified retirement plan. The services are exempt from income and Social Security taxes on the business owner or co-owner when they are made available to other employees who normally receive retirement information from the business.

The entrepreneur may deduct the cost of business-related counseling, including legal counseling and services, as a business expense. Costs of personal financial and tax counseling services you receive are deductible as itemized expenses to the extent total itemized expenses exceed 2 percent of adjusted gross income. This includes estate planning legal counseling and services related to taxes or income-producing property. These deductions can offset all or part of the compensation income arising from the business's payment, to that extent reducing the entrepreneur's income tax. These deductions would not reduce Social Security tax.

Portable electronics

I mean laptop computers, cell phones and their hybrid offspring: smart phones and personal digital assistants. These, with their accessories, are commonly found in entrepreneurs' pockets or briefcases, furnished, along with their operating costs, by the business.

Business deductions for such items provided to entrepreneurs or their family members are limited. Purchase costs don't qualify for immediate writeoff or accelerated depreciation, even for business use. Users are taxed as compensation on the entire value of using the item, unless they establish the personal portion of such use, in which case only the personal portion is compensation. As this book goes to press, the IRS is working on easing these rules for cell phones.

Relocation

Moving your business is a business expense, as everyone knows. And it remains so when you move it for personal reasons—say because the new place is warmer, or more exciting, or less exciting, or whatever.

Now consider your personal move, to a new residence in the area of the new business location. Business payment of these costs—which may run in the tens of thousands of dollars—can be a perk.

A business can pay reasonable expenses of moving to a new residence in the area where you've moved the business. The business payment is a deductible business expense, but not compensation to you—in other words, it is a tax-free perk—if you meet the conditions below. The business bears the cost of the move, less the tax value of its deduction, at no tax cost to you. You could also award this perk to family members working in the business who are moving near the new business location, but you aren't obliged to offer it to other employees.

Reimbursement is tax-free only for reasonable expenses of travel to the new residence (but not meals costs), and of moving household goods and personal effects (including cars).

You must give the business a detailed accounting of your expenses, and return any reimbursement in excess of proper expenses. Reimbursement for other, personal, expenses is compensation, subject to income and Social Security tax (including self-employment tax), if not repaid to the business.

Spouse Travel

Business travel looks less like work and more like a vacation when your spouse goes along. That's how it looks to the tax authorities, whatever your idea of a vacation may be. Vacations are nondeductible, and even if you can prove it's all for business, the business can't deduct expenses of a spouse tagalong unless he is an employee and the trip is relevant to his work.

Not that I see this as much of a problem when it's your business. Elsewhere—and why not here too?—I've cited benefits from making your spouse an employee with useful work to do. Doing so lets the business deduct for his business-related transportation and entertainment costs and meals, plus any extra hotel costs of accommodations for two.

Maybe your spouse is a co-owner of the business. That's not enough to support deduction for his expenses. He must work in the business, and the trip must be relevant to that work.

Tax reimbursement

Taxes on perks are sometimes paid for retiring entrepreneurs. Here, the tax cost is effectively borne by those who own the business after the entrepreneur's retirement. It occasionally applies for perks and other benefits during the entrepreneur's working life, and to perks or relatively small amounts of compensation received by working family members. (Tax reimbursement is rare for partners.)

When a business pays a worker's tax on a perk or other compensation, that is further compensation, subject to further tax. The tax pyramids: tax on tax on tax, etc. You might think that this would discourage businesses from agreeing to such a pyramid, or workers from asking for it. It does, in some businesses; it doesn't, in others.

Travel in Style

The limo from the airport. A deluxe suite at the town's grandest hotel. Haute cuisine at its finest restaurant. All for you on your business trips.

The rules say the business can't deduct travel expenses that are "lavish or extravagant," but tax authorities don't see lavishness or extravagance in the luxury we've just described. There's no restriction—short of the ridiculous—on what your business can spend on your business travel.

Except, of course, what you *want* your business to spend on such things. A $4,000 trip may be no less deductible than one to the same place, for the same duration, that costs $1,500. But after taxes the $4,000 trip still costs the business a net, say, $2,600, while the $1,500 trip costs, say, $975 after taxes. You'll need to decide whether the extra $1,625 is worth it.

Postretirement Perks

You may have heard that General Electric CEO Jack Welch's postretirement piñata included— for a while—personal use of a company jet, a $50,000-a-month New York City apartment, chauffeur/bodyguards for his speaking engagements and book promotions, a box at the opera, VIP seating at Wimbledon, and dozens of other items like flowers, wine, groceries, and periodic haute cuisine dinners out.

This was to be at the expense of tens of thousands of General Electric stockholders. The negative publicity—it would be hard to imagine any other kind—drove him to back off, despite his claims that he deserved it all.

I don't see you in this picture. When you retire from your family business, your "severance package" will come out of what you still own of the business, and what the next generation owns.

The small business post-retirement perks I see mostly continue selected perks the business already provides, with maybe a few extras. These are the most common at retirement:

Cafeteria Plans. Retired C corporation entrepreneurs supposedly can participate in their businesses' cafeteria plans, allocating a portion of their severance pay to tax-favored benefits. This rarely happens.

Car. For retirees, this perk is giving the entrepreneur ownership of a company car she has been using. The entrepreneur will be taxed on its fair market value at that time, or on the leased value if the business continues to lease it.

Charitable gifts. This perk is usually a business match of contributions the retired entrepreneur makes personally. This is not taxable.

Club memberships. These are taxable.

Financial counseling. The entrepreneur can be taxed on company payment for this, with a possible offsetting deduction by the entrepreneur for costs related to income-producing investments.

Group-term life insurance. Retired entrepreneurs in C corporations can continue to participate in such plans. Coverage up to $50,000 is tax-exempt; amounts over $50,000 lead to tax under favorable rules.

Health care. Health care in retirement, including disability and long-term coverage (not technically health care), is covered in Chapter 4.

Low-interest loans. Outstanding loans may be forgiven (cancelled) at retirement. The cancelled amount is taxable.

Portable electronics. The business assumes such devices in the entrepreneur's possession are his already; the perk is the offer to cover operating costs (mostly, connection charges). This is taxable.

Relocation. Severance contracts may agree to cover the cost of the entrepreneur's move to a retirement location (often, a low-tax location). Taxable.

How Small Businesses Justify Postretirement Perks

Small businesses pay postretirement perks as *deferred compensation*—which means the entrepreneur should have been receiving compensation before he retired. Sole proprietors don't qualify.

Items received at around the time of retirement (such as loan cancellation) may be current (rather than deferred) compensation. Also, an entrepreneur who stays on as a consultant to the business may receive the perk as current compensation for his services as independent contractor. (Former sole proprietors serving as consultants to a business with a successor owner or co-owners can qualify here.)

Strategy Review

Your goal here is to exploit, reasonably and realistically, the opportunities to use business perks to enhance your personal and family lifestyle. Perks are most often provided to C corporation entrepreneurs, and to entrepreneurs' family members who are employed in the business, whatever the form of business. These are the leading options:

1. Making others pay. The individual entrepreneur may arrange for co-owners, often family members, to share the cost of the perk.
2. Cafeteria plans. An entrepreneur's working family members, and C corporation entrepreneurs, can benefit personally. Businesses of all types, if they have employees, can benefit through FICA tax savings.
3. Charitable gifts. Making one's charitable contributions through one's business is better economically than taking distributions from the business that the entrepreneur then contributes to charity.
4. Group-term life insurance. This is a modest tax-favored perk to an entrepreneur's employees and to C corporation entrepreneurs when a group of employees participates and other requirements are met. When offered to employees through a cafeteria plan, the business may save FICA taxes.
5. Relocation. Business-paid expense of moving your residence when you move your business is a tax-free perk for entrepreneurs and family members in the business.

Your Business Location

WEALTH CREATION STRATEGIES 28–32

Vornado Realty Trust is a giant real estate investment trust that started life as two brothers with a discount store. In time they added more stores, in good locations. The stores had their ups and downs, but their land values soared. The day came when developing the real estate became Vornado's major business. The message here is that, in the right circumstances, a business should own its own real estate.

Why Buy When You Can Rent?

In the rent-or-buy dilemma, renting will often be the smart choice. Renting costs less than buying, so it builds wealth faster than buying. But when there's a reasonable economic case for buying, consider these factors:

1. If you own it, you can borrow against it.
2. If you own it and its value increases over time, as often happens with buildings and land, you can sell it at a profit.
3. If you own it, it can be an income-generating asset in your retirement, or for your heirs.

The best time to acquire real estate for your business isn't the business's early stages but after it's prospering. The business should be throwing off income that depreciation deductions from your real estate acquisition can shelter from tax, income that can help pay for the real estate itself, or other wealth-building investment.

Bootstrap the
Business Building

I know a husband-wife team of lawyers whose estate and retirement nest egg is the office building where they practice. They borrowed to buy the building, and they rent out the extra space to other professionals. Rents from tenants go to maintain the building and service the mortgage debt. Here's how that could work out in cash flow—rental income and cash outlay:

Rental income $85,000
Less
Maintenance, real estate taxes, insurance. $30,000
Mortgage interest $45,000
Mortgage principal. $10,000
Total. $0

Mortgage principal payments build the couple's equity in the building, and reduce the interest cost. If the value of the building can be expected to rise (and theirs has already done that handsomely), this is a fine wealth-creation plan. The couple sees the building as a rental income stream for their retirement, and maybe later, for their two daughters.

Depreciation for Tax-Free Cash

You'll note that so far I haven't discussed what income taxes can do to this wealth creation strategy. Federal taxes wreck many a good plan, but not this one. The tax drawback—that mortgage principal payments aren't tax-deductible—is countered and often bettered by the tax benefit: the deduction for depreciation.

In the previous example, income exactly equaled outgo. The couple spent $10,000 of rental income on mortgage principal. This expenditure is taxable (because principal payments aren't deductible). The couple had $85,000 of cash income from the property, less $75,000 of deductions. This results in a tax on the $10,000 balance—say a tax of $3,000—so the building causes more outgo ($88,000) than income ($85,000).

How can the couple counter that? By depreciation, an expense with no "outgo." Assuming the building's depreciation was $10,000, the building now has $85,000 in deductions to offset the $85,000 in rental income, resulting in $0 tax. ·

The numbers just cited show an increasing equity (from mortgage principal payments) in a growing asset, with no new cash investment and no tax cost. Change any of the numbers and you change the deal. But depreciation is a number you can, somewhat, control for your own financial advantage.

If your building produces a positive cash flow, you can take out the excess cash tax-free, to the extent of the depreciation, as you can see in this example:

Items	Tax Treatment	Cash Flow Treatment
Rent received $90,000	Income $90,000	Cash in $90,000
Maintenance, real estate taxes, insurance $30,000	Deduction $30,000	Cash out $30,000
Mortgage interest $45,000	Deduction $45,000	Cash out $45,000
Depreciation $15,000	Deduction $15,000	Cash out $0
Mortgage Principal $10,000	Deduction $0	Cash out $10,000
	Taxable income $0	
Result	**Tax** $0	**Net cash return** $5,000

Your building can show a tax loss even with a positive cash flow or a cash breakeven. Even so, such a tax loss—*if available*—can free up further tax-free cash, where the loss can be offset against salary, other business profits, or investment income.

EXAMPLE

Take the facts of the above example except assume that rent is $87,000. The building has a $3,000 loss for tax purposes but $2,000 positive cash flow. The $3,000 loss can reduce taxable business profits by that amount, yielding an additional $1,000 or so in cash.

For many entrepreneurs, tax losses from rental real estate aren't available—meaning can't be currently used. See "Your Stealth Business." in Chapter 8, for more on this problem.

Payback—maybe

Though depreciation can generate tax-free cash, you'll have to "pay" for that benefit, eventually, when you part with the depreciated property.

Depreciation reduces the property's tax basis. Profit or loss on a sale is selling price less basis. Basis, a key tax concept, is usually what an item cost, including any capital improvements (and minus depreciation deductions). A reduction in basis—from depreciation deductions—will increase your taxable gain (or reduce your loss) when you sell the property. So depreciation used to your tax advantage today is "recaptured" to cause tax pain later.

But that's okay: That's still a wealth-building strategy, in most cases, for two reasons:

- Even when today's tax saved and the future tax to be paid are the same dollar amount (which is often the case with equipment), future tax is usually paid with cheaper dollars, because of intervening inflation. Meanwhile, you have your earnings (also eventually subject to tax, of course) on the dollars saved today.
- Future tax on real estate is usually at capital gains rates—meaning the dollar amount of future tax is less than the tax saved today.

EXAMPLE

Grant bought a business building with land for $450,000, allocating $400,000 to the building and $50,000 to the land. Over ten years, Grant has taken $100,000 of depreciation (reducing total basis to $350,000), which saved $35,000 in tax. Now, after ten years, Grant sells land and building for $585,000, representing around 2.66 percent appreciation annually over ten years. Of Grant's $235,000 taxable profit, $100,000 is recapture of prior depreciation. Total tax on sale is $45,250: $25,000 on the recaptured depreciation and $20,250 on the remaining gain.

Depreciation saved $35,000; its recapture cost only $25,000, so sale with recapture was worth $10,000 to Grant.

The depreciation deduction is a tool of great power in building wealth. It does not depend on the *value* of the building; depreciation is allowed, and should be claimed, even while the building is increasing in value.

You take the deduction against the full purchase price of the property, even if you have borrowed most or all of the price. For example, you borrow to buy a $2,000,000 building with $200,000 down. Your depreciation deduction is a percentage of $2,000,000, not of $200,000.

You take depreciation on a building over the building's "life." Except in rare cases, depreciation is considered to occur each year and depreciation deductions are to be taken each year; you will not be allowed to skip one year and double up the next. You must use an IRS-approved depreciation system.

ABOUT DEPRECIATION

Depreciation on your business financial statement reduces its (stated) profitability, so you'll usually want to show low depreciation and higher profit. Depreciation in your tax return reduces the tax you owe, so you will often want to show high (large) depreciation, for lower taxable profit and lower tax. You can use one depreciation method for financial reporting and a different method for tax reporting.

Do a Cost Allocation That Builds Wealth

Buy a building and you're usually also buying the land it's on for a single price. You'll take depreciation deductions on the building; land isn't depreciable. It's somewhat up to you to decide how much of your purchase price went for the building. The more of the purchase price you can reasonably allocate to the building, the bigger depreciation deduction you get.

EXAMPLE

On a $1 million building purchase, $200,000 might be a reasonable allocation to the land. But so might $120,000. Using $120,000 increases your depreciation deduction by $80,000 over the life of the building.

ACTION POINT

Beware of using real estate *tax* appraisals. The appraisal may not in any case reflect the price you actually pay, but it will allocate value between land and building. Beware of using that proportion in allocating your actual purchase price. In my experience, tax appraisers tend to overstate the relative value of the land.

And be wary of signing on to a seller's proposed allocation, if there is one. The seller's tax interest conflicts with yours.

Your purchase contract can and usually will avoid any allocation, leaving it to you to make your own allocation based on market values. Your own judgment of relative values may be adequate; your tax advisor's judgment may be better. You or your advisor may want to engage a real property appraiser for the allocation job. The IRS seldom challenges an allocation made by an experienced professional appraiser.

Deconstruct Your Business Building

There's a rule that (most) business buildings are to be depreciated over a period of thirty-nine years. This means that generally only 2.56 percent of their cost can be deducted each year as depreciation.

How to increase this percentage? Deconstruct your building. Not clear? Would it be better if instead I said: *Virtually* deconstruct your building?

Your building is bricks and mortar, or concrete and steel, and so on, and these materials have long lives. But it's also wiring and valves and a host of other components that the IRS recognizes have shorter lives. So the way to larger current deductions is to assign the appropriate (long) life to the building frame and the appropriate shorter life to things inside, like electrical wiring, room partitions, carpeting, and so on, and even to some outside work, like grading for sidewalks and parking areas.

Virtual deconstruction is my euphemism for identifying shorter-lived components and allocating portions of the building's cost among them. This doesn't increase total depreciation over the life of the building. But it can greatly increase the depreciation *rate*, the proportion of total cost that you can take in the early years of ownership. And it may be available to you now, to increase your depreciation rate for buildings you already own.

Virtual deconstruction is optional; most owners settle for 2.56 percent, applied to the whole building. Making the appropriate allocations is a job for your tax professional, who might bring in a construction engineer or other advisor. This can be costly and would have to be weighed against likely benefits of "virtual deconstruction"—which might, for example, double depreciation in an early year.

Residential buildings

These qualify for faster depreciation: over 27.5 years, meaning a 3.64 percent annual rate. By "residential" they mean long-term occupancy— apartment or room renters, not hotels (which use the commercial 2.56 percent rate). Deconstruction can be done for residential buildings too, and often involve such shorter-lived equipment as refrigerators and window air conditioners, and even furniture.

Prepare for Mortgage Pain

In a traditional self-amortizing mortgage, each year's cash outlay for mortgage payments is the same, but the proportion going toward interest falls and that going toward principal rises. Your equity in the building is rising, but your interest deduction is falling.

For example, on a twenty-year loan at 6.5 percent interest, the nondeductible equity (principal) portion in the first year is 28 percent of the mortgage payment; in the tenth year it's 50 percent. Depreciation of real estate, which may offset and more than offset the cost of equity in early years, is fairly constant each year for most owners, and so offsets less each year. Your cash outlay stays the same but results in higher taxable income.

Disaster? No. It just means that tax encouragement for real estate acquisition is front-loaded. Planning can take care of it, in these ways:

1. Invest some of today's savings for possible future cash needs. This doesn't happen in any business segment as much as it should. But it's a little more likely, and more necessary, for holders of rental properties than when the real estate is your business premises.
2. Arrange a different kind of loan, one that doesn't self-amortize:
   - An interest-only mortgage. These are interest-only for just a few years, converting to fully amortized over a relatively short period.
   - A mortgage with a balloon payment. These will have a relatively short term—maybe fifteen years—and modest principal payments (say 1 percent of principal) are made each year, up to the balloon payment year.

3. *Use* the equity you've built. A sale or sale–leaseback can give you back your investment, tax-free, with appreciation (taxed at favorable rates). Or, you can borrow out the equity and appreciation, tax-free.
4. Muddle through. Real estate acquisition can build wealth now. The cash crunch, if any, will come later when, I hope, your business spins off cash to cover it.

Use Tax-Free Swaps to Grow Real Estate Holdings

Tax later is better than tax now. We saw in Chapter 2 how this truth builds retirement plan fortunes. It's also the backbone of this wealth creation strategy. Suppose you have real property that has risen in value in your hands, but you want some other property in its place. Business property sold at a profit is taxable; the tax you owe on the sale reduces what you have to spend on your next property.

EXAMPLE

You own property worth $460,000 that you'd like to spend for replacement property. If you sell it and owe tax of, say, $75,000, you have only $385,000 to put down—which reduces what you can afford as a replacement.

Avoiding tax, therefore, keeps more of your wealth working for you—the full $460,000, in this case.

How to escape the tax?

There's no tax on an exchange of one piece of business property for another of the same general type—a "like" property.

So does that mean you should wander the earth looking for that special someone who has the property you want, who wants to part with it and take yours in its place, in a tax-free exchange? No; something a lot more practical—use a *deferred exchange*, which may look complicated but happens every day.

Here's how it can work:

1. You find a, well, allow me to call her a "buyer" for the moment, someone who wants to own your property and can pay what it's worth.
2. You find the property you want—call it the "target" property, whose owner wants to sell it.
3. Your "buyer" buys the target property and swaps it to you, tax-free, for yours.

This transaction is usually handled by a "qualified intermediary" (an independent service provider, somewhat like an escrow agent) who handles all aspects of the transaction for a fee, using the buyer's money.

For you, this is a sale in all but name. The name (deferred exchange) lets you escape tax if the deal fits certain requirements, one of which is that no more than 180 days can elapse between transfer of your current property and receipt of the target property. (There are ways around this limit.) Construction work on the target property, before the exchange and to suit your needs, can be arranged.

It's also okay, using an arrangement somewhat similar to that with a qualified intermediary, to acquire the target property first and thereafter transfer what you presently own.

Tax Later?

As always: *Tax later is better than tax now.* So you've saved the tax "now." What's the tax "later"?

The tax saved is in theory to be recaptured, more or less, when and if you sell the property you got in the exchange. There may never be a recapture if you own the property at your death. Meanwhile, if what you got is depreciable, your depreciation deductions on it will be limited to the remaining amount allowable on the property you gave up.

These recapture rules don't disturb the truth that tax later—in cheaper dollars—beats tax now.

State tax now

Swaps that save federal income tax almost always save state *income tax* too (though not always where the properties are in different states). But a state real estate *transfer tax* could hit transfers exempt from income tax. And where a mortgage is involved, there may be a state mortgage tax.

Cash and debt can cause tax now

Swaps can be taxable now when you receive cash or shed mortgage debt. Here, you can be taxable on gain (profit) *up to* the amount of the cash you receive, or the amount of mortgage debt you owe that the "buyer" assumes (agrees to pay); the law equates this with cash, received by you.

EXAMPLE

You want to reduce your real estate holdings and exposure, in favor of more modest space. You swap property worth $300,000, with a basis of $180,000, for property worth $250,000 plus $50,000 cash from the "buyer." Though your profit is $120,000 ($250,000 plus $50,000 minus $180,000), you owe tax currently on only $50,000, the cash received. Tax here could be $7,500.

The result would be the same if the property had a $30,000 mortgage, and the buyer assumed the mortgage and gave you $20,000 in cash, instead of $50,000.

Using your real estate as a down payment

Say your target property is worth $1,000,000, while what you own is worth $300,000 with a $180,000 basis. The deferred exchange we describe effectively lets you use your real estate for its full $300,000 value (though your "investment" is only $180,000) as a down payment on the target property.

How an ESOP Helps Finance Real Estate Acquisition

You're not supposed to use your company retirement plan to grow your business assets. But one type of retirement plan can, within limits, be used that way, and it especially suits the acquisition of business real estate. It's the employee stock ownership plan (ESOP) and it's *available only to corporations.*

The strategy is built on your corporation's long-term commitment to fund the ESOP plan, so it's not cost-free.

At its simplest, the corporation contributes cash to the plan, and the plan uses the cash to buy stock in the corporation, stock the corporation newly issues for that purpose. The cash goes out from the corporation and comes right back. This may look like nothing much has happened. But the ESOP is really a unique financing device for the corporation, and this device gives the plan an investment asset.

CASE STUDY

Andy Wye owns 80 percent of Wye Corp., which earns about $750,000 a year. Andy plans to grow Wye Corp. through acquisition of real estate to be used in the business. The first step is a Wye Corp. contribution of $100,000 to the Wye Corp. ESOP. The ESOP spends that $100,000 to buy stock Wye Corp. newly issues for the purpose, stock that is now an investment asset for the ESOP.

What happened? Wye Corp.'s $100,000 cash contribution to the ESOP is tax-deductible, a deduction that saves, say, $35,000 in Wye

Corp. tax. Wye Corp.'s stock sale to the ESOP, through which it got the $100,000 right back, is tax-free. So the corporation is $35,000 richer than before.

Of course, more has happened than that. If the Wye Corp. stock just bought represents 2 percent of total Wye Corp. shares, Wye Corp. stockholders have just transferred 2 percent of future Wye Corp. income and Wye Corp. assets to the ESOP. Andy's 80 percent of Wye Corp. is now 78.4 percent, though as an ESOP plan participant he can share in the plan's 2 percent stock interest.

If we assume that Wye Corp. before this transaction had $100,000 to invest in real estate, now it has $135,000 (tax saved and cash coming back from the stock sale to the ESOP). That could be the entire cost; more likely, though, it's just the down payment.

Much business real estate will cost more than could be paid for out of a simple ESOP contribution. That's why so much real estate is bought over time with a down payment and a big mortgage.

Just as the ESOP helped with the down payment, it can help with the mortgage.

How ESOP Covers Your Mortgage

The ESOP can borrow the money your corporation needs.

Not that it takes on the mortgage. The building will be owned by, and depreciable by, your corporation; it's your corporation that's liable on the mortgage. The ESOP buys further new stock issued by your corporation in an installment sale. In its installment purchase, it is effectively borrowing the unpaid purchase price from *your corporation*. The ESOP pays this installment debt off over time out of future ESOP contributions from your corporation, contributions used in fact to add wealth to the corporation's business.

CASE STUDY (CONTINUED)

Say Wye Corp. is buying a building (with its land) for $1 million, using $135,000 down and a ten-year mortgage loan for $865,000, at 6.5 percent interest. And say that the ESOP contracts with Wye Corp. to buy a further $865,000 of newly issued Wye Corp. stock, to be paid for over ten years at 6.5 percent. Assume the mortgage and the installment debt are each to be amortized in periodic installments over the period.

Wye Corp. pays the bank $120,326 each year. Over ten years that's $1,203,260, of which $865,000 is principal and $338,260 is interest. Wye Corp. contributes $120,326 each year to the ESOP, but that comes right back to Wye Corp. as principal and interest on the installment loan. In other words, Wye Corp.'s contribution to the ESOP comes back to pay Wye Corp.'s mortgage, leaving behind a big tax deduction for each Wye Corp. contribution.

Using the ESOP device can give Wye Corp. huge leverage in buying the building. Without the ESOP, Wye Corp.'s net after-tax cost of buying the building, using reasonable assumptions, could be $1,112,510. With the ESOP loan, it's $805,084.

We can't guess what having and using the building might do to augment Wye Corp.'s profits over the ten years. But it could be a conservative guess that the building's value has increased 20 percent over ten years, to $1,200,000. Looking only at the building's cost and value (and disregarding the unknowable effect on Wye Corp.'s profits), buying without the ESOP yields a return on investment of 7.77 percent over ten years. Buying with the ESOP, the investment return is 49 percent.

Newly issued stock shares dilute the value of all shares. Assuming the shares in the ESOP's installment purchase give the ESOP a total interest of 16 percent of Wye Corp., Andy's interest drops to 67.2 percent—though maybe of a much richer company, and also enhanced by the interest he has as an ESOP participant.

Need the money up front?

Instead of an installment purchase, the ESOP could take out a bank loan, pay Wye Corp. the full stock purchase price up front, and pay off the bank loan over time. Wye Corp. would facilitate the deal by guaranteeing the ESOP's loan repayment. Wye Corp. now has the cash from the ESOP's stock purchase, and won't need a mortgage. But that wouldn't eliminate its financing costs, which are reflected in Wye Corp.'s future contributions to fund the ESOP's loan payments.

ACTION POINT ✓

Don't try this at home. Their use as financing tools is a key reason ESOPs exist. But actually using them for such a purpose is tricky and complex, calling for professional guidance from a retirement plan specialist.

Strategy Review

Your goal in this chapter is to build long-term wealth in the form of real estate used in your business. Your opportunities:

1. Rent as an acquisition tool. Consider buying more space through the business than you need and renting out the excess.
2. Earn tax-free cash flow. Your depreciation deductions generate positive cash flow.
   - You can maximize depreciation with savvy allocation of the price paid for land and building.
   - "Deconstructing" a building into components with shorter lives can augment depreciation even further.
3. Trade up. Use "deferred exchanges" to preserve full asset value when replacing business properties.
4. ESOP financing. Incorporated businesses can use ESOPS to help with purchase down payments and long-term financing.

Chapter 7

Your Business Equipment

WEALTH CREATION STRATEGIES 33–36

Asset acquisitions can add wealth to one's business. In the tax deduction for depreciation, businesses have a mighty instrument that helps them acquire business equipment. Depreciation generates tax-free cash flow, which can effectively cover part of the cost of the equipment, and is available for other business uses.

Should Your Business Buy or Lease?

Some advisors note that equipment, especially high-tech equipment, quickly becomes obsolete. That, they argue, favors leasing, so you don't get stuck holding (and maybe still paying for) obsolete equipment when it's time to shift to newer technology. That's often true, in specific cases. But remember that the equipment owner who leases to you knows the obsolescence risk as well as you, or maybe better, and has factored that into the lease rent charged you.

Some lease, rather than borrow to buy, thinking they can't afford the interest cost of the loan. Maybe so. But consider that the equipment owner has borrowed to buy what's being leased to you and is passing on that interest cost, and then some, to you.

Leasing may be the only option in start-up settings when the business may lack the credit for a major purchase. So be it. Consider the purchase, and borrow-to-purchase, strategies in this chapter for future purchases once the business gets established.

Borrowing to buy

Equipment loans to small business are often over the expected useful life of the equipment—five years, seven years, sometimes longer or shorter. The borrower's credentials are important in getting the loan: how long in business (less than two years can be a problem); business income; projected business income, taking into account what the equipment can do for the business. Loans can be for a large part of the cost (say 90 percent) or the entire cost, sometimes with preferences for Armed Service veterans or their spouses.

Loan terms may call for full amortization or partial amortization with a balloon payment at the end. Some lenders require borrowers to make financial covenants (commitments), such as to maintain specified equity-to-debt ratios and working capital balances. Business borrowers may have to subordinate their owners' claims to the lender's claims—so that, for example, owners can't withdraw capital until non-owner loans are repaid. Owners may be obliged to personally guarantee the loan.

Depreciation: Wealth-Building Tool

You take the depreciation deduction against the full purchase price of the equipment, even though you have borrowed most or all of the price. For example, you borrow to buy $200,000 of construction equipment, with $20,000 down and $180,000 borrowed. Your depreciation deduction is a percentage of $200,000, not of $20,000.

You take depreciation over the equipment's "life." A short life means larger annual depreciation over fewer years. Except in rare cases, depreciation is considered to occur each year and depreciation deductions are to be taken each year; you will not be allowed to skip one year and double up the next. Generally, you must use the life the IRS prescribes for the type of item in question. You can of course dispose of the item before its life ends.

Though stuck with the IRS "life," you can still choose "method." The straight-line depreciation method gives the same amount every year (except for the first year, where the law won't allow a full year's depreciation even for items bought January 1, and the final year). The *declining balance* method somewhat frontloads your depreciation deduction, taking a larger part of the allowable total into the first few years of ownership, and less later. In later years you must switch from a declining balance to a straight-line amount when switching will give you the same or a greater deduction.

Depreciation works best for you when it can offset current income. When depreciation and out-of-pocket expenses exceed business income, the operation is running at a tax loss. This can be useful in some cases, but it's no goal for wealth-builders.

It's sometimes said that depreciation deductions "recover" the cost of the depreciable property. This isn't so. For every dollar you put down or owe on a building purchase, you may eventually be allowed a dollar of deduction, but that's only worth a part of the dollar—35 cents on the dollar, if your effective tax rate is 35 percent. It's more useful to see depreciation as reducing the tax due on the profits the depreciable property helps generate, or sometimes—if it's not yet generating profits—the tax on your other income.

Use Instant Equipment Writeoffs to Build Wealth

It's a basic principle of business and tax accounting that a business's tangible assets—real property and business equipment—decline in value over time. This decline is recognized by periodic depreciation deductions against the asset's cost as shown on the balance sheet. These deductions reduce business financial and taxable income.

But small businesses get a special tax benefit for equipment purchases. They can often write off—treat as a current expense—the entire cost of an equipment purchase in a single year. The amount "expensed" exempts from income tax an equivalent amount of business income, even when there is no equivalent cash outlay or, indeed, any current outlay. Depreciation generates tax-free income. Expensing does it faster.

CASE STUDY

Gene, who had been leasing delivery vehicles, decides to buy three qualifying vehicles for a total of $75,000, effective July 1. Business income for the year, disregarding these purchases, is $250,000. Expensing these purchases cuts business income by $75,000, saving $24,750 in federal tax costs, and maybe another $6,000 in state tax costs.

The cost expensed is the amount Gene put down in cash to buy the equipment (if anything), plus whatever he borrowed to buy the equipment. So if Gene paid $7,500 down and borrowed the rest, his federal and state tax savings of $30,750 is more than four times his down payment.

If the business is buying the equipment from its owner or co-owner, a close family member of either, or a related business, full writeoff is not allowed.

The loan is to be repaid out of business earnings generated through the equipment he bought. The business can't deduct payment of loan principal—though the $30,750 in tax savings helps generate money to make principal payments. The business can deduct interest on the debt, against business income.

Expensing is optional. Some entrepreneurs skip it in their business's early days, when income is slight. Some, even later, prefer to take depreciation, to get more or less equal writeoffs over the equipment's life.

You can also choose to expense part of an item (sometimes to offset a spike in income in the year of purchase) and depreciate the rest. Most entrepreneurs, of course, expense as much as their dollar and income limits allow.

Limits on equipment expensing

Dollar limits. The dollar ceiling (indexed for inflation) on what can be expensed is often increased by financial tax stimulus legislation. It's scheduled at $134,000 for 2010. Small businesses rarely exceed the ceiling. Amounts in excess of the ceiling must be depreciated.

Income limits. You can't expense more than the year's business income (after all other business deductions). Here's how to work within that limit:

EXPENSE SOME AND DEPRECIATE THE REST

Say your income after all business deductions is $60,000 but you must get equipment costing $100,000. You could expense some of the $100,000 cost and take deprecation up to the maximum allowed for first year depreciation on the property's basis left after expensing.

How much expensing and how much depreciation? We have a formula for that.

You want to take the maximum allowable deductions. The year's income is $60,000. The first year depreciation rate is, say, 10 percent of the item's cost (an IRS depreciation rate table would tell you the percentage). X is the amount to be expensed.

The formula is:

$$X + 10 \text{ percent of } (\$100,000 \text{ cost minus } X) = \$60,000.$$

The answer: The amount expensed is $55,555, the amount depreciated in the first year is $4,445 ($60,000 minus $55,555), and $40,000 remains to be expensed or depreciated in future years.

You can decide how much you can expense and how much to depreciate after the year is over and you know what your business income is.

BUY SOME EQUIPMENT THIS YEAR AND THE BALANCE BEGINNING NEXT YEAR

Unlike the case with depreciation, expensing doesn't turn on when during the year you buy, or first use, or prepare to use, the property. Thus, with $60,000 expected income this year, you could buy two vehicles this year (expensing $50,000) and the third the next year (expensing $25,000), assuming adequate income each year.

Generally, only corporations are allowed to expense property they buy and then lease out. This would eliminate expensing when a business owner, or the owner's family, buys equipment to lease to the owner's business, unless the buyer-lessor is a corporation.

What's a small business

Expensing is only for small business. "Small" is defined by how much equipment the business buys. Broadly, the amount a business can expense phases out once its total purchases in a year exceed three to four times the dollar ceiling.

CASE STUDY

Henry's single member LLC bought $200,000 worth of manufacturing equipment three-and-a-half years ago, paying $80,000 down with a $120,000 self-amortizing seven-year loan for the balance. He expensed $100,000 of the cost and has taken $73,657 in depreciation. Labor and maintenance costs total $50,000 for the period. He has paid interest of $26,763 to date and still owes $73,657 in loan principal. The equipment could be sold today for $60,000, which would yield a $27,205 taxable profit on the sale.

This recitation has omitted the key fact: What adding the equipment did for his business. Only Henry can know, or reasonably guess, the answer in advance, though I know cases where the entrepreneur got business, got contracts, because he could deliver a finished product that only the added equipment could make possible. Here, the added equipment increased Henry's annual business receipts by 45 percent of the cost of the equipment, or $90,000 for each of three years plus $45,000 for the half year. In this case, equipment purchase, operation, and sale generated positive cash flow of $110,997, specifically: cash receipts from equipment operation and sale, less cash outlays for operating expenses, principal, interest, and taxes.

Use Corporate Low-Tax Shelter to Help Buy Equipment

Most types of small business entities pay no federal income tax. Owners of the businesses are taxed directly on business earnings, in the years earned, whether or not currently paid out to them by the business.

C corporations, on the other hand, are taxed directly on their earnings, but their owners aren't taxed until earnings are paid out to them. This difference makes the C corporation a modest tax shelter, and make the sheltered funds a mechanism for acquiring business equipment.

When a C corporation's income is $50,000 or less, its tax rate is 15 percent. So it can serve as a tax shelter for owners whose *personal* federal tax rate might be up to 35 percent. By tweaking corporation income—and we'll see ways to do that shortly—the corporation can save, say, $10,000 a year. This tax shelter can help in our project to build wealth through acquiring and operating business equipment.

You'll need capital for equipment down payments, for loan principal payments, for purchases on credit, or to purchase money loans. Such payments are not tax-deductible. They don't reduce your taxable business profits; you are paying for them after tax. But you can get part way to tax deduction, with depreciation and expensing your purchase. These do reduce taxable business profits, and the tax saved can go to meet capital requirements—funding purchases, down payments, and loan principal payments.

The corporation tax shelter helps too. The tax saved through the shelter provides additional money for principal payments.

Income Tweaking

For right now, your goal is to keep corporation income under $50,000, but not much under. Going over $50,000 is no disaster, but a higher rate applies to the next $25,000 of income (and a blended rate can apply even to the first $50,000, if income exceeds $100,000).

But don't suppose we're trying to keep what you the entrepreneur get out of the business to $50,000 or less—just what the corporation pays tax on.

We can picture a business like this: Your corporation borrowed to buy heavy equipment some years back and is currently taking depreciation on it and paying off the loan. This year's gross receipts are $800,000, and after expenses—including depreciation and interest on the loan, but nothing, yet, for you—there's $300,000 left. You might pay yourself $250,000, allocated among your salary, retirement, and health benefits, and the corporation's Social Security taxes on your salary.

All of these are deductible by the corporation. You owe income tax only on the salary, at your individual rate, plus your own share of Social Security tax on your salary. The corporation has taxable income of $50,000. The $42,500 left after the $7,500 income tax goes to pay down principal on the equipment loan.

Depending on business income and transactions for the year, you calibrate toward $50,000 of taxable income by increasing deductible expenses (say, prepaying some expenses, to the extent prepayment is deductible, or increasing your salary or benefits) or by decreasing expenses (postponing some to next year or decreasing your pay).

Other uses

Maybe you won't want to tweak income of your main business, year in and year out. Or maybe your main business isn't a corporation at all. A corporate tax shelter could still serve your *leasing* corporation, if you have one.

Personal service corporations—usually incorporated professional practices and consultants—don't get this tax shelter. They pay tax at the top corporate rate, on all their corporate income.

Trade-In and Up

Equipment wears out or becomes obsolete. To replace it, entrepreneurs may use money saved for the purpose out of business profits that were received tax-free thanks to depreciation. Since the entrepreneur borrowed to buy the equipment, some of that money would instead have gone to pay down loan principal.

The old equipment, though today worth nothing close to its original price, is often worth more than its basis—that is, its original cost plus capital improvements minus accumulated depreciation and expensing. Sale for more than basis generates a taxable profit, and the tax will reduce what you'd otherwise have to apply toward a suitable replacement.

Use Tax-Free Swaps to Upgrade Equipment Holdings

A trade-in avoids tax and lets you spend the equipment's full value toward the replacement. There's no tax on an exchange of one piece of business property for a "like" property—that is, another of the same general type. This concept was covered in detail—for real estate swaps—in Wealth Creation Strategy 31. It applies the same way here, with these additional considerations when you're swapping equipment expensed under Wealth Creation Strategy 34.

You can depreciate or expense the new replacement equipment (or depreciate some and expense some). Yes, I know I said you could only expense property you purchase. But the law treats the extra amount you put up (on top of the value of property you trade in) as a purchase. And another break: Ordinarily you must pay tax on some of what you expensed if you stop using it in your business. That doesn't apply if you trade it away for "like" property.

If you still owe debt on the old equipment, the lender may still have a security interest in the old equipment, which must somehow be discharged or transferred. Maybe the loan balance must be paid now—which may require sale of the old equipment after all. Or, the lender on the old equipment may lend on the new, and transfer the security interest to the replacement equipment.

What's "like" property?

Almost any piece of equipment you'll likely use in your business will be "like" business equipment you give up. And you can exchange one item for several or several for one.

161

How ESOP Helps Finance
Your Equipment Purchase

You may remember this financing device from Wealth Creation Strategy 32. It's the employee stock ownership plan (ESOP), *for corporations only*. It would work the same way for a big-ticket equipment purchase.

Strategy Review

Your goal in this chapter is to build long-term wealth through equipment used in your business, and through satellite operations and businesses. Your opportunities:

1. Depreciation is a mighty tool to build wealth, through its power to generate positive cash flow for use in acquisitions. Expensing is a form of "instantaneous depreciation," uniquely available, at your option, to small business.
2. Sums that small business corporations can shelter from full corporate tax can go far to help acquire equipment or pay down equipment loans. Entrepreneurs sometimes manage (calibrate) corporate income to maximize the modest shelter.
3. Trade-ins and trade-ups, maybe including sophisticated "deferred exchanges," can preserve full asset value when replacing worn or obsolete equipment.
4. Incorporated businesses can use ESOPS to help with purchase down payments and long-term financing. Getting this right is extremely complicated.

8 You, Conglomerated

WEALTH CREATION STRATEGIES 37–40

Asset acquisitions can add wealth to one's business, as we know. But the acquisition techniques in this chapter are used to build wealth *outside* the business, and therefore outside its tax and ownership structure. Wealth planning can put asset ownership directly in the hands of the business owner individually, or members of the owner's family, or separate family owned business or investment entities.

Buy and Hold Business
Assets Outside the Business

People of my generation remember shipping magnate Aristotle Onassis. He had a wealth strategy that worked for him. When he wanted to add another tanker to his fleet, he offered some giant oil company a long-term lease on his yet-to-be-built ship. Big banks were eager to lend Onassis money to build the ship on the secured income stream flowing to him under the oil company lease.

Don't see yourself in this picture? Okay, so you're no almost-billionaire ship owner. You can still use part of Onassis's strategy to acquire real estate or equipment for business use—assets that *you* rather than the business can own, and pass on to your heirs.

The arrangement calls for an owner and a lessee. The owner is you or some entity such as an LLC that you create and own. The lessee is your business, a separate entity. The business lessee pays the owner a reasonable rent for the space or equipment, which it deducts for tax purposes, avoiding tax to that extent on its business income. The rent is business or investment income to the owner, offset by operating expenses and depreciation deductions.

Can we do "The Full Onassis" here? That would be a bank loan for the purchase price on the security of rent to be paid under a lease between "you business" and "you owner." Banks wouldn't offer this deal to the likes of you. You should expect to put money of your own down on the purchase, along with a mortgage or other debt for the balance. Such a lender may seek the owner's personal liability, maybe through a personal guarantee where the owner is a limited liability entity. But rental income can fund debt service, and depreciation may in effect fund principal payments and may help recover the down payment, tax-free.

EXAMPLE

Denise forms a single-member LLC to buy a business condo for $1 million, with $100,000 down and a $900,000 mortgage to be paid off over twenty years at 6.5 percent interest. The LLC then rents the space to Denise's business—say that's a corporation—for $98,000 a year.

The LLC's monthly mortgage payments total $80,522 for the year, of which $22,690 is mortgage principal the first year and $57,832 is interest. The LLC's upkeep expenses, taxes, and insurance total $12,000 for the year and depreciation the first year (it's higher later) is $24,610.

The LLC's taxable income the first year is $3,558, with a $5,478 positive cash flow (before income tax).The tax on $3,558 is around $1,070 (assumed), leaving $4,418 net cash after tax. The $4,418 could be applied toward recovery of the down payment, and the LLC at year's end has $122,690 equity in the condo space.

Results can be much the same if the business already owns the real estate, or Denise does. The LLC could buy the real estate on mortgage and lease it back to Denise's business.

Why LLC?

Onassis's ships were separate corporations, to insulate every other ship and Onassis, personally, from liability for damage one ship might do to other parties. The corporate entity type still offers that protection, but there are other good options. Today's trend for property holdings is toward the LLC.

Real property owned and sold by the corporation is subject to two income taxes: on the corporation's profit (imposed on the corporation) and on the corporation's distribution to the stockholder (imposed on the stockholder). Sale by a non-corporate owner, such as an LLC, is taxed once under federal law, to the owner or co-owners.

Real estate owned by an individual—say, the business owner—gets a basis step-up when the owner dies. This can eliminate all or most income tax on the heirs' sale of appreciated real estate. Basis step-up, explained below, can also be arranged on death of a partner or LLC member. Basis step-up doesn't happen to real estate held within a corporation, though the basis of corporate *stock* steps up.

Real estate morphs into personal property when it's put into an entity (a corporation, LLC, or partnership). This can sometimes be used to escape state death tax. Here's what I mean:

State death taxes tax real property—where the property is and personal property where the deceased owner resided. What you own in an LLC, partnership, or corporation is personal property even though *it* owns real property. So New Jersey real property put into a New Jersey LLC escapes state death tax everywhere if the now-deceased LLC owner had validly established residence in a no-death-tax state like Florida.

And holding real property through an LLC, instead of personally, can save state/local real estate transfer taxes: You sell your LLC ownership interest, not the real estate itself.

How to Hold Business Assets

Most U.S. businesses are sole proprietorships—which don't limit the owner's liability. Businesses conducted as partnerships—"general" partnerships—don't limit the liability of any partner, even (with some exceptions) for acts or defaults by other partners.

But any entrepreneur with ambitions to grow her business as a wealth creation instrument must consider getting protection against personal liability to business creditors or claimants.

Limited liability essentially means that business creditors can reach no more than the assets of the business plus the assets the owners have committed themselves to provide but have not yet provided.

All limited liability entities require some kind of registration with the authority (state) granting the limitation, at some cost and effort. The state typically imposes annual re-registration fees, and may subject the entity to income or franchise tax, in addition to taxing the owner.

The following business entities, recognized in every state, limit owners' liability:

Corporations. These have highly developed and elaborate rules intended to: inform potential creditors; protect business funds or assets on which creditors may be relying; and protect the interests of minority stockholders against over-reaching by majority owners ("corporate governance" rules).

Statutory close corporation rules in some states simplify corporate governance. Stockholders can agree by contract (a shareholder agreement) to run things through designated managers, with minimal formalities and—if they choose—distribute earnings otherwise than proportionate to stock ownership. A business headquartered elsewhere can be incorporated in a state with statutory close corporation rules, and then qualify that corporation to do business in the state where it's headquartered.

Corporations are generally subject to a federal corporate income tax. Such corporations are called "C" corporations, after a chapter of the federal tax code.

Most corporations can qualify to *elect exemption* from federal income tax (there are some exceptions to exemption). Corporations electing this tax exemption are called "S" corporations, after another chapter of the tax code. An "S election," as it's called, for federal tax purposes, has no effect on the corporation's liability protection under state business law. A statutory close corporation can be an S corporation.

Limited partnerships. These are partnerships with one or more general partners—whose liability is not limited—and limited partners, whose liability is generally limited to the amounts they have invested or committed. General partners typically run the business; limited partners are typically passive investors. A person can be both general and limited partner, in which case she is liable as a general partner.

A general partner can effectively limit liability by holding the general partnership interest through a limited liability entity, such as a corporation, which she controls.

Limited Liability Companies (LLCs). These can operate more or less like general partnerships, where all or most of the owners ("members") have authority to act in the business—called "member managed"—or like limited partnerships, where one or a few owners are authorized to act (or a non-owner manager acts) and the rest are passive—called "manager managed." Liability is limited for either type.

LLCs with two or more members are treated as partnerships for federal tax purposes unless they elect tax status as a corporation. By so electing, they can make the further federal tax election of S corporation status.

Under federal tax law, single member LLCs are treated as sole proprietorships unless they elect tax status as corporations (which allows further election of S corporation status). Thus, a single member LLC that doesn't elect corporate tax status can't protect its owner against federal tax claims against the business.

Federal tax status of an LLC does not affect its treatment as an LLC under state business law, nor does it determine state tax status.

Most state income tax laws follow the federal rule taxing the single member owner unless corporate tax status is elected. But in some states there's no election: some tax the owner, others tax the LLC. Federal *employment* tax law taxes the LLC (no election), as do most states. Unemployment tax problems arise in states that tax the owner.

Professionals generally may practice in LLCs or under a counterpart professional limited liability company law.

Limited liability partnerships (LLPs). These are general partnerships each of whose general partners has limited liability. They are widely used for professional practices; in some states they can only be used by professionals.

State taxes

Five states have no corporate income taxes; six states have no personal income taxes (so no tax on passed-through income); a few states tax S corporations, partnerships, and LLCs.

With professional guidance, you can change your current business entity to one that suits you better (a change subject sometimes to income tax, state transfer tax, and co-owner and creditor issues). Change might be done to qualify for a Wealth Creation Strategy unavailable in your current business form.

Multiple entities

Each significant separate activity can and often should be a separate limited liability entity: building, laboratory, studio, treatment center, consultancy operation, equipment rental operation, or other sideline businesses. There's some protection—and also lots of complication and expense—in putting assets into differing entities in differing states (or countries).

ACTION POINT ✓

Be scrupulous in keeping separate entities apart, acting carefully in a representative capacity for each, and maintaining separate books and records, registrations, bank accounts, and tax filings. Treat each entity's assets and money as belonging to the entity, not you personally. Failure to maintain the entity's separate integrity allows the IRS and other creditors to ignore or defeat protections for family limited partnerships, family corporations, and family LLCs holding personal assets.

And don't overdo it. Multiple entities cost money and, maybe more important, require attention. The more complicated your ownership structure, the less likely you are to maintain it.

How Liability Limitation Fails

Limited liability entities offer substantial, but not total, protection for the business owner. The owner's personal assets can be reached by creditors of the business in these cases:

- When the owner assumes liability, directly, or secondarily as a guarantor of the business's debts.
- When the owner acts directly rather than as a representative of the business, in a manner leading the creditor to believe that the owner, rather than the business, is the obligor, or when the owner effectively disregards the entity, treating its assets as his own. A limited partner may lose limited liability as to outsiders (customers, suppliers, etc.) who reasonably believe, from his activity in the business, that he is a general partner.
- For the owner's own malpractice or negligence (though liability is limited as to liability for a co-owner's malpractice or negligence).
- For capital contributions to the business that the owner was obligated to make but has failed to make.
- When the owner takes a distribution from the business, or directs a distribution, to defraud business creditors.

- When the owner takes distributions that must be returned under state law. This can apply when the distribution (such as a dividend) would make the business insolvent.
- When the entity failed to observe due formalities and procedures in organization or operations, in some cases. State law may excuse such foot faults, and continue limited liability protections. Operating through a statutory close corporation or an LLC forestalls such attacks because such entities run with fewer formalities and procedural routines.
- Under various other statutory obligations imposed directly on the business owner, such as for willful failure to pay payroll taxes, or failure to pay employee wage claims.

Rentals That Enrich
the Family

You may have heard the term "family income shifting." It means putting some of a parent's income into a child's hands and thereby saving tax on the rate differential between parents' and child's tax brackets. Most income-shifting opportunities suggested at tax time are trivial, worth a couple of hundred dollars at most. But with business, and business assets, opportunities can be huge: shifting tens of thousands of dollars of business rent to lower-taxed hands within the family.

Say that your business could profit from new or added sales space, or warehouse space, or a processing facility, or a studio. Such space could cost your business $30,000 a year to rent, but you mean to buy what you need, which will be cheaper in the long run. Instead, your *family* could buy and operate the new space, directly or indirectly, and you could put that $30,000 of rent into their hands, year after year.

Or say that your business needs a high-tech machine that could cost the business, say, $20,000 a year to lease. Your family could buy and lease out the new machine, directly or indirectly, and they could collect that $20,000 rent each year. Just how many dollars that saves depends on total deductions available for the building, and family tax brackets, but $5,000 a year for real estate rent could be reasonable—more when rent is higher.

When operating deductions and depreciation are higher in relation to rent, such a move may not save much income tax. But that can still be okay, because the moves to shift annual family income also build permanent family wealth, in ways not possible when the real estate assets are held *in the business*.

Building Family Assets

Here, the aim is to put business real estate, a major item of personal and family wealth, in the hands of your children or other heirs, a move that your business income can indirectly finance. This can be done in a way that avoids probate headaches and federal estate taxes on your estate.

CASE STUDY

Ted's business needs more space: office space, warehouse, assembly area, whatever. A business entity, preferably an LLC, is formed to acquire and operate the space, to be owned by Ted's two sons. They provide what the LLC will put down as a down payment. The LLC borrows the rest against the security of the purchased space and the promised income stream of rent to be paid by Ted's business. The LLC leases the newly purchased property to Ted's business.

The result is that Ted's sons have a major investment asset, paid for largely out of business income. Rental income the real estate earns goes to the children through their LLC and they will owe income tax on the income. Ted escapes tax on business profits paid out as rent.

Rent is income to the LLC, and therefore to Ted's sons, but reduced by operating expenses, depreciation, and mortgage interest. The balance is tax-free cash, to the extent of depreciation deductions minus mortgage principal payments.

This saves federal or state death taxes, or both, in Ted's estate (assuming throughout that Ted otherwise owns enough to leave a taxable estate). If Ted's business is a sole proprietorship or single member LLC, real estate in the business is directly subject to death tax. If he had some other business entity, the value of Ted's share in the business, including his share in its real estate, would be subject to death tax. This death tax is avoided when (as in Ted's case) the real estate is owned by other family members, directly or through an LLC or other entity.

This also avoids probate problems and expenses. Some expenses and fees of probating an estate are based on the size of the probate estate. So some part of those expenses is saved if assets that might otherwise be in your estate pass to heirs before your death.

And it protects the real estate from creditors of Ted's business.

We're assuming here that what your family gets in these arrangements belongs to *them*. *They* own it, not just sort of own it until you want it back. But there can still be trust and custodianship arrangements and other limitations on their interests that can tie their hands, especially if they are minors, see chapters 12 and 13.

Dealings between the business and the LLC should be businesslike, at arm's length.

ACTION POINT ✓

Implementing this strategy will take the following steps:

1. Have an LLC formed under state law, with an operating agreement describing what it's intended to do.
2. Have family members buy LLC memberships. For those who are minors, interests would be held by a custodian or trustee.
3. Appoint a responsible adult as manager. In this plan, you, the entrepreneur, are not a member or a manager.
4. Provide funds for the LLC. These are paid in by or for the members as the price of their membership interests. Typically the money would come from your gifts to the members. The money involved should be adequate to cover the down payment and operating expenses until rents received can do that.
5. The purchase of the property to be rented back to the business. This would be a formal purchase by the LLC, usually also involving a mortgage loan.
6. Rent to the business entity. Rent and other terms should be commercially reasonable. That means they shouldn't be unrealistically generous to the LLC, which might look like siphoning business funds off to the sons. And they shouldn't be so little as to cause a significant tax loss to the LLC (and therefore the members). Costs of operating the space—real estate taxes, insurance, maintenance—could of course be made the tenant's responsibility under the lease, though this would reduce what could be charged as rent. Alternatively, the space could be operated for a fee by a real estate managing agent.

Hold through a leasing corporation

Another possibility is that the owner-lessor could be a corporation, making use of the corporate shelter described in Wealth Creation Strategy 34. The corporation could acquire and lease one item to the business, or a package of items, for a sizable—but reasonable—rent. The corporation would deduct depreciation or expensing, or both, plus interest on any purchase money loans, and operating expenses. Net profits under $50,000 from these rental activities are taxed at 15 percent; the remaining 85 percent can go for loan principal.

One time only

If one corporate tax shelter is good, are two better?

Not really. The $50,000 shelter is shared among all corporations owned by the same, or related, persons. So if you own two corporations, the 15 percent rate applies to the first $25,000 for each corporation. And remember, each corporation has a cost, in setup and maintenance, including state/local registration and reporting.

Your Stealth Business

Real estate or equipment held for rental to your business is in itself something of a business. It has assets, liabilities, income, and expenses. Rents charged the business should be reasonable (about what would be charged by parties dealing at arms' length).

The typical business entity for such holdings is the LLC, for its limitation of liability and management characteristics and because its income and deductions, including any tax losses, pass through directly to the LLC owners.

Tax losses are when expenses and depreciation exceed income, which can happen even when the real estate is producing a positive cash flow. Owners want to use the tax loss to offset (effectively eliminate tax on) taxable income from elsewhere—from another business, or investments, or salary.

Most entrepreneurs should try to avoid rental tax loss situations (for themselves or other family owners) where they can. And they often can, through reasonable calibration of the rent charged the business.

What lies behind this advice is the tax law's restrictions on the owner's use of such losses. Individuals renting equipment can't deduct such losses in the year they occur, except to the extent of taxable income from other rental or similar activities. Lacking such "similar" taxable income, they are condemned to long postponement of such losses, until they dispose of their properties or their ownership interest in the properties.

Individuals renting real estate, with adjusted gross income (AGI) below $150,000 can deduct up to $25,000 of such losses if they are actively participating in the property management. This could apply to you as owner-manager, depending on what you do as manager, but it's seldom available for children owning through an LLC.

Satellite Businesses Can Add Retirement Wealth and Other Benefits

Many entrepreneurs create satellite businesses—businesses spun off from their main business. I've described arrangements whereby an entrepreneur personally or through a business entity leases space or equipment to the entrepreneur's business. That leasing operation can be a business, and one that can expand to lease equipment or space to others. But let's look farther:

A business may be created to provide further services to existing customers. We see this often among medical/dental professionals—for example, a physical therapy service for orthopedic patients. Another example is the mortgage lender who added businesses to do property appraisals, title work, and insurance.

The added business may represent what business school professors call "integration"—owning the next business step back toward the raw material, or the next step closer to the consumer. I saw integration with two different publishing companies that created and own their printing operations, and now do printing work for other, noncompeting, publishers.

Business spinoff should be done sparingly. A lot can go wrong. You'll need to understand your new business thoroughly, and you'll be taking time, energy, concentration—and maybe assets—from your main business, which is plenty challenging already. If you can make the new business work, it will deliver expanded wealth potential:

Self-financing. Funding you provide the business may come cheaper than from commercial lenders. Make some of the funding as a loan and you may have standing as a creditor if the venture is unsuccessful—and as a *secured* creditor, if you take a mortgage or security interest in a business asset.

Early, start-up losses. You can deduct these against the income from your main business, in effect netting modest losses from the new venture against taxable profits from the main business. This is true whether you own the new business personally, or through the main business—assuming neither main business nor satellite/spinoff is a C corporation.

Of course, losses, start-up or otherwise, are no path to wealth. But with a cushion of income from your successful business, you're better equipped to take the early hits in a new business than your more lightly financed potential competitors, and so may have a better chance at long-term success.

Purchasing/bargaining economies of scale. These are sometimes possible.

Retirement plans and other employee benefits. These can represent an additional wealth opportunity if the new business is profitable. I relentlessly urge tax-favored retirement plans on all entrepreneurs whose businesses make money: They are the first, the essential, business wealth creation tool.

Counting the earnings in your next business may allow additional tax-deferred investments. However, total contributions and benefits from all the businesses you control can't exceed the overall limits on benefits and contributions.

The new business may also offer other employee benefits. Health insurance options depend on the size, type, or location of the business, and of the work force. Your participation through the new business may enhance your overall coverage or reduce your costs.

More or richer perks—business-paid lifestyle expenses—may be possible with a second business. And more generous plans of all kinds may be possible in a new business with no co-owners, or more agreeable co-owners than you have in the main business.

None of this is possible, though, unless you're an active worker in the new business, not just an investor. Remember that you may have to make benefits in one business available to employees of the other, where you control both businesses.

What Not to Do with the New Business Entity

Each new business entity should, like the main business, be a limited liability entity. Resist any impulse to enrich one particular business through arbitrary or unreasonable transactions (or, of course, on-paper-only transactions) between your businesses.

This is sometimes done to get some business opportunity or preference, often under a government program. But mostly I see devices to shift income or tax deductions from one to another (often to reduce federal or state income taxes), or shift assets (maybe to avoid state franchise or property taxes), or sales (to avoid sales taxes). Federal and state laws often effectively combine business entities that are under common or related ownership, refusing to recognize transactions between them, or imposing on all members rules that some individual members might otherwise escape (say, through a size exemption).

The imaginations of the entrepreneur and the professional advisor are fertile, and some ways around some prohibitions will be found. But here I want the focus to be on satellite businesses that will be run, as well as they can be run, as true businesses and not as tools to confuse or disguise.

Family Satellite Businesses Enhance Family Wealth

You can use your business, your business smarts and contacts, and your personal assets, to grow serious family wealth through your family's own satellite business. Family members active in profitable sub-businesses can enjoy major wealth creation opportunities of their own—especially, retirement plans. Many family estates own several small businesses. Some get that way by splitting single enterprises run by the founding entrepreneur into several, run by the children.

Business Expansion

Think of what your family can do, when you consider expanding your business. For example, a retailer or other provider of goods or services expands by opening another location. There may be an opportunity there for a family member.

One option is for the entrepreneur to help family members own, build, fit out, and lease the location to the entrepreneur's business. Lease rentals from the new location could shift substantial income from the entrepreneur's business to his family members, with overall favorable income and estate tax results.

Another option would be to have a family member run the new location. The entrepreneur could be co-owner and general manager (hands-on or otherwise), sharing profits from the new site, or taking supplier and management fees, as with a franchise.

Helping the new business

The successful entrepreneur has much valuable input to offer a family member starting up a business, whether a satellite of the entrepreneur's business, or something different. This help is usually at some cost or risk to the entrepreneur, which need not mean the entrepreneur is reluctant to offer it.

ACTION POINT ✓

The parent who is an entrepreneur and who wants to help her family members set up a business should consider these steps:

Sweetheart loans. Parents often fund their children's ventures with low-interest or no-interest loans, reducing the start-up costs. Loans up to $100,000 have no tax consequences if the borrower has less than $1,000 of investment income. This works fine when the loan is used in business, but the rule punishes loans intended to shift investment income from parent to child. Such a loan can save, say, $10,000 a year over what a commercial lender would charge for a $100,000 loan to a new venturer with no long-term credit history.

Where this break won't apply (as where the loan exceeds $100,000), charge interest at the Applicable Federal Rate (AFR). The lowest AFR rates are for short-term (e.g., demand) loans. The child deducts interest paid to the parent; the parent reports it as taxable income.

How things go if the child defaults is between parent and child. But the IRS won't allow the lender a tax deduction for the bad debt unless it can be convinced that the parties intended a true loan, which the lender really intended to collect. Some entrepreneurs use their credit instead of their cash, taking out a loan at commercial rates, based on their own credit history, and in turn lending that to their children.

Guarantees. Entrepreneurs often guarantee loans third parties make to family members. The guarantee—by itself—has no tax consequences. If the family member defaults, the lender expects to collect from the entrepreneur. The entrepreneur's attempt to deduct his payment under the guarantee, as a bad debt, faces something of the same obstacle as bad debt deduction for the borrower's default on a loan by the entrepreneur.

ACTION POINT

Business smarts. Entrepreneurs have skills their children may lack, and may put those skills to use for the child's business. Services performed free in a business the child owns have no tax consequences. If the entrepreneur is a partner, or an S corporation stockholder, in a profitable business co-owned with the child, the entrepreneur should collect something that reflects "reasonable" compensation for his services.

Business opportunities. An entrepreneur may be able to steer her business customers to providers of related services—services her children's businesses could provide. I mentioned physical therapy services (steered from medical orthopedic practices) and appraisal fees and the like (steered from a mortgage lender). The entrepreneur will often be a co-owner of such satellite businesses.

Strategy Review

Your goal in this chapter is to build long-term wealth by holding business assets *outside* the business, and through satellite operations and businesses. Your opportunities:

1. You can personally own or control business real estate or equipment and use rents from the business to pay or reimburse your acquisition costs.
2. Consider how a spinoff or satellite operation from your main business can enhance wealth, especially through additional retirement and other tax-favored benefits.
3. When family members own and lease equipment to the business—
   • High-taxed rental income can be shifted into low-taxed hands and
   • The family estate can avoid or reduce estate taxes, expenses and creditor risks.
4. Family satellite businesses can expand family wealth opportunities, especially when helped by your skills, smarts, and contacts.

Chapter 9

The Home-Based Business

Here I'll consider things an entrepreneur can do in the home that contribute, in a modest way, to a wealth creation program. There's nothing wrong with home office deductions. But tax deductions alone don't build wealth. However, you can create wealth by putting a tax deduction together with some other opportunity or benefit:

- A deduction you can get without parting with cash—like depreciation.
- A deduction you get for something you're doing anyway—like heating and lighting your apartment, or repairing the roof of your house.
- A deduction that does double duty—as where what for most people is an ordinary itemized deduction for real estate taxes or mortgage interest becomes a business deduction that saves self-employment tax and escapes itemized deduction limitations.
- Where qualifying for one deduction unleashes other deductions, possibly more valuable—as with car expenses and other transportation costs.

Home office deductions do one or more of these things. And a business office in a home can do more for wealth building than one outside.

Qualifying for Home Office Deductions

To qualify, some space in your home must be your principal place of business. For most entrepreneurs, this is essential. Luckily, "principal place of business" isn't a difficult test to meet if you work exclusively from your home and are self-employed.

It's your principal place of business if you use it exclusively and regularly to manage your business and have no other space where you do that. If you have an office at home and an office elsewhere for the same business, move business management and administration to your home.

You can get home office deductions even if the home *isn't* your principal place of business, when:

- You use the place to *meet patients, clients, or customers* in the normal course of business. This suits professional practitioners such as physicians, therapists, and lawyers.
- You use it to *store inventory or product samples* in a retail or wholesale business, and it's your only fixed location for that business. You can carry on personal as well as business activities in that space.
- You work out of a *separate structure*, such as a renovated garage or a greenhouse. This need not be a principal place of business or a place to meet clients, etc.

Then there's the space you use. It must be a specific, identifiable part of your dwelling, you must use it exclusively for business, and it must be regularly so used. "Exclusively for business" doesn't mean you can't read a personal e-mail message you might get along with the business stuff.

The space can be a room or more than a room. It can be *part* of a room and need not be separated, say by a screen, from the rest of the room—though the smaller the space the less the tax relief. People tend to overuse the term "home office." It need not be *office* space. Any business use—such as a laboratory or a studio—qualifies, if the other tests are met.

ACTION POINT ✓

Once you've identified the home office space, move out any personal use items (say, a TV) and move all your business-related items in.

Business percentage

You'll need to express your home office space as a percentage—called a "business percentage"—of your total dwelling space. You can do it by room or a part of a room, where rooms are of about equal size—one room in a seven-room dwelling is 14.28 percent; half of such a room is 7.14 percent. Or you can do it by square feet of floor space: If the home office is 80 square feet out of 1,000 square feet, home office space is 8 percent of the total. Take whichever gives you the larger deduction.

Direct expenses of your home office are such things as decorating and repairs specifically for the office space. These are deductible in full. (Of course, office supplies, postage, etc.—business items that have nothing to do with your dwelling—are also deductible in full.) A separate office phone is deductible, including the cost of putting in the extra line. But if there's just one phone in the home, you can only deduct business long distance charges.

You use your business percentage to take home office deductions for a portion of your *indirect* expenses—meaning expenses for the home as a whole, including the home office. Such expenses are:

- Deductible mortgage interest
- Qualified mortgage insurance
- Real estate taxes

These are items homeowners are allowed to deduct in any case, whether or not connected with business, but status as "home office expenses" enhances their value, for self-employed entrepreneurs. (Casualty losses, say from fire or flood, also allowable in any case, may be direct or indirect expenses, depending on what the casualty damages.)

Status as a home office expense also allows a partial deduction (the business percentage again) for other items otherwise not deductible:

- Homeowner's insurance
- General repairs, including painting, of the dwelling
- Security system costs
- Utilities (electricity, gas, home fuel)
- Services such as condominium fees and trash removal (but not lawn care or landscaping)

- Rent, for renters
- Depreciation, for owners

EXAMPLE

Tina has the following home expenses: real estate taxes $6,000; mortgage interest $4,000; insurance $600; utilities $3,400; general repairs and maintenance $1,400. Her business percentage is 14.28 percent. Her home office deduction is $2,200 (14.28 percent of $15,400). She could deduct the interest and taxes portion of this amount ($1,428) anyway, with no home office, though in a less favorable way, as itemized deductions. She has an additional deduction for home depreciation (see "Depreciation" later in this chapter).

Rent

This is a big-ticket item, normally not deductible. A business percentage of rent, especially apartment rent, is often a fairly sizable number. A small apartment, renting for $2,000 a month, might generate a yearly $6,000 home office deduction for rent alone. You can also deduct insurance and utilities.

Should you rent rather than own your home, since you get a relatively larger deduction for your home office if you rent? No. Home ownership offers wealth creation opportunities that transcend deductions. See Wealth Creation Strategies 42 and 43.

Storage

The more space you can dedicate to business, the greater your (still modest) deduction—the more you're sheltering from tax. Usually you maximize deductions with storage space—often to store business records. We've seen this with investment advisors and with lawyers.

EXAMPLE

Paul has his law office in two rooms in his home—one as office space where he works and the other as space for meeting with clients. He also uses a third of his unfinished basement exclusively to store files and law books. He used the square foot measure to figure the deduction. The basement space added 272 square feet.

Depreciation

The first step in the home office deduction for depreciation is to find the basis of the dwelling—of the apartment, or of the building excluding the land if it's a single family home.

Usually this is the original cost, plus capital improvements, minus past depreciation deductions if any, with special rules for property acquired by gift, exchange, or inheritance.

The next step is to determine the fair market value of the dwelling. If there's no doubt that value exceeds basis, you can stop there. Otherwise, get an estimate of the value. Maybe the real estate tax valuation is a good guide; maybe a broker can tell you.

Value is relevant here only because home office depreciation is based on the lower of value or basis. Depreciation is taken over thirty-nine years, so effectively it's one-thirty-ninth a year or 2.56 percent (less the first year; the amount depends on the number of months the home is used in the business that year). Since only part of the dwelling is used for business, you get only the business percentage of that depreciation number. For example, the property's basis is $200,000. Depreciation for a full year of space used entirely for business is $5,120 (2.56 percent of $200,000). The business percentage is 14.28 percent. The home office depreciation deduction is $731. No big bucks here.

No deduction is taken, and no reduction in basis is made, for the remaining 85.72 percent, the "nonbusiness" part of the depreciation.

Capital improvements to the home qualify for separate depreciation on the same principles.

Business Income Limit

Your home office deductions can't exceed the income you derive from the business you conduct from home. If you conduct business in more than one place (for example, you regularly meet clients in an office downtown and in your home), you must allocate the business income between the two offices.

 ACTION POINT ✓ Make the allocation in a reasonable way, based on how much time you spend in each place, how much you have invested in each location, and so on. You can improve your allocation to the home office by holding more meetings there and doing more work there.

Nothing but the Best Office Equipment and Furnishings

Highest quality equipment and furnishings—especially furnishings—are lifestyle expenses. They're a form of wealth you get others to share the cost of, through your tax deductions. If your conscience needs easing over this, remember, you as a taxpayer are already sharing the costs of other entrepreneurs who are doing the same thing.

There's no obstacle—affordability aside—to paying and deducting whatever it takes for any needed high-tech equipment or any other tools to improve office or business efficiency.

Many who work at home also invest substantial sums in their home office furnishings. Quality and comfort are prized, and may be seen to pay off in personal well-being on the job and—where this applies—with business clients or prospective clients received in the home office.

So maybe for you, only the finest will do. Does that mean that you can take tax deductions for whatever the finest costs?

Well, often, yes. Remember we're talking about equipment and furnishings used exclusively for business. So what can prevent, or limit, deduction for what it costs?

There's a dollar ceiling. The system treats items that will be useful for more than a year as property to be depreciated over their useful life. But you can take an immediate writeoff—full deduction, called "expensing"—for purchases during the year of business equipment and furnishings (not real property). The dollar ceiling (indexed for inflation) on what can be expensed is often increased by financial tax stimulus legislation. It's scheduled at $134,000 for 2010. Small businesses rarely exceed the ceiling. Amounts in excess of the ceiling must be depreciated.

There's an income ceiling. You can't expense more of such equipment costs than your business income for the year (the excess can be carried to following years).

You can't deduct upscale antiques or other art. Your expensing allowance is a substitute for depreciation deductions over time. Art works don't depreciate, the tax law says, so there's no depreciation or expensing deduction for them.

Expensing's downside

You'll be taxed on sale of expensed items. Profit on the sale, up to the amount expensed, is ordinary income. Profit is, roughly, what you get on the sale, minus the item's cost as reduced by expensing and depreciation.

And you'll be taxed on these items even if you don't sell them but convert them to personal rather than business purposes. Here you have a tax to pay even though your conversion to personal use doesn't generate cash with which to pay the tax. (Of course, your prior expensing generated the cash saved through lowered taxes on your business profits.) The taxable amount is the amount expensed minus the depreciation you would have been allowed.

Home Office Sale Is a Tax-Favored Payday

I say much in Chapter 6 about wealth creation through business real estate: you invest in business real estate that is likely to increase in value, taking depreciation deductions, which generate tax-free cash out of business profits.

When you cash in on the property's increased value by selling it, you get favorable treatment, even for the "recaptured" prior depreciation. (Depreciation reduced your tax by what was your top tax rate at the time—say, 35 percent. The "recapture" tax on sale is less than what the deduction saved you, and is imposed later, in cheaper dollars.)

There's all that and more with a home office. For most business real estate, the "favorable treatment" is capital gains, at a low rate (for the recaptured depreciation it's a higher rate: 25 percent).

But on sale of the business part of your dwelling (the home office part), most profit is *completely exempt from tax*—though there's a tax on the recaptured past depreciation like that for other business property.

Profit on sale of a personal residence is generally tax-free up to $250,000 (often $500,000, on husband-wife joint returns). But if you're selling a residence that has a home office, or had one, depreciation accumulated since 1997 is taxable, generally at 25 percent.

CASE STUDY

Frank bought a house and land for $300,000 six years ago. He allocated $60,000 to land, and used one-fourth of the house exclusively for his business. The property is now worth $450,000, and he's taken $9,230 in depreciation on the business part ($60,000, divided by 39, times six years).

Disregarding sales expenses, and assuming no capital improvements, Frank would net a profit of $159,230 on the sale for $450,000. Profit on the business (home office) part is $39,230 but only $9,230 is taxable (at 25 percent, for a tax of $2,308). For the same profit on business space outside the home, *all* is taxable: $30,000 at 15 percent and $9,230 at 25 percent. Frank's use of a home office yields $4,500 more after tax. The "dwelling" portion of the profit—$150,000—is completely exempt.

Sale of very pricey residences may be mostly tax-exempt (exempt, that is, up to $250,000 or $500,000 of profit) and taxable at capital gains rates on the balance. The rate for "recapture" of depreciation is 25 percent.

A home office isn't for everyone. Some entrepreneurs can't do their business from home; others don't want to. But when you can make a home office work for your business and your personality, you'll keep greater wealth on sale of a home office than on sale of comparable business space outside the home.

Profit allocable to a separate structure used in business on residential property—a garage, for instance—doesn't qualify for tax exemption on sale. The profit is allocated between the two categories of capital gain that apply on sale of business property that's not part of the seller's residence.

Exchange Your Home Office, Tax-Free

You can exchange the dwelling you own, with a home office or other business-use space, for another dwelling with space you *intend* to use as a home office (or other business use). You can make that swap tax-free, despite any depreciation deductions you've taken, and even if you've received cash in addition.

Tax-free swaps postpone tax. Postponing tax builds wealth. Consider this:

CASE STUDY

Ray, a consulting engineer, uses one-third of his house as his home office and has taken $30,000 of depreciation on the home office (business) portion. The value of the whole property has risen substantially (about $150,000 over what he paid). He now arranges to exchange his house for another dwelling, part of which he intends to use for his business. Though the value of the two properties is about equal, the business space he's getting is worth somewhat less than the business space he's giving up. So he asks for and gets $10,000 cash to make up the difference.

The IRS ruled that "the taxpayer" (Ray) owed no tax on the residence portion of the swap, no tax on the $30,000 of depreciation (which had reduced past business taxes), and no tax on the $10,000 cash received.

It didn't matter whether any of the property Ray *received* had been used as a home office or other business space. And that the tax-free treatment here was granted based on what Ray *intended* to do with the space he acquired. In effect he said that he planned business use for $110,000 worth of the property he was getting.

Such an exchange involves all the transactional expenses and paper-work you'd expect: transfers of deeds, maybe old mortgages paid off and new mortgages created, transfer taxes, and maybe mortgage taxes. Such a transfer might even be a deferred exchange of the kind described in Chapter 6. There, cash can be paid as in a sale, but held aside to be spent later on what the "seller" wants in exchange.

A taxpayer swapping a dwelling with office or other business-use property reports that to the IRS. The IRS gets to see what the taxpayer thought the intended business space was worth (though the tax form asks for no details). It would be wise for one reporting such a transfer to make a contemporaneous record of what space is intended for business use, should the IRS later ask.

A Home Office Converts Commuting into Business Transportation

You'll have heard that commuting expenses—costs of trips from home to work—aren't deductible. But things change when your home office is your principal place of business. Now transportation costs from home to another place you do business—to see clients, make a sales presentation, shop for business equipment or supplies—*are* deductible.

Many will be able to deduct a large part of their car operating expenses and leasing costs. A larger deduction is allowed when you own the car: for expensing or depreciation (within the dollar limits that apply for cars). I know cases where the car deductions authorized by this rule exceeded the home office expenses. But the deduction is allowed for business trips from home using public transportation, too.

Here you must make your home your "principal place of business." For how to do that, see "Qualifying for Home Office Deductions" at the beginning of this chapter. You won't qualify without that, even when you can deduct home office expenses because, for example, you meet clients there.

Home Offices for Partners

Business partners qualify for home office status under the rules for self-employed persons. Some partners occupy the same dwelling—husband-wife or family partners—but this isn't necessary. Partners living in different locations can qualify, based on the expenses and uses of their separate homes.

Have the partnership agreement require partners to provide space at their own expense (without reimbursement by the partnership) for conducting their activities in the partnership business.

Home Office Limits for Corporate Owners

The law discourages home office deductions for employees. Entrepreneurs who are corporate owner-employees can overcome some of these obstacles but can't get to parity with self-employed persons.

On the plus side, it's about as easy for a corporate owner-employee to qualify for home office as it is for a self-employed business owner. An employee's home office must be for the employer's convenience, meaning the employer should not provide space for the employee on separate business premises.

The corporate owner-employee passes this test if her only fixed business location is at home. The home is her principal place of business.

Many owner-employees have employment contracts with their corporations, which help on issues such as employee health care and corporate compensation deductions. The contract can cement the fact that the home office is for the employer's convenience by including a contract provision along these lines:

The employer corporation does not provide the owner-employee with office space. He must provide space at his own expense. Pay and benefits the corporation provides are intended partly to compensate for that expense.

If you use the office to meet clients or store inventory or samples, as described in "Qualifying for Home Office Deductions" at the beginning of this chapter, you could get home office status without meeting the "convenience-of-the-employer" requirement.

Some employers have paid their employees rent for the space in the employees' homes that the employees use for business. But the owner-employee receiving rent for space in her home can't take a home office deduction, except for rent paid for space to store inventory or product samples. Of course she can deduct home interest and taxes that are allowable in any case.

Now for the downside of employee status, even for the corporate owner-employee: All allowable employee home office deductions are "miscellaneous" itemized deductions that are reduced by a 2 percent floor—meaning deduction is allowed only for the excess over 2 percent of adjusted gross income (AGI). So if your miscellaneous deductions total $5,000 and your AGI is $150,000, only $2,000 is deductible—the amount over $3,000 (2 percent of AGI).

The deductions don't reduce Social Security taxes that you (and the corporation) must pay, unlike the case with self-employed business owners, whose business deductions reduce their self-employment taxes.

Car expenses are an exception. The corporation can pay the entrepreneur's expenses for business use. With adequate reporting by entrepreneur to corporation, these costs, deductible by the corporation, are tax-free to the entrepreneur, and exempt from Social Security tax. This outcome is about the same as when the self-employed business owner deducts business car costs from his or her business profits.

ACTION POINT ✓ To get this tax-free treatment, you must substantiate (prove time, place, and business purpose of) each expense the corporation is paying, and must return any excess amounts advanced by the corporation that aren't substantiated.

Strategy Review

This chapter is for those who conduct business in their residence, through a home office or other business space. Home office status can increase wealth, modestly, in these ways:

1. You can enhance your personal/business lifestyle with fully deductible, top-of-the-line, business equipment and office furnishings.
2. Sale of your home office can leave you with more wealth than would a sale of comparable business space located outside the home.
3. You can exchange one residence with a home office (or other business space) for another residence with space you intend to use as a home office (or other business space), tax-free. This can be done in a sophisticated way that is in effect a sale and purchase, and that can also let you withdraw cash tax-free.
4. If your home is your principal place of business, business trips from home lose their "commuting" taint and are fully deductible—sometimes worth more to car owners than home office deductions.

10 Cashing In—Sort Of

WEALTH CREATION STRATEGIES 45–51

When Ted needed a down payment to buy his summer place, he had no trouble raising the money: He borrowed it from his business. The firm's cash was working, not just sitting around waiting to be borrowed, but he had plenty of fund-raising options. The business could take out a mortgage, or increase a mortgage, on its real estate. Or it could draw on its line of credit, or borrow against receivables. In any case, Ted would be able to raise cash from the business using its assets or income stream, and borrow it personally, to help expand personal assets.

Many businesses build up capital, and entrepreneurs sometimes want to withdraw some of it, periodically or for special needs, without terminating the business. There are many reasons to do this; one we see a lot is spreading part of the wealth suspended in the business among family members. And there are many ways to withdraw capital besides borrowing. Withdrawal techniques should avoid or reduce taxes for the business, the entrepreneur, or both, and should preserve credit worthiness and preclude possible creditor challenges.

What it costs to take capital out of the business depends on the form of business entity you're using, and the rights of your co-owners, if you have any. Covering all that here, as I do, makes for a long chapter. You'll be able to see how a given wealth creation strategy works for business entities other than your own. Skipping these saves time, of course, but reading them could lead you to an entity form that could do better for you than what you're using now.

Taking Cash Out of Your Corporation or Co-Owned Business

Small business cash. Almost an oxymoron. It's no news to you that small businesses *need* cash, they don't *have* cash.

Many sole professionals—doctors, dentists, solo lawyers—make lots of cash each year, but they have it personally. It's not kept in the business, or not for long. For solo proprietors and single member LLCs, cash withdrawal of accumulated earnings shifts money from one pocket to another—a nonevent, and this strategy is not for them.

But there's much to be said about cash withdrawals from a corporation, or from an unincorporated enterprise with co-owners.

Not *Allowed* to Withdraw? Says Who?

Co-owners of the business may have the right to prevent withdrawal, or dictate withdrawal terms, which could include changing your proportionate interest in what's left, and often your share of future income. Here are the general rules:

Partnerships. The partnership agreement is all-powerful. It can specify what withdrawals can and can't be made or can leave the decision to a vote, or to designated partners.

It's common (but not necessary) for the agreement to require all or a majority of partners or members to agree to any withdrawal, including withdrawal of current profits. Some agreements more or less automatically allow withdrawals (distributions) at a level high enough to cover a partner's taxes on current profits. Sometimes such distributions are made to depend on the amount of cash on hand, as determined by a manager or management group.

Conditions for withdrawal of firm property often differ from those for withdrawal of cash.

LLCs. Those with two or more members are treated as partnerships for tax purposes, unless they elect to be taxed as corporations. All strategies and rules for partnerships in this chapter apply equally to LLCs treated as partnerships, unless we expressly say otherwise.

Corporations. If your corporation has other stockholders, they are entitled to share dividend distributions in proportion to their stock ownership (with some exceptions for C corporations with more than one class of stock and for statutory close corporations). The stockholders can legally overturn a dividend distribution that goes to you alone, and make you repay it, or share it proportionately with them. (Also, state laws may prohibit dividends exceeding designated ceilings.)

S corporations, like some partnerships and LLCs, may authorize distributions to cover stockholders' tax on current profits.

C corporations are taxable. S corporations generally aren't taxable; owners are taxed directly on S corporation earnings (generally as *un*incorporated business owners are taxed on business earnings).

Creditors. These occasionally can restrict one's right to withdraw. That's rarely a problem for prospering businesses, but if that's a concern, see "Creditors and Other Naysayers," later in this chapter.

Withdrawals from C Corporations

C corporations are more likely to have accumulated cash than other business forms. This is because they can, to some degree, accumulate money at low tax rates.

Cash withdrawals (distributions) from current or accumulated earnings are dividends to the stockholder, taxable at a preferred capital gains tax rate. This could be a good deal. You could keep more of your earnings than in an unincorporated business—depending on what the corporation's tax rate was.

CASE STUDY

Assume corporate net income (after salary, benefits, and other expenses) of $50,000 a year for each of four years. At the end of year four, the corporation distributes $170,000 of accumulated profits to Jack, its sole owner, whose federal tax on it is $25,500. Jack keeps more this way ($13,500 more) than if he were unincorporated, in the 33 percent bracket. (State corporate and individual rates would affect this result, as would state tax, if any, on the type of unincorporated business entity Jack might use instead.)

Withdrawals called "pay"

What you take out as pay for your services is usually fully deductible by your C corporation, reducing to that extent its taxable business profits. And what you collect in pay ("compensation") is usually fully taxable to you. You can't claim the tax relief for dividends for anything the C corporation can deduct. But there are exceptions:

1. You're not currently taxed on pay in the form of retirement plan investment contributions and not taxed on health care and selected other benefits you get for your services. Here, the C corporation's taxable profits are reduced at no tax (or no *current* tax) to you.
2. The IRS bars deduction for that portion of your pay which it considers excessive (unreasonably large) for the value of the services you provide. The matter may be resolved by negotiation or compromise with the IRS, or by a court, which may rule for one side, or partly for each.

"Pay" in these cases is defined broadly, technically including retirement and other tax-favored benefits (though the IRS doesn't often fuss about these). It can include other items or transactions, such as corporate property given the entrepreneur, or sold to him or her at a bargain (or even used free by the entrepreneur).

One discourages the IRS from making such a challenge by leaving *some* income taxable and paying out *some* dividends. The IRS challenge is also somewhat blunted where the pay level is fixed before the year's profits are known. And the IRS generally doesn't bother incorporated professional services providers whose pay is entirely traceable to their own personal services.

Many tax advisors are skilled in handling—and anticipating—pay deduction issues. It would be good to consult one when considering taking a large sum in pay (say, several hundred thousand dollars) that would leave little corporate income.

S Corporation Withdrawals

Cash withdrawals are tax-free to the entrepreneur-stockholder, up to the basis for his or her stock. (The amount withdrawn in excess of the entrepreneur's basis is taxable gain.)

An exception to tax-free treatment arises when the S corporation was a C corporation before electing S corporation taxation. Here, tax can apply when the S corporation holds accumulated profits from its C corporation days. Withdrawals treated as made from these profits are taxed at the favored capital gain rate.

Withdrawal from a Partnership

One way a partner cashes in is by taking a withdrawal (distribution) of some partnership asset or assets. Here our focus is partnership cash, but a distribution could be of anything the partnership owns.

The partnership agreement, or partners' vote, controls your right to withdraw. Thus, there will probably be a price tag on the distribution. If you get something, other partners may demand the same thing or a different thing. Or, if you're getting a distribution, co-owners may require a reduction in your partnership interest—your share of other partnership assets, or of future profits, or both. Distributions of partnership assets, including partnership cash, are often tax-free. In this chapter we're considering only partial cash-ins, as opposed to complete liquidation of the partner's interest or of the partnership, in chapters 12 and 13.

A distribution of cash is tax-free up to the amount of the partner's basis for his or her interest. "Partner's basis" means primarily what the partner paid or put in to acquire the interest, plus her share of partnership debts, plus her share of partnership earnings, minus previous distributions to her of cash or property (including reductions in her share of partnership debt), and minus her share of partnership losses, if any.

A partner in a prospering partnership typically has substantial basis, from accumulated assets or cash.

CASE STUDY

Joan and Julia are 50-50 partners in a successful art dealership. Each put up $50,000 to start. They took out what profits they needed to live on and to pay taxes on partnership earnings, and have used the rest to build inventory and cash reserves. The partnership today is worth $600,000, each has a basis of $120,000, and Joan wants to take out some of what she's accumulated.

She'll need Julia's okay as to what she can take out if she wants the partnership to continue. But assuming she has that okay, she could take out up to $120,000 cash tax-free. (For what happens on property distributions, see Wealth Creation Strategy 49).

The distribution reduces her basis dollar for dollar. If she takes $120,000 now and more later, the later amount is taxable unless she has added more basis. One adds basis by leaving some of one's partnership earnings in the partnership, by contributing more property or money, or by assuming more partnership debt.

"CASH"

When I speak of "cash" distributions or withdrawals, I mean withdrawals from business bank accounts or the equivalent. A firm's debt or equity investment holdings should not be distributed in kind. The holding should be sold or redeemed, the proceeds paid into the firm's account, and the withdrawals made from that. (This nicety could be skipped for sole proprietorships.)

Borrowing from Your Corporation or Co-Owned Business

If you're a sole proprietor or single member LLC, the borrowing is a non-event. The money is yours already. You may tell yourself you're borrowing. No one else cares, except maybe creditors, would-be creditors, or potential investors.

Borrowing from Your C Corporation

Most loans come from wholly owned or family C corporations. C corporations can accumulate income taxed at low rates and so are more likely to have accumulated capital than any other business type. But to be able to borrow it out tax-free, the borrowing must look and feel like a real *loan*.

Real loans are tax-free, but that's because loans are supposed to be repaid—there's an *obligation* to repay.

All the same, a loan, especially a long-term loan, is a form of cashing in your business capital. The $150,000 you take down now—toward a cabin cruiser or a ski lodge or to invest in another business—is no less a loan because repayment will happen years hence, when you sell the business or when your estate or heirs inherit it.

To avoid legal and tax troubles, you must make sure that what you call a loan won't be called a dividend by others. A *dividend* is a formal or informal distribution of corporate profits; after a dividend, the corporation is poorer. A *loan* converts one corporate asset (cash) into another (a debt from the borrower).

If your corporation has other stockholders, they could challenge a sweetheart loan to you as being in effect a dividend that you must pay back to the corporation or share with other stockholders. Some states require stockholder approval for loans to corporate officers.

But tax trouble lurks even for sole stockholders. Tax authorities tend to presume that any major stockholder's withdrawal from a prospering corporation, whether the withdrawal is formal or casual, is a taxable dividend, unless there's a sound alternative explanation.

ACTION POINT

To be *sure* the IRS won't treat your loan as a dividend, do these four things:

1. Put the loan in writing, as a formal loan from the corporation to you.
2. Set a repayment schedule and keep to it.
3. Have the document charge interest at commercial rates, and pay it.
4. Post security for the loan.

These, in combination, give certainty, but you can do somewhat less without much risk:

Put the debt in writing. None of this taking out a bunch of cash, or drawing a check on the corporate account, with a mental note to pay the money back eventually. And don't think a simple "IOU" is enough. Do a loan agreement as a corporate document, with a promissory note. But you can be more relaxed about the other requirements such as:

Repayment. A repayment schedule that amortizes the debt periodically over the life of the loan is good evidence that a true loan is intended. But a balloon payment due on a specified date, with little or no amortization, can suffice. And it can be okay to renew the loan for a new term on or before the balloon due date.

Interest. A commercial interest rate is good evidence that the loan is a valuable corporate asset, and hence not a dividend to the purported borrower. Any interest you pay goes to *your* corporation. For an allowable minimum interest rate, see "Below-Market Interest," below. Pay interest when due.

To ease the pain of interest payments, you could take a dividend from the corporation equal to your interest cost. You can be allowed an interest deduction if the interest is on a debt for your residence (your principal residence or one other residence) for investment, or for another business. Your deduction for interest paid could reduce your tax by, say, 25–35 percent of what you pay, while the dividend is taxed at 15 percent. Assuming an annual interest cost of $25,000, this saves you $2,000 to $4,000 a year. The corporation can't deduct the dividend and has $25,000 of taxable interest income.

Or consider increasing your pay to cover the interest payments. You will be taxed on increased pay, but you may qualify for an offsetting interest deduction under the rules just mentioned. The corporation would generally deduct the increased pay, which would offset its interest income. The result is that the corporation is poorer by the amount of the extra pay, but you're not taxed on the pay because of your offsetting deduction for the interest.

Security. Posting security (collateral) helps but isn't absolutely necessary. For entrepreneurs with balloon payments, I suggest you post some of your stock in the corporation.

Seeking forgiveness?

You can have the corporation forgive (cancel) the debt later. You may want or need that, some day, but it's not the way to withdraw capital tax-free. The amount you owe when your debt is cancelled is usually income you're going to have to pay taxes on. Of course, if there are other stockholders, they may object to the cancellation.

Borrowing from Your Partnership

Borrowing from your partnership is a way to cash in, as is borrowing from your corporation—assuming your partners agree to this. A partnership loan is tax-free to the borrower, as a commercial loan would be. But still observe the niceties used in corporate borrowing, or at least these: The loan is in writing, with interest at least at the AFR. Do this to avoid triggering the partnership version of the below-market interest rule. The below-market rules apply if the firm separately compensates the borrower for her services to the firm. Such compensation (which is in addition to the borrower's share of firm income) is common for managing general partners.

Borrowing from Your S Corporation

There's usually no danger that loans from your S corporation will be treated as dividends. S corporations have no previously untaxed earnings, unless they were once C corporations and carried over their earnings. The IRS often tries to treat the loan as disguised compensation for services.

S corporations sometimes underpay owner-employees as a tax move. This doesn't save income tax, since owner-employees are taxed currently on any pay they get and on their share of S corporation profits left over: lower taxable pay only means higher taxable profits. But it saves Social Security taxes, which are imposed on pay.

The IRS (understandably) answers that S corporation owner-employees are cheating the Social Security tax system (and sometimes the unemployment compensation system) by paying themselves too little.

No, I didn't forget I was talking about *loans* from one's S corporation. My point is that the IRS will get on your case if you're borrowing from your S corporation instead of taking "reasonable" compensation. The problem won't be the loan; it will be the low or no pay. The IRS will consider your loan a disguised withdrawal of pay and impose FICA tax on your S corporation profits as if you had received what it considers reasonable pay. On the other hand, if you've paid yourself reasonable compensation, borrowing from your S corporation is tax-free.

What's "reasonable" pay? There's no definitive answer. Some tax experts say solo S corporation owner-employees should pay themselves 60 percent of S corporation earnings. Some tax experts say that S corporations with relatively high earnings should pay at least the Social Security old age earnings ceiling ($106,800). For pay above this ceiling, only the Medicare portion of Social Security tax can apply (at a rate of 1.45 percent each on employer and employee). So that tax is saved if pay that stops at the old age ceiling is considered reasonable.

Retirement plan risk

Contribution/investments in qualified retirement plans are allowed only against the entrepreneur's or employee's compensation for personal services (which includes self-employment earnings). Taking only modest compensation can limit the amount you can put in your retirement plan.

BELOW-MARKET INTEREST

The tax law can conclusively presume there's an interest charge, for tax purposes, at the U.S. Treasury's Applicable Federal Rate (AFR), if your loan sets no interest rate, or sets one below the AFR. This rule applies when the borrower's outstanding loan balance with the lender is $10,000 or more.

The rule makes you the IRS's plaything, and must be avoided. Under the rule the lender is assumed to pay the borrower an amount equal to the interest foregone (the amount less than the AFR rate), and the borrower is assumed to make an equal payment to the lender. The two would-be transactions leave the parties' immediate cash positions unchanged, but with tax owing from one or the other. That's because one party or the other has taxable income without an offsetting tax deduction. The corporate lender suffers if its presumed payment is considered a dividend. The borrower suffers if the loan is made to him as an employee.

You can avoid this whipsawing by setting the interest rate at least equal to the AFR on the date of the loan. That way, no interest is *presumed*. Actual interest is used and the borrower doesn't risk automatic denial of the interest deduction. AFRs are posted at the IRS website: *www.irs .gov/app/picklist/list/federalrates.html*.

Sell, Then Lease Back, Business Property

It's a common situation: You own business premises that have shot up in value, thanks to neighborhood development or the location's popularity. You'd like to cash in on (meaning take out) that appreciation, but you don't want to move your business. How to unfreeze the asset, and take out the appreciation, at minimum cost?

Consider selling appreciated business real estate to a bank or real estate firm and immediately leasing back. This is fairly common. International Paper did that with its building in Stamford, Connecticut, tweaking the deal so that it leased back *part* of the space. For you as a sole proprietor, a sale-leaseback could deliver a bundle of cash—reduced by tax on your profit. But you'd now have to pay market rent for your space, a rent based on the exalted value of what you just so profitably sold.

This could be your best choice, but consider these other options:

Borrow out your equity. This avoids tax on your real estate's appreciation, and there's no rent to pay—but there's an interest cost. You still own the space and can gain (or lose) if values go up (or down).

Sell-lease back to a family member. See Chapter 8 for assets held by family members or a family entity and leased to the business.

Single Member LLC

Sale and then leasing back are done in the name of the LLC. The results are the same as described above for a sole proprietorship.

Partnership

This depends on the terms of the partnership agreement or LLC operating agreement. Generally, the partnership will have a gain on the sale portion of a sale-leaseback equal to the net selling price minus the partnership's basis for the property. How much any partner collects out of what the partnership gets on sale is determined by the partnership agreement. The partnership won't be taxed on the sale. Partners who get cash distributions from the sale will be taxed the way they would be on any other cash distributions, with this further consideration:

Usually, a sale-leaseback of property subject to a mortgage or other debt shifts the debt obligation to the buyer. This relieves partners from their share of the debt. Relief from debt is treated as the receipt of cash, so some partners who get no real cash are taxed as if they did.

How the rent expense of the leaseback is shared among partners would also be determined by the partnership agreement. In effect, an agreement may direct sales profits disproportionately to one partner or group and leaseback burdens disproportionately to another.

How these generalizations affect you depends on the partnership agreement. Most entrepreneurs will need to consult with a partnership tax specialist.

Borrowing out the equity could be less complicated, but that's one more generalization that might not work in your case.

S Corporation

An S corporation's gain (profit) on a sale-leaseback is its sales proceeds less the basis for its property. If a stockholder contributed the property to the S corporation, the S corporation's basis is generally the contributing stockholder's basis, plus later capital improvements and minus later

---

THE GOOD AND THE BAD OF S CORPORATIONS

What's good about S corporations is that co-owners share income and losses proportionately to their stock ownership. But to business and tax planners, that's also what's *not* good about S corporations. I often prefer partnerships (and LLCs) because the agreements can—to some degree—distribute income and tax burdens disproportionately: cash and tax benefits more to my clients; tax burdens more to the others.

depreciation. The S corporation pays no tax, but stockholders are taxed on the S corporation's gain as part of S corporation taxable income, in proportion to their stock ownership during the year. Tax applies whether or not the proceeds are distributed.

Exception for converted C corporation. If the S corporation was formerly a C corporation, property that was worth more than its basis (appreciated property) when acquired from the C corporation gets special treatment: The S corporation pays corporate tax on sale gain to the extent of the appreciation acquired from the C corporation within ten years before the S corporation's sale. It's called a tax on "built-in gain." That corporate tax reduces dollar-for-dollar the amount taxable to the S corporation stockholders.

ACTION POINT ✓

Have the S corporation hold the property until the 10 years is up if you can. Doing so reduces the 35 percent tax rate on "built-in gain" to 15–25 percent.

C Corporations

C corporations often do sale-leasebacks, but not as a way for their owners to cash in on frozen equity. C corporations are taxed at full rates on sales of appreciated property. They don't get the capital gains relief that's available to proprietors, partners, LLC owners, and S corporation stockholders.

Borrow Out Equity in Business Property

Businesses often borrow against their assets—that is, borrow using the assets as collateral. This can be a growth strategy, as when the business borrows against current receivables to fund new purchases or activities that generate future receivables. On the other hand, sometimes it's because the business is in trouble.

But in this wealth creation strategy you're borrowing out equity as a way to cash in.

CASE STUDY

Phil is a sole proprietor with valuable assets contributing strongly to his profit stream. In Phil's case it's real estate—land and a building, for his assembly plant—now worth $800,000. Basis after depreciation is $350,000, and his mortgage, which he's been paying down regularly, stands at $300,000.

As Phil sees it, the real estate represents $500,000 of frozen value ($800,000 minus the $300,000), value he owns but can't use. He knows about Wealth Creation Strategy 47 (sale-leaseback) but he doesn't want to sell the building. In any case, the sale will trigger a tax, which will eat into the proceeds. But he can borrow out that frozen value, or almost all of it, tax-free.

Phil renegotiates the mortgage to borrow, say, $750,000. This would give him $450,000 cash immediately—that is, the $750,000 loan less the $300,000 already owed. The deal could be interest-only for, say, ten years, with a balloon payment at the end. Say the interest rate is 6.5 percent. That's $48,750 a year but would be offset by what he would save in interest and principal on the former $300,000 mortgage (around $31,900 a year, assuming fifteen years remaining at 6.5 percent).

With this new loan, his equity in the building has dropped from $500,000 to $50,000, and his cash has gone up by $450,000.

The $450,000 comes to Phil's business entirely tax-free and remains tax-free to Phil if he pockets it.

Compare this outcome with sale-leaseback, using reasonable assumptions about past depreciation and future rent. Sale-leaseback generates cash of $500,000 ($800,000 value less $300,000 mortgage). After taxes, that's $422,500. Phil saves the annual $31,900 in mortgage payments but now pays, say, $80,000 in rent (at 10 percent of the property's $800,000 value).

Phil must also plan for the future:

- Annual interest payments of $48,750, which, based on these facts, is about $17,000 more than he was paying already, deductible by the business.
- Continuing annual depreciation deductions, based on the building's original cost.
- The looming $750,000 debt, against the (current but maybe fluctuating) value of $800,000.
- The property's value may continue to rise. Phil still owns it and can cash in on the rise by renegotiating another loan or selling it. Or, value may not rise.

Since Phil's new loan has siphoned most of the cash out of the property, he could face a cash crunch on a later sale. Taxable *profit* on sale is sales price less basis; the *cash* he'll get is sales price less mortgage. So tax on the profit, at rates between 15–25 percent, could exceed the cash.

How Other Business Entities Borrow Out Frozen Equity

With business entities other than sole proprietorships, the entity owning the property borrows out the equity and then arranges how the entrepreneur gets the funds.

Here is what happens with each type of entity:

Single member LLC

Here things go just as they do with sole proprietor Phil, except that the loan is done in the name of the LLC. Funds the LLC owner then borrows from the LLC are fully available for the owner's use.

Partnership

Partners can borrow out frozen equity. The partnership does the borrowing, so you'll need other partners to agree to the borrowing, and on how much of the borrowed funds can come to you.

Added partnership debt increases the basis of individual partners, under rules that depend on a partner's personal liability for the debt.

Here there's a major difference between general partnerships and LLCs. Unlike general partners, LLC members aren't personally liable for firm debts (though they can make themselves liable by personally guaranteeing the debt).

What happens to partners when the partnership adds or reduces debt is too complicated for exploration here. Leave with this message: Partners *can* agree to borrow out frozen equity. And loan proceeds can go to one partner, some partners, all partners, or stay within the partnership, as they arrange. But what to do in your own case is something you should put to a tax pro specializing in partnership rules.

Corporations

Funds that C corporations and S corporations borrow out of equity are tax-free to the corporations.

Distribution of these funds to C corporation stockholders is taxable as a dividend up to the corporation's accumulated profits. Any excess is tax-free up to the stockholder's basis; any over that is capital gain.

Distribution to S corporation stockholders is tax-free up to the basis of their stock, and capital gain for any excess. Unlike what happens with partnerships, the increase in an S corporation's debt does not increase its owners' (stockholders') basis. So cash coming out is more likely to exceed basis and be taxable capital gain.

If the corporation was once a C corporation and has accumulated profits from that time, distribution in excess of basis is taxable as a dividend up to accumulated profits; any excess over that is capital gain.

49 Take Out Appreciated Property

Have appreciated business property distributed to you? So you can sell it yourself, or hold it for rental or other income? You can do this tax-free, depending on the form of your business entity. Broadly, it's *always* tax-free (a nonevent) with sole proprietorships and single member LLCs, *generally* tax-free with partnerships and LLCs, *often* tax-free with S corporations, and *not* tax-free with C corporations.

I'll explain further, but remember our focus: a prospering, continuing business, in which co-owners, if any, are willing to allow the entrepreneur to take out an appreciated business asset, with or without conditions.

Partnerships

The general rule is that distributions of property to partners aren't taxable to them and don't generate taxable income to the firm.

Tax can result in these specific cases: distributions of money; when the recipient's share of firm debts is reduced; certain liquidating distributions; special types of property, usually receivables or inventory, disproportionately distributed; certain property originally contributed to the firm by a firm member. In the last two cases, the transaction may generate income to the firm as a whole. Firm members will be taxed on that income. Tax-favored distribution to one partner now can have negative tax consequences to other partners later on—say, on complete liquidation. The firm as a whole can alleviate this through tax elections involving the tax basis of partnership assets.

Partnership rules are too complex for easy summary here. Take away from this strategy the thought that tax-free property distribution can be achieved with professional tax help.

S Corporations

Property distributions as dividends are tax-free to the entrepreneur up to the basis for her stock. Excess of the distribution's value over the entrepreneur's basis is taxable gain.

Exceptions to tax-free treatment arise if the S corporation was a C corporation before electing S corporation taxation. Here, tax can apply when the S corporation holds profits from its C corporation days. The *S corporation* is taxed on appreciation in property transferred from a C corporation within ten years of its distribution to an S corporation stockholder. The S corporation's tax here is like that imposed on an S corporation's sale in a sale–leaseback.

C Corporations

There are several problems here. The distribution is usually a dividend to you, and so is probably taxable at the property's full value. Yes, many think that the current favorable capital gains tax rate on dividends isn't so bad.

Taking the property in redemption of some of your stock (reducing your proportional ownership) lightens the tax load. Here only the property's value in excess of the basis for your stock will be taxable. The problem here is that the redemption must substantially reduce the combined stock interest of you *and your family.* We don't see that often among entrepreneurs who mean to preserve their businesses.

Use Exchanges to Diversify Your Business Holdings

The better your business does, the more you'll hear this word from business and investment advisors: Diversify. Because no business prospers forever, and no business *lasts* forever. A serious program to build enduring family wealth will have you reduce some of your commitment in your main business and move some of that wealth into other businesses. Many who do this simply invest the funds in securities or real estate. But some choose to put the funds into a sideline business, often involving rentals, of space, vehicles, other equipment, or intangible assets such as trademarks.

How to Diversify

Your first thought may be to *sell* assets your business doesn't need, and put the proceeds to work in investment, or another business. For those expecting a big profit, income taxes are a deterrent, since they will cut down on what's available for new investment or for business.

The ideal solution would be to exchange part of your business assets for marketable securities or the equivalent. Ideal, yes, but you can't do that tax-free. A transfer of a business holding for a marketable security currently saleable to the public is taxable. But there are devices that can achieve a kind of diversification tax-free. Consider these examples:

- Exchange funds—where you transfer your stock in your business corporation.
- Umbrella partnership real estate investment trusts (UPREITs)— where you transfer your business real estate.

Exchange fund

An exchange fund (sometimes called a swap fund) is a limited partnership. Entrepreneurs transfer stock in their incorporated businesses to the fund and get limited partnership interests in the fund in exchange. This is diversification, since the other limited partners are also transferring in their corporate business interests, and each limited partner shares the proceeds of the partnership's businesses. The greater the number and variety of participant businesses, the greater the diversification. And the exchange is tax-free, though you may need to transfer cash, too, which the fund may use to buy real estate assets.

Because of securities law rules, participants generally must meet minimum net worth requirements.

Income earned on fund investments is paid to, and taxed to, fund participants. When the fund liquidates, participants receive tax-free distributions of fund stocks. Since a sale of such stock is taxable, the participant may instead consider putting stock received into another exchange fund, tax-free.

UPREITs

For you, the entrepreneur, an UPREIT is the way to diversify your real estate holdings.

You and other real estate owners contribute real estate to a common pool, and each thereafter shares in the pool's income and asset values. The pool is a limited partnership. Contributing partners receive limited partnership interests, called "units," tax-free, for the property they contribute.

An UPREIT is an "umbrella partnership" real estate investment trust (REIT)—that is, a REIT invested in and controlling the limited partnership just described. The REIT has raised money through a public share offering to investors. It puts that money into the limited partnership in exchange for a general partnership interest therein and some limited partnership units.

You as a limited partner will have achieved investment diversification: the limited partnership will hold a variety of properties, maybe from different parts of the country.

You and fellow limited partners, and the REIT stockholders, can have a steady (taxable) income from the limited partnership properties the REIT manages.

Your UPREIT arrangement will allow you to convert your limited partnership units into REIT shares.

Conversion of limited partnership units to REIT shares is taxable, taxing your real estate's appreciation in your hands, plus any later appreciation of the limited partnership units you got in exchange.

 ACTION POINT Before you transfer your real estate, get the REIT's commitment that REIT shares received in the conversion can be publicly traded.

A borrower be?

Remember Wealth Creation Strategies 47 and 48, on borrowing. That's a path to diversification. Money borrowed by you or through your business can come out to you tax-free for use in diversified investment or another business.

Put Family Members on the Payroll—Productively

Lots of people—tax pros, financial advisors, business page columnists— tell the entrepreneur to put his kid on the payroll. It's a way, they say, to shift tax on what the kid is paid from parent to kid.

This is true, as far as it goes. But let's get real about what it's worth. The tax saved is trivial in most cases, because the kid's work is trivial, and what the kid can justifiably be paid for it is trivial. Do that if you want to, but read on for the bigger opportunity:

Take on family members who are capable of really useful service to the business, who could do work you'd otherwise pay someone else for: like the doctor's wife I know, and the dentist's wife I know, who manage their husbands' six-figure practices and are paid accordingly. Or the computer-savvy son just out of college, who can set up and run the business sales tracking system while he prepares for a bigger job elsewhere.

Your business can enrich your family, putting tens of thousands of dollars in the pockets of family members who do real work, at no (or little) cost over what the business would pay strangers.

Pay could include retirement contributions, health care, and business perks. Of course, the biggest rewards are likely to go to a spouse, son, or daughter who makes the family business a career. Amounts paid the family member should be reasonable for the work, and be actually paid to the member, or used (as with retirement contributions) for his or her benefit.

> ### EXAMPLE
>
> Say your business earns $250,000 before deducting what you would pay your deputy manager. You might pay an outsider $50,000. Your daughter might be worth $60,000, considering her knowledge of how you want things done and your ready access to her. But suppose she's equipped to make an extra contribution to your business that could bring in something extra to your business, say an extra $25,000 (to $275,000 in business earnings), before her pay. You might share this extra with her. So instead of $250,000 kept in the family ($190,000 to you and $60,000 to her), it could be $275,000 thanks to her extra skills, divided $195,000 to you and $80,000 to her.

Your business as employer would have federal and state law duties toward the family member, as it has toward other employees (there's some modest relief from these duties for family member employees, in a few cases). For requirements and exemptions in your state, consult the state Labor Department.

If short-term or temporary employment is planned, consider treating the family member as an independent contractor. This rules out some employee benefits and in effect puts employment taxes entirely on the independent contractor—which can justify a higher rate of pay. A parent in retirement could be a candidate for some temporary or part-time projects.

Training

It can pay to train or groom a family member for work in your business. Training you provide could be invaluable. Likewise for some training away from you. In some fields—hotel and restaurant businesses come to mind—sons and daughters get training by working in a similar business in another city or country, and then join their parents' business with wider knowledge of competing practices and standards.

A family member's training that your business pays for—say in a technical school—can be deductible by the business and not taxable to the trainee. The training should be to improve skills in the trainee's current work, and should be available to other similarly situated employees.

Selling Part of Your Interest

Why haven't I mentioned this before? It's because such sales aren't the way the group I serve cashes in. They don't want to sell partial interests outside the family—diluting family control, and at high tax cost to the seller. Okay, sales to venture capitalists are outside the family. So are the occasional sales to key executives, to keep their talents in the business. But these are part of a growth or continuity plan, not what I consider cashing in. Cashing in when you have co-owners often means you have a smaller share of what's left of the business—of its assets, and its future income. That's a form of selling an interest in your business that's considered in this chapter's other wealth creation strategies.

Creditors and Other Naysayers

Co-owners of the business will care what you're pulling out of your business, and you'll have to square withdrawals with them. And these other parties may care:

Current business creditors

Withdrawing cash or property from a business has a wealth protection side, by reducing the business assets that business creditors can reach. In this chapter I assume throughout a prospering business and withdrawals by a business owner or co-owner that—

- Don't render the business insolvent (an act that could be considered constructive fraud) or,
- For corporations, don't violate state law prohibitions against dividends exceeding designated ceilings (usually, earned surplus) or,
- Aren't "bulk" transfers of most of a business's assets, transfers that must under state law be reported to business creditors before they take place.

Creditors occasionally require the business to maintain certain minimum working capital balances or debt-equity ratios. If the property you pull out serves as collateral for a loan, you may need to pay off the loan, substitute other collateral, or otherwise square things with the lender.

There's this problem if you borrowed from the business: The unpaid loan is an asset of the business. Even if yours is a limited liability entity, its creditors can reach the business assets—including your debt to the business. Be especially wary of taking a loan instead of reasonable pay. Yes, the pay will be taxable. But creditors who could come after you on your debt to the business would have no claim to recover reasonable pay you took when times were good.

Tax Authorities

Some of the strategies described in this chapter are subject to taxes, to some degree, and must of course be duly reported, and the tax paid. Even some nontaxable transactions are reported—such as loans from corporation to stockholder.

Prospective lenders and investors

Withdrawal of business cash or property reduces business assets and your equity in the business. Diminished business assets may make your business less attractive to lenders and investors. A loan from your company to you doesn't reduce the company's total assets, on paper, but prospective business lenders and investors won't think your promissory note is as good as hard cash or tangible property.

Of course, assets you take out may improve your personal balance sheet when you come seeking a personal loan. But remember you got there by reducing another asset you had: your equity in the business. If you borrowed from the business, prospective lenders who see your personal financial statement will need to learn about the loan.

"Prospective lenders" here is shorthand for anyone, such as landlords, who will examine your financial status before making funds, goods, or services available.

Strategy Review

Your goal in this chapter is to take out some of the wealth suspended in your business, without terminating or risking the business. Your opportunities:

1. Withdraw accumulated business cash. For most business entities with such cash, this can be tax-free, because of prior taxation. It usually won't be tax-free for C corporations, but its owner's overall tax burden can be less than if unincorporated.

2. Borrow from the business. True loans are tax-free, but the strategy best suits C corporation sole owners.

3. Sale-leaseback can extract frozen appreciation in business real estate, while continuing to use the asset. This comes at a sometimes-acceptable tax cost.

4. Borrow out frozen appreciation to generate funds while postponing taxation.

5. Withdraw appreciated property, to sell or rent out personally. This risks double taxation for C corporations and some S corporations, but is worth considering for other entities.

6. Diversify business holdings. Business stock interests and business real estate can be pooled with those of other entrepreneurs, tax-free, in exchange funds (stock) and UPREITs (real estate).

7. *Share* business income with productive family members to build family wealth in a tax-favored way.

Chapter 11

Wealth Creation
Graduate School

WEALTH CREATION STRATEGIES 52–59

When Richard's retirement plan account reached seven figures, he began to think about how he could pass on to his children and grandchildren the amounts he wouldn't need for his retirement.

The money is all his—or his and his wife's, depending on the kind of plan he has. But there are rules on what can be done, when, with sums not used in retirement.

Many of these options will be available to you; we'll also consider which are *right* for you.

By the time you reach this chapter, you already know that your business retirement plan investments can grow tax-free until withdrawn. So if you're aiming to build an estate, your first move is . . .

Don't Withdraw Funds from the Plan if You Can Help It. If you *must* withdraw, take as little as possible.

The longer withdrawal is postponed, the more there will be when withdrawal occurs. The less you withdraw now, the more there will be when and if you must withdraw again.

You will use both these principles—and others to be mentioned shortly—in building an estate for your heirs. And what works for you, to magnify what you have, will also work, to a large extent, for your heirs, magnifying what they can realize from your retirement plan after your death.

ESTATES AND ESTATE TAX

When you hear the word "estate," your first thought should be Tara or Mt. Vernon, or some twenty-first century equivalent, not an estate *tax*. The federal estate tax, which some enjoy calling the "death tax," merits respectful interest, not fright. Only about half of one percent of Americans leave an estate large enough to owe any federal estate tax at all. Should you be, er, lucky enough to be one of the chosen few, the federal estate tax to be borne by your beneficiaries and heirs will be, on average, about 8 percent of the estate.

Sure, estate planning helps some estates to pass untaxed and others to go lightly taxed. But no entrepreneur need throttle back a drive to build and transfer family wealth from any fear of a death tax. It's a myth that small businesses are targeted by, much less devoured by, estate tax.

The law says you can postpone withdrawal until you reach age seventy and a half. But it permits this postponement only if the language of your plan allows it.

ACTION POINT

Some plans say plan distributions begin at age sixty-two or age sixty-five or at retirement. If you don't want your distributions to begin before seventy and a half, you may need to have the plan amended to allow postponement.

For example, if the plan now calls for distribution beginning at age sixty-five, have it changed to *allow* distribution at that age, for participants who want it then, but *require* distribution to start no earlier than age seventy and a half.

Any downside to such a postponement?

Generally not. For all plans except defined benefit plans, your account at age seventy and a half (assuming no withdrawals) is your account at age sixty-five plus all net investment growth to age seventy and a half, plus any amount added for work after sixty-five plus net investment growth on that. (If there are employees in the plan, your account might also include amounts forfeited by employees who leave.) Of course, your account would reflect net investment loss, should that happen.

Defined benefit plans are set up to pay an annuity or a lump sum at retirement. Plans will make an "actuarial adjustment" if you postpone withdrawal. This increases the annuity amount you'll get once payout begins, to reflect the fact that payout is over a shorter period when withdrawal is postponed. Such postponement doesn't help make you or your beneficiaries richer.

As an answer to that problem, for entrepreneurs in defined benefit plans, there's rollover. You should act on your option at retirement age to take out your money in a lump sum and roll that amount over to an IRA. That will let you postpone withdrawals with the same opportunities just described for plans that aren't defined benefit plans.

If you're married and in a defined benefit plan, you'll need your spouse's okay to take a lump sum instead of an annuity.

What if you need the money?

Your plan investments are a tax shelter. Any money you take out loses its tax shelter forever, except for loans.

Of course, you may have no choice. Important personal and family needs come first. But try to spend your share of business or investment earnings or other assets before dipping into the retirement plan.

Once you reach age seventy and a half, you must thereafter take out a prescribed minimum percentage each year from your account. Your plan must distribute that minimum amount to you, and all or most of it will be subject to income tax.

Yes, the tax shelter your investments have enjoyed for years and maybe decades in the retirement plan ends for these distributions. You're free to reinvest what's left of the distributions after taxes somewhere outside the tax shelter, or spend it.

What's the minimum withdrawal?

It's figured under an IRS table that's based on, but is longer than, your life expectancy. The table favors those who want to maximize their estate by minimizing withdrawals. For example, life expectancy at age seventy under a standard table is seventeen years. The IRS table number is 27.4. The higher the number you can use, the less you must withdraw:

EXAMPLE

You have $850,000 in your account and you must start to withdraw. Using standard life expectancy, you take out $50,000, which is $850,000 ÷ 17, or 5.9 percent. Using the IRS number, 27.4, you take out $31,022, which is $850,000 ÷ 27.4, or 3.6 percent, almost 40 percent less.

Your number is re-projected each year as you age. Though it declines each year, it's always much more than your life expectancy at that age. The law will never make you take out *all* your money. Assuming you have other money to live on, you will always be able to leave some of your tax-sheltered money to your heirs—and usually a lot, if you had a lot at age seventy and a half.

Minimum withdrawal from a defined benefit plan is figured a bit differently. Take the advice earlier in this chapter to rollover, out of the defined benefit plan, when you reach retirement age.

Why just the minimum?

You can take more than the minimum if you wish. But of course, the less you take, the more remains in the fund to grow, tax-free. Even withdrawals need not prevent future growth, since investment earnings often exceed withdrawals.

The amount you must withdraw for a year is based on the account total at the end of the preceding year. By taking withdrawal at year-end, rather than earlier, your plan in effect invests the withdrawal amount tax-free for the full year, building your fund.

<table>
<tr><td>WEALTH
CREATION
STRATEGY

53</td><td># Keep Working,
Adding Money</td></tr>
</table>

Where I have my weekend home there's a father-son law firm, and the old man, in his late eighties, comes in every day.

We all know entrepreneurs like that, business owners and professionals who just won't quit working. As long as what they do makes money, they can if they wish put some of it—and sometimes all of it—tax-free into their retirement fund, piling up additional wealth for their heirs.

 ACTION POINT ✓ Make sure your company's plan doesn't require paying out the account balance once the participant reaches the plan's retirement age. If it does, have the plan amended to allow continued plan participation regardless of age.

Social Security Consequences

Working beyond full Social Security retirement age won't cut your Social Security benefits, though earnings are subject to Social Security or self-employment taxes. Such taxes paid late in life rarely help increase your future Social Security benefits.

Defined Benefit Plan Participants Can Build More in a New Plan

In Wealth Creation Strategy 52 I advise entrepreneurs in defined benefit plans to leave the plan at retirement age. If you intend to continue working for serious money after retirement age, you would do well to start or join a different plan—say a 401(k)—for post-retirement age earnings. If you're still the employer, you can set up another plan, and might even terminate the old plan, but don't touch anyone's benefits already earned, including yours. This works best when you have a small work force. An employer is free to terminate a solvent plan more or less at will.

ACTION POINT

- Have the plan amended to terminate the plan.
- Give adequate notice to participants, a reasonable time before termination. If it's an insured defined benefit plan, give adequate notice to the insurer as well.
- Make adequate provision for paying benefits earned up to the date of termination. Broadly, the amounts earned are the amounts in participants' accounts in the trust (including amounts due but not yet paid in for the final year); the determination is more complicated for defined benefit plans.

You can shut down the plan at your retirement, or it may shut down should your business end at your death. The trustee distributes assets owed participants or beneficiaries according to the plan's terms. If the business goes on after you leave, the plan can go on under the new management, or be changed, or terminated, as the new owners decide—assuming benefits already earned are protected.

Which Beneficiary?
The Answer Decides How
Much Gets Passed On

You will need to make major decisions about who will get your money. The first decision is easy. Naming an individual beneficiary—a human being or, if carefully done, a trust for a human being—to take your account at your death is necessary to pass the largest amount possible of your retirement account. You can name more than one such beneficiary, to receive equal or unequal shares, if you like.

Filling out a beneficiary designation form is routine in any retirement plan. But all too many plan participants name their estate, expecting to specify who gets what later, in their wills. This can be a costly mistake. Failing to designate an individual or appropriate trust as beneficiary forces more-rapid-than-necessary distribution of the account. For one dying before age seventy and a half, distribution may have to be over the five years after death. On death after age seventy and a half the distribution is based on your remaining life expectancy. (Yes, they really mean the life expectancy of someone dead, but they look at the *statistical* life expectancy.) The distribution will be subject to income tax in that period to whoever gets it (except when it goes to charity).

Naming your estate is costly in another way, by adding to probate costs. Some expenses and fees of probating an estate are based on the size of the probate estate. So part of that expense is saved if you have assets passing to beneficiaries outside probate.

Who you choose as beneficiary can determine how much of your wealth gets passed on (though I don't say that consideration should override who you *want* to get the money).

Naming Your Spouse

This can eliminate estate tax on your estate if that's a concern. Also, if your spouse is more than ten years younger than you, choosing your spouse can reduce the amount to be withdrawn during your lifetime. This leaves more for your spouse, if he or she survives you, and, maybe, more for whoever takes your spouse's assets after his or her death.

EXAMPLE

Your fund at age seventy and a half is $850,000. With any other beneficiary you must withdraw $31,022. By designating a spouse age fifty-six as your sole beneficiary, the required amount drops to $28,053. The younger your spouse, the smaller the required withdrawal.

If you should die before age seventy and a half, your spouse could arrange to put off withdrawing until you would have reached age seventy and a half, or until his or her own age seventy and a half, whichever is later.

Even when your spouse is adequately provided for and your real aim is to pass retirement plan funds on to another, such as a child, it may work out best overall if your spouse gets the money first (free of estate tax) and then makes gifts to the child.

Another common approach: Pass part of your assets, including retirement assets, to a child or children, up to the dollar amount exempt from estate tax (broadly, $3,500,000), and the balance to your spouse (which gets the estate tax exemption for amounts passing to the spouse).

ACTION POINT ✓ Create separate accounts, designating who is the beneficiary of what in the beneficiary designation form. More on separate accounts shortly in "Naming a Child or Other Beneficiary" and "Your Other Will."

You might, of course, name your spouse beneficiary regardless of these considerations. Or, you might want to pass the money on beyond your generation by on of the following methods.

Naming a Child or Other Beneficiary

Whom you choose doesn't affect the withdrawal period while you live (except when it's a spouse more than ten years younger than you). But after your death, the child or other beneficiary has the right to spread withdrawal based on the beneficiary's own life expectancy.

Of course, the younger the beneficiary, the longer the withdrawals can be spread and the longer the tax shelter lasts. But you may want a trustee or custodian for the money, especially for a minor who may not yet have reached maturity at your death.

EXAMPLE

Say your total fund of $800,000 passes at your death to your grand-daughter, age fifteen. She can spread withdrawals over a life expectancy of 67.9 years. Assuming the fund earns a constant 7 percent, it would continue to grow, earning more than she has to take out, until she reaches age sixty-nine.

She could be free to withdraw any amount at any time, depending on the terms of the plan or IRA.

A beneficiary can name her own beneficiary to take amounts in the account at her death.

Your retirement assets may well be a major portion of the wealth you leave behind. As your fortunes change, you should periodically review what your retirement assets (along with your other assets) have grown to, and how the distribution of retirement assets fits with your overall intentions for your estate.

You can have separate accounts for individual beneficiaries, or assign equal or unequal percentages of an account to selected beneficiaries, or designate one or more persons to take over if a designated beneficiary should die before you, and so on. You can, subject to certain conditions, make the beneficiary a trust for one or more designated individuals—commonly done for younger beneficiaries.

You can change beneficiaries at will, with final determination made at or after your death. Changing a beneficiary doesn't affect the period over which your withdrawals are to be made (or the percentage to be withdrawn), unless changing to or from a beneficiary spouse more than ten years younger than you.

Spousal override

Your spouse will sometimes have the power to block your designation of a beneficiary other than your spouse. Specifically, he or she may be entitled to the balance in your account at your death, even though you have designated someone else. A spouse has such rights if your plan is a money purchase pension plan, a 401(k) or other profit-sharing plan, or a stock plan.

He or she can waive these rights, in a written document, and allow your account to pass to your designated beneficiary or beneficiaries. If getting such a waiver proves difficult, consider rolling your account over to an IRA. Your spouse has no rights to your IRA under federal law (though may have or acquire such rights under state domestic relations law). And your spouse has no such override rights in:

- SEP or SIMPLE plans, which in this respect operate under IRA rules
- Defined benefit plans, when a spouse has a right (unless waived) to a specified annuity, but not to an account balance

---

ESTATE TAX ON RETIREMENT PLANS AND IRAS

Broadly, federal estate tax, where it applies, is collected up front, on the assets' value at death. It's not postponed until distributions are made.

Plan benefits and IRAs *can* be hit by *both* income and estate tax—in the rare cases where estate tax applies. Even so, this burden is often exaggerated. Estate taxes, where due, average around 8 percent of the estate. Spreading distributions over the beneficiary's lifetime tends to avoid the highest progressive income tax rates.

The generation-skipping tax is a backstop to the federal estate and gift tax system. Essentially it applies to transfers totaling more than $3.5 million that skip a generation—for example, from grandparent to grandchild while the grandchild's parent is living. It can therefore apply where a grandchild beneficiary receives a huge amount of plan funds at the grandparent's death.

Annuities

Pension plans pay out their benefits in the form of an annuity starting at normal retirement age, or maybe at an early retirement age. For married participants, it's supposed to be a joint and survivor annuity, for the plan participant and then the participant's spouse if he or she outlives the participant.

Plans that aren't pension plans can also provide annuities, though this is less common.

We've shown in depth how the entrepreneur as plan participant builds retirement wealth and a family estate through postponing plan distributions, and by making minimal withdrawals once distributions are required.

There's some opportunity to do that with annuities, too, but not enough. Fortunately, one can escape or work around annuity limitations, as further explained below.

Some retirees place their own retirement security uppermost and choose annuities, to be sure they won't outlive their money. That's a respectable view, and it's not for us to criticize, but it won't maximize the assets that can pass to one's family.

Another reason some like annuities: State laws make proceeds (collections) under annuity contracts completely exempt (or, more often, partially exempt) from creditor claims against the annuitant (annuity beneficiary), even where the annuitant bought the annuity.

Roll it over

If you don't want an annuity, you can arrange to have the money that would otherwise be spent on an annuity rolled over to your IRA. You could instead have the money distributed directly to you in a lump sum, but I don't advise that. The lump sum is immediately taxable (entirely or mostly), and forfeits the tax shelter for future investments.

Annuity for Your Spouse

A joint and survivor annuity is what a married participant in a pension plan is to get unless both spouses choose something else. The most common form is joint and 50 percent survivor. Under this form, if a participant collects $80,000 a year for life, the surviving spouse gets $40,000 (50 percent of $80,000) for life after the participant's death.

An IRA rollover will get you out of an annuity, and let you leave more to heirs or beneficiaries. But for retirees who really want annuities, see Wealth Creation Strategy 56.

Magnify the Surviving Spouse's Annuity

In Chapter 2 we built a defined benefit fund to pay you the largest allowable annuity on retirement. The typical pension plan assumes an annuity on the participant's life alone—a single life annuity. Thus, to be able to pay, say, $175,000 annually over a given life expectancy from age sixty-five, the fund would build to, say, $2,066,750.

But a joint and survivor annuity for a given amount at a given retirement age costs more than a single life annuity at that age—because it expects to pay out over a longer period. And you can't get a joint and survivor annuity that pays $175,000 over *two* lives if all you have to spend is $2,066,750. The $2,066,750 you have to spend on, say, a joint and 50 percent survivor might buy only, say, $155,000 a year during joint lives and half that ($77,500) for the survivor's remaining life (depending among other things on your spouse's life expectancy).

The path to greater retirement wealth is to deliberately build toward the maximum annuity allowed. And that's a joint and full survivor (also called joint and 100 percent survivor). It means the survivor gets the same amount after the participant's death that the participant received during their joint lives. On the assumptions here, that would let you build to a fund of $2,635,545, almost $600,000 more.

You're not locked in

Remember the option to take a lump sum. With your spouse's agreement, you could withdraw the entire $2,635,545 that was built on the assumption of funding a joint and 100 percent survivor annuity, and roll it into an IRA.

ACTION POINT

You won't get the maximum (joint and 100 percent survivor) fund unless the plan specifically provides for that. To get that, amend your plan to specify such an annuity; of course your business as employer must put in enough to pay for it. Do this well before retirement age. Remember that new or additional benefits for you, such as this, must be made available to other participants as well, which would increase the company's cost for those participants.

Life Insurance

Life insurance—an investment designed to provide wealth or comfort for one's heirs—merits priority consideration when planning a family estate. Consider these advantages:

- The life insurance investment portion (cash surrender value) grows tax-free.
- Life insurance proceeds can be exempt, or partly exempt, from both income and estate tax.
- Proceeds escape the expenses and delays of probate.
- Proceeds are generally exempt from claims of the insured person's creditors and, in some states, the beneficiary's creditors.

Buy Life Insurance with Plan Distributions

Retirement plan assets that grew fat for your retirement through tax-free growth can be made still larger for your heirs when used to buy life insurance.

Not that I'd advise most entrepreneurs to cash out their plan assets and put them all, or mostly, into life insurance. Plan withdrawals are taxable, with only the after-tax remainder available for insurance investment. So my wealth creation strategy advises buying insurance with money that has already lost its plan's tax shelter, the required minimum amount you must withdraw. Amounts you don't have to withdraw continue to grow in the plan, for you or your beneficiaries or heirs.

Of course, the later in life you start your insurance, the greater the annual premium cost per dollar of insurance (with a further possibility that cost or even availability may be affected by negative health factors in later life).

Use Your Plan Annuity

If your plan pays an annuity you won't need to live on, you can spend that annuity on insurance.

EXAMPLE

Your plan will pay you an annuity of $42,700 a year from retirement at age seventy. Income tax on that amount may be, say, $10,700, leaving $32,000. A $32,000 annual premium will buy, say, $1.25 million

> in life insurance (a $1.25 million death benefit under a guaranteed
> universal life policy). The amount, of course, varies depending on
> health and the company chosen. If estate tax is a concern, have the
> life insurance held by an irrevocable life insurance trust.

What about larger withdrawals?

Some entrepreneurs may be advised to take larger withdrawals—
more than the required minimum—to spend on life insurance. The
idea is to incur the extra income tax now to save estate tax on what's
left (at higher rates) later.

I don't thrill to the idea of paying tax now that you don't owe, hop-
ing to save future tax. It's even less appealing when you can, and want
to, leave your fund to your spouse—which would avoid estate tax in
your estate if he survives you.

IRREVOCABLE LIFE INSURANCE TRUST

Estate tax, where applicable, taxes what one owns at death, and sometimes what one once owned but gave away. So estate tax can apply to
life insurance proceeds payable at one's death, if one owned the policy
at death or within three years before death.

The *irrevocable life insurance trust* is a device to avoid estate tax on these
proceeds. It exploits the standard estate planning technique of shedding
one's assets, or paying for another's assets, in order to become poorer
and so avoid estate tax, or anyway minimize the tax. If this sounds a lot like
King Lear's estate plan, you can understand why I do little of this work.

You create (grant) the trust, you make the trustee the owner and beneficiary of the insurance *policy*, and you name those you wish to enrich—
usually family members—as beneficiaries of the *trust*. You are the insured,
but you surrender all rights to the policy, however small, and all rights to
change the trust. The transfer is subject to federal gift tax, based on the
policy's value at that time, but no gift tax need be paid unless and until
lifetime gifts exceed $1,000,000. Grantors typically make periodic gifts
to the trust for the trustee to use to pay future premiums. These may
themselves be taxable gifts, but *can* escape gift tax where trust beneficiaries have, but don't exercise, fleeting rights to withdraw these funds.

If all this is done right, the trustee collects the proceeds when the insured dies and distributes them to the trust beneficiaries. There's no income tax on the beneficiaries and, if at least three years have passed since the policy was transferred to the trust, there's no federal estate tax either. Life insurance is subject to death tax in some states; few states have gift taxes.

Life Insurance Already in the Plan

Most plan participants don't have life insurance in their plans. Those who do already know approximately how much their beneficiaries will get from their insurance at their death—to which will be added the balance from the non-insurance portion of the plan.

When a person with life insurance in his plan dies while still working, the proceeds are paid to the plan trustee, to be distributed to the beneficiaries. The insurance beneficiary is subject to income tax on part of the proceeds (the part that equals cash surrender value) and exempt from tax on the balance.

EXAMPLE

The plan owns a $700,000 policy for Ann, the business owner. At Ann's death, when the policy has a $240,000 cash surrender value, the $700,000 is paid to the plan trustee, who distributes it to Jack, Ann's son and beneficiary. Jack owes tax on $240,000 (paying a tax of, say, $72,000), netting $628,000 after tax.

When insurance proceeds are very large, or the insured's estate is otherwise very large, estate tax can be a concern. The usual techniques for avoiding estate tax (such as irrevocable life insurance trusts) don't apply to insurance in a plan—because the insured can't effectively give up rights to that insurance.

So much for what happens with plan life insurance when the entrepreneur dies while still working.

The plan won't hold life insurance on you after you retire. The policy must come out of the plan, and you must make a choice:

You can take the policy itself, or have it converted to an annuity. Take the policy and you must pay tax immediately on its fair market value (which can be more than its cash surrender value). That tax will deplete your current funds, but the policy proceeds at your death will go in full, free of income tax, to your beneficiary. If estate tax is a concern, use an irrevocable life insurance trust to avoid that tax.

Or you can have the trustee convert the life insurance into an annuity, which avoids current tax. (The policy's value buys an annuity of equal value.) This is favored when the cash surrender value is large.

IRA Rollovers

If you're nearing retirement or are planning for your heirs, you should consider rolling your business retirement assets over to an IRA.

As you know, rollover moves money from one tax-sheltered account to another. And you also know that there are two kinds of IRA: a Roth IRA and the traditional IRA.

Traditional and Roth IRAs are worth our attention as serious wealth only when they hold money rolled over from a business retirement plan.

Rollover to Traditional IRA

Rollover to a traditional IRA doesn't *create* wealth, but it effectively *protects and preserves* wealth, and can save trouble. I recommended rollover for entrepreneurs in defined benefit plans. Here are reasons to roll over in other situations:

If the business will go on after you retire, your successors may choose plan trustees or other fiduciaries whose investment policies won't suit you. To avoid that problem you can withdraw your account from their control and put the money into an IRA, where you will completely control the investments. Consider this also if for any other reason you lack confidence in those who will run the plan when you leave.

If you're the only one in the plan and your business is no longer very active, you can shed continuing plan reporting duties and technical responsibilities if you terminate the business and roll over the assets. This move would also avoid problems after your death if you were to die unexpectedly as plan trustee, with no designated successor trustee.

The best way to roll over is via a transfer by the plan trustee to the trustee or custodian of the IRA.

Rollovers that aren't done between trustees are subject to tax withholding at 20 percent. If you're your plan's trustee and withdraw as trustee, tax withholding doesn't apply if everything you withdraw reaches the IRA within the sixty-day deadline.

Downsides to rolling over

- Unlike the case with business retirement plans, federal law gives your spouse no rights in your IRA. Making him or her a beneficiary of your IRA is up to you. Thus, an IRA owner is free, under federal law, to leave the entire amount to a child or a friend—something not allowed for a retirement account, if the spouse objects. (State law may grant one spouse rights in the other's IRA.)
- The IRA can't hold life insurance policies. So it can't buy any, and life insurance held in a retirement plan can't be rolled over to the IRA, and must instead be distributed or converted to an annuity as described in "Life Insurance Already in the Plan," earlier in this chapter.
- You can't be trustee or custodian—the terms are legally equivalent here—of your IRA. This doesn't affect your power to direct investments, but investment and control of the assets is done through another entity. Most IRA owners get their IRAs by signing a boilerplate IRA agreement from a financial institution, and selecting their IRA investments from what those institutions make available. But you *can* use a self-directed IRA, and be able to choose out-of-the-way investments such as real estate and individual businesses.

IRAs are exempt from creditors' claims against the IRA owner, with minor exceptions.

Your Other Will

It will take thought and effort to make your plan or IRA a fully satisfactory tool for distributing your wealth. Here's what I mean: Most people with sizable business and personal assets—home, investments, and so on—have carefully drawn wills covering who gets what after their death, and under what conditions. Plans and IRAs give you virtually none of the options for your retirement assets that your will can provide for your other wealth. (From here on my comments will focus on IRAs, which through rollovers become major repositories of plan funds after retirement. But what I say is generally applicable to funds remaining in plans, after your retirement and for your beneficiaries.)

IRAs typically give the beneficiary—the person who takes your IRA assets at your death—the same rights you have over IRA funds. You may want to change that. For example, *you* can withdraw everything, at once. You may not want a young beneficiary to have such a right.

You and your lawyer need to know exactly what rights your beneficiaries are getting under your IRA. That means studying the IRA document's wording and that of the beneficiary designation form, and making sure they can suit what you want. It will often mean getting the brokerage firm or other provider of your current IRA to change its boilerplate language, into a separate IRA contract just with you.

This can be done, though it usually requires perseverance, and may be best done by your lawyer. Getting agreement sometimes requires the gentle threat that you'll otherwise move your assets elsewhere.

It's possible, as an alternative, to have an IRA tailor-made, and independently administered, while still making IRA investments using the investment or brokerage firm you use already.

Many of us have several IRAs. Once you have a single IRA document and beneficiary form that suits your needs, you can use them for all your IRA funds, without moving the funds from where they're currently invested.

ROTH IRA

Unless you've done a Roth IRA *conversion*, there's not much money in the Roth, and there won't be unless you *do* a conversion. A Roth IRA conversion is where you convert (essentially, roll over) your traditional IRA investments into a Roth IRA, in a transaction carrying a big tax bill. If your money is now in your business retirement plan, you can convert directly from your business retirement plan to a Roth IRA. Your big tax hit today buys tax exemption for future withdrawals, by you or your beneficiaries.

Roth IRA Conversions to Buy a "Tax-Free" Future

Roth IRA conversions come up when people with large sums in business retirement plans or traditional IRAs start thinking, as we're doing, of enhancing those assets for their later retirement and for the next generation.

Roth IRAs beat traditional IRAs in these ways:

- Where you can pay the conversion tax with other, not tax-sheltered, funds. You'll earn more over time leaving tax-sheltered funds intact and spending other funds.
- Roth IRAs can, and traditional IRAs can't, receive new money after the owner is age seventy and a half.
- The annual ceiling on new money, which is the same for traditional and Roth IRAs, in effect favors Roths.

Where tax rates on withdrawal will be higher than tax rates now, conversion now is preferable, avoiding higher rates.

Roths for Beneficiaries

The economics tend to favor Roth conversions when planning for beneficiaries. Beneficiaries the same age in traditional and Roth IRAs must withdraw at the same rate. But the Roth IRA withdrawal is tax-free while the traditional IRA withdrawal is entirely or mostly taxable. For traditional and Roth IRAs of equal size, the traditional IRA beneficiary therefore nets less from the IRA than the Roth IRA beneficiary, *always*.

Roth IRA conversions are even more favored when the IRA owner lives beyond age seventy and a half. From that age one must start withdrawing from a traditional IRA, but need withdraw nothing from a Roth. Since withdrawal reduces the amount available to pass on to the owner's beneficiaries, the traditional IRA beneficiary *starts out with less* than the Roth beneficiary.

A Roth's income tax exemption doesn't extend to the estate tax or generation-skipping tax. Some estate tax planning aims to reduce one's wealth, often by making lifetime expenditures to benefit those we'd otherwise take care of in our wills. Applying this reasoning, some rejoice that the tax money you part with on a Roth conversion (to buy income tax exemption for your beneficiary) may reduce your estate enough to avoid an estate tax, or reduce its amount.

ESOPs and the Stock Sale from Heaven

If your business retirement plan is an employee stock ownership plan (ESOP), you have been building many years for the moment you will retire and sell your stock to the plan, the ESOP.

Okay, so selling to the ESOP is not the only reason you set it up. The ESOP has other wealth-building uses, as in acquiring business real estate or business equipment (see chapters 6 and 7).

But the ESOP is a great device for cashing in your stock, or some of it. The ESOP is a ready market that already knows the stock's worth. And, if the plan doesn't have the wherewithal to buy the amount of stock you want to sell, it can borrow what it needs, at little or no risk to you.

But your stock sale is just the first step in maximizing your ESOP wealth. In a truly successful business, your stock is worth a lot more than it cost you. That, as you'll quickly realize, means that the seller will have a large capital gains tax to pay, which can cut significantly into what the seller nets on sale. And here's where ESOPs come through with a further wealth creation feature specifically crafted for entrepreneurs intending to pass their wealth to their families.

Make Tax-Deferred Diversified Investment of Sale Proceeds

Take the proceeds of your stock sale to the ESOP and put them into "replacement investments"—that is, stocks or bonds of U.S. corporations. You'll probably take care that investments are diversified, though that's not required. You'll pay no immediate tax on your gain, to the extent that the proceeds (not just the gain) are invested in qualified replacements. Tax will apply only when, or if, you sell your replacement investments.

You achieve your aim to maximize what your family collects after your death if you hold on to the replacement investments until death. Such a move eliminates capital gains tax on all profits in the stock sale and—an added benefit—on any investment gain thereafter to the date of death.

CASE STUDY

Lou is co-founder and 25 percent owner of a garment business. Counting the cash and property he invested over the years, his stock interest cost him $650,000. He now sells that stock to the corporation's ESOP for $4,000,000. His capital gain is $3,350,000 and his tax (depending on rates at the time) could be $502,500, which cuts his take on sale to $3,497,500.

But if he puts the $4,000,000 into replacement investments, there's no tax now, and won't be until he sells a replacement item.

He may decide to sell, or need to sell, a replacement item. If so, he'd owe tax from the stock sale based on the proportion of replacement property sold later. For example, if he sold 10 percent of the replacement property at what it cost him, he'd owe tax of $50,250 (10 percent of the $502,500 tax deferred on sale to the ESOP).

To avoid the need to sell, Lou should select investments likely to pay him the dividends and interest he expects to need to live on—and thereby be able to hold all the investments for the next generation.

Suppose the investments are worth $4,900,000 at his death. His heirs will get all of it—the $3,350,000 gain on sale to the ESOP, the later $900,000 gain, and return of the original $650,000 investment—free of income tax. (This will be subject to federal and state death tax, if applicable.)

Is it that easy?

Making this succeed takes work. Here are major hurdles you must overcome:

Someone needs to continue the business. This could be co-owners who remain after you are bought out. Or it could be new owners, such as key employees of the firm. Departing owners often sell some stock to the ESOP and some to others (with no capital gains relief on sale to others).

The ESOP, which holds mostly company stock, needs to raise the cash to buy your shares. So it must borrow, but from whom? Leading candidates would be interested parties—a major stockholder, or the employer (the company)—or a bank or other financial institution. How does the ESOP repay the loan? Out of the future cash contributions the employer is committed to make to it, and out of dividends on the stock it holds. The employer takes tax deductions for the contributions and the dividends, so in effect the stock purchase is funded with pre-tax dollars.

The replacement investment transactions must be done right, with careful and timely reporting of stock or bond purchases intended to serve as replacements.

Never Too Late

There's nothing to prevent a corporate owner or co-owner nearing retirement from having the corporation form an ESOP, which can, by arrangement with those who will continue or succeed as owners, buy out her interest.

Strategy Review

Your goal in this chapter is to maximize the retirement plan wealth you mean to pass to your spouse or other family members. These are your richest opportunities:

1. *Retained and New Investment.* Retirement plan investment wealth will grow, in almost all plans, even beyond retirement age, if you can:
   - Postpone withdrawals as long as possible.
   - Make required withdrawals as small as possible.
   - Keep working, to add further investments and investment earnings.

   These programs fare less well for those in defined benefit plans. For such plans:
   - At retirement age, roll your account into an IRA.
   - If you will work beyond retirement age, have your business adopt a new plan that can include you.

2. *Beneficiary Choices.* To preserve wealth creation opportunities for your family, you must name one or more individual beneficiaries or one or more trusts for individuals. No one can tell you who should get your money, but where economic factors matter:
   - Naming your spouse is favored in larger estates.
   - Naming a child or other family member may be the choice in other cases.

3. *Annuities.* Annuities usually put safety ahead of wealth creation, and don't serve well to pass wealth on, but:
   - Building toward a joint and 100 percent survivor annuity can maximize funds in a defined benefit plan—which may be rolled over.
   - Annuities can fund large life insurance premiums.

4. *Life Insurance.* Life insurance is a major source of tax-free family wealth. Buy it with taxed funds from
   - Plan withdrawals
   - Plan or IRA annuities

5. *Rollovers.* Rollover to a traditional IRA preserves wealth. Rollover (conversion) to a Roth IRA is a high-cost means to increase wealth, especially for the next generation.

6. *Stock Sale to ESOP.* C corporation owners and co-owners can cash in by selling their stock to the corporation's ESOP. Sale proceeds properly reinvested can pass to heirs free of income tax.

12 Keeping It in the Family

WEALTH CREATION STRATEGIES 60–68

This isn't true for every entrepreneur, of course, but many feel a strong drive to pass the business they've built to their children. We see it in the business press when Hugh Hefner passed Playboy Enterprises operating control to his daughter Christie, and when Leonard and Ronald Lauder succeeded to their mother's Estee Lauder empire. But we also see it in the neighborhood, when sons and daughters succeed parents in the fruit and vegetable store or the fuel supply business.

This chapter focuses on increasing the business wealth of the family members who will succeed to the business. Their increase is mostly at the expense of you, the older generation, usually the original entrepreneur who founded the business. You might wonder how *transfer* of wealth becomes *creation* of wealth. My answer is that you will be doing transfers—something you want to do anyway—in ways that make the whole family unit better off than it would be without those strategies. That's because the strategies will conquer, frustrate, or minimize the centuries-old systems by which federal and state governments reduce through taxation the wealth that can pass from the older to the younger generation.

How to pass your business on to the next generation is the decision of a lifetime. There are many options and, like most major decisions, they need to be worked out in steps.

First, answer these two questions:

- Do you expect your estate to owe federal estate tax? Broadly, federal estate tax applies if net worth at death (not counting amounts passing to the surviving spouse and charity) exceeds $3.5 million.
- Does your business use substantial capital assets, currently owned by the business itself, or wholly or partly by you?

If you answer yes to both questions, you should especially consider Wealth Creation Strategies 60 through 62, strategies designed to minimize or avoid estate tax on business assets. They're based on gifts of business interests you make while living—*gifts*, since gifts reduce your taxable estate. Later strategies in this chapter guide sales of the business interest directly or indirectly to the next generation, which in a particular family may be following a gift program. Corporation owners may want to transfer stock as pay, along with a gift or sale program (Wealth Creation Strategy 63). The insurance program described in Wealth Creation Strategy 68 should be considered by owners of sizeable businesses facing a strong likelihood of estate tax liability.

Getting your business valued is an essential early step in any program to transfer business interests. Ideally, a professional will do the appraisal, which is costly (not always costly for personal service businesses). Valuation may need to be done more than once, during your program, depending on how you decide the interests are to be transferred.

- You'll want to know what the business would sell for—the business's market value or, if you're a co-owner, the market value of *your* interest.
- You'll want to know if your business holdings, together with your other assets, are liable for federal estate tax and state death tax.
- You may want to know what partial interests are worth—interests you might give or sell. This value can reflect discounts that can facilitate tax-free transfer.
- Where transfers are to be made over a period of years, you may need frequent or annual valuation.

The firm you choose to make this appraisal will want to know how the appraisal will be used. It's an open secret that some appraisers tailor their valuations high or low according to what the client wants to hear—a secret so open that others affected by the appraisal (prospective buyers, the IRS) may challenge the results.

So it can be good to select a respected firm, especially when you may need to return to it for follow-up valuations. You professional advisor—lawyer or CPA—can recommend a reputable firm.

If a professional business appraisal is more than you can afford—as it will be for many—get a written document of valuation from a CPA. A professional appraisal can be done later, when a question arises about valuation.

Estate Taxes

I'll do a lot in this chapter to tell you how you can minimize estate or other death taxes. This isn't because federal or state death taxes break up small businesses. That's a myth. At current exemption levels, nearly all small businesses and family farms will escape federal estate tax.

But then, most small businesses aren't applying my wealth creation strategies. Since you are, your holdings are more likely to grow and risk estate tax. Even so, virtually all estates subject to estate tax can pay the tax out of cash on hand. Of course, most estates have more claims on their assets than just estate taxes. To cover estate taxes and other debts, they usually must use other liquid assets.

Funds passing to a person's surviving spouse aren't subject to estate tax at that person's death. This effectively exempts thousands of large estates from federal estate tax. With the spouse's inheritance removed, the remaining wealth, passing to others, is below the taxable threshold (for example, is less than $3.5 million). It will often happen that estate tax avoided in the first person's estate will be imposed on the spouse's estate. Often, not always. The spouse could remarry—allowing a second escape, for amounts passing to the new spouse. Or, the spouse might spend down the inheritance below the taxable threshold. Or the threshold might rise.

What forces some small businesses to break up when the owner dies is the owner's failure to provide, outside the business, for heirs who don't join the business. Here the liquid assets may not be enough to cover bequests to those persons, on top of the estate tax and other debts—and so the business gets sold. See Chapter 13 for wealth creation strategies to prevent that outcome.

Federal Gift Tax

No giver (donor) owes tax on a *taxable* gift until the total of such gifts reaches $1,000,000, after which tax is due on gifts exceeding that $1,000,000 total. All taxable gifts must be reported to the IRS, and prior taxable gifts count as part of the estate in determining whether the estate is large enough to be subject to estate tax. If tax was paid on any gifts, that tax reduces dollar for dollar any estate tax you might owe.

Sometimes estate planners urge giving that incurs gift tax, to get the *gift tax* amount out of the taxable estate. This move, if made more than three years before death, can save money where estate tax will apply in any case.

> **EXAMPLE**
>
> A $100,000 gift incurred $20,000 of gift tax. The $100,000 is subject to estate tax, but the $20,000 gift tax paid is offset against estate tax due. Had there been no gift, $120,000 would be subject to estate tax, with no offset.

Gifts made within 3 years of the donor's death are included in his estate, with any gift tax paid. Certain gifts are "exempt," and don't count toward gift tax or estate tax. They are gifts of cash or property that don't exceed a specified dollar amount per year, per recipient (donee). One can give the exempt amount to any number of recipients. The amount—$13,000—rises with the cost of living. (Exemption isn't available where the recipient has no current right to use or enjoy the gift.) Also, payments of another's medical bills or education expenses are exempt gifts, assuming the payments go directly to the provider of medical services or the educational institution.

Gifts to your spouse and to charity are also, in effect, exempt.

Follow a Gift Program That Avoids Gift Tax and Estate Tax

Most entrepreneurs seeking to avoid gift and estate tax on transfers of business interests to family members do so by means of exempt gifts. That is, they make gifts of business interests valued at less than the exemption dollar amount (e.g., less than $13,000). Since the exemption amounts aren't large, you might think it would take a lot of years to pass on serious business wealth. That can make it a good idea to start early, to have more years to make the gifts. But there are several tools that help speed it up:

- Valuation discounts
- Get your spouse, if you have one, to join in the gift. This doubles the amount you can give tax-free each year, whether or not your spouse owns an interest in the business.

> ### EXAMPLE
> You own an interest worth $600,000. You get your spouse to join you in a gift of $28,000. A gift of not more than $13,000 from each donor is exempt.

- Make a larger gift that stays below your $1 million lifetime total. (This can risk the gift's inclusion in your estate.)
- Combine a gift program with other techniques, such as sales for value; see "Selling the Business to the Next Generation," later.

Valuation Discounts

Your business is worth $1,500,000. So a one percent interest in it is worth $15,000, right? Not in a small business, such as a family limited partnership or a family corporation. It's a minority interest, so the minority stockholder or limited partner has little or no power to get at the assets or to require a distribution of earnings. And it's a family entity, which virtually no outside investor wants to buy into. So the percentage interest should be discounted, below $15,000, for the limited minority participation and its limited salability—called "minority discounts" and "marketability discounts."

Discount amounts vary with circumstances. With family entities, as much as a 40 percent discount might apply, making the one percent interest worth, say, $9,000. With an exempt gift ceiling of, say, $13,000, an entrepreneur and his or her spouse could give each child, tax-free, a 2.89 percent interest in a single year.

The value of an interest changes with the value of the business. Exempt gift ceilings also change (increase) with inflation.

A discount too far

Sometimes the donor tries deliberately to drive down the value of the interest she is transferring by loading on restrictions or limitations on the recipient's rights and powers. Why? The lower the value, the more of the business can pass to the kids now, free of gift tax. Entrepreneurs in family businesses tend to be especially aggressive in trying to maximize valuation discounts. Some planners go the extra mile to depress the value of interests being given by: authorizing the donor general partner to require additional capital contributions from limited partners, and requiring unanimity among all partners before the limited partnership can be dissolved (and its assets distributed)—additional limits intended to make the donated interests worth even less.

This gets overdone. The value the donor uses for today's gifts risks getting revalued upwards later, by the IRS, with unfortunate future consequences. The IRS doesn't like family valuation discounts much, especially those of family limited partnerships, and finds ways to block or punish them:

- When family limited partnerships are used to hold non-business assets, such as marketable securities and personal residences. The

IRS thinks such family limited partnerships have no business purpose—they're just shams to avoid gift tax by dragging down values of transferred assets. The IRS won't recognize the family limited partnerships and their discounts. If a family limited partnership holds both business and non-business assets, discounts for the non-business portion of family limited partnership assets won't be recognized.

- When the entrepreneur gets back an interest in the family entity worth less than the assets she transferred to it. The IRS attack here is that what the entrepreneur transferor "lost" on the exchange is a taxable gift by the entrepreneur to the other family business members.
- When the limited partners' rights are "too" limited. To the IRS, this could mean that the recipient limited partner got no current rights from the gift, only a potential future benefit. This invalidates the gift tax exemption (see "Federal Gift Tax") and the transfer is taxable (at a discounted value, if appropriate). Or that the limitations on the limited partner go beyond what state limited partnership law allows. This invalidates any discount based on the limitations.
- When the entrepreneur doesn't live up to the agreement. For example, suppose an entrepreneur consistently treats, as his own, items supposedly transferred to the family entity. The IRS will consider the entrepreneur still the owner and put the "transferred" items in his estate, subject to estate tax, at the entrepreneur's death.

Use discounts, sure, but reasonably. You'll need a skilled professional to advise you on how much discount to claim; you should be conservative.

Remember, the IRS is watching

You must say on the gift tax return if you're claiming a valuation discount, so the IRS can review the discount. If you fail to file a gift tax return because you think the discounted gift is within the dollar exemption, there's no statute of limitations on the IRS. That means that if the IRS later learns about the gift and disputes the discount, it can seek to collect the gift tax at any time, with ripple effects to the estate tax on your estate.

ACTION POINT ✓

To preclude long-after challenges to your discount, report the gift on the return, and the discount, even if you claim the gift doesn't exceed the exemption ceiling (for example, for less than $13,000).

Gifts can postpone tax

Neither donor nor recipient owes income tax on a gift, even of appreciated property. The recipient will owe income tax on sale of property received, but this may happen years later, after the donor's death. If the recipient had inherited the property instead, its value might have been cut down by estate tax at the donor's death.

Gifts to children

Recipients of the donated property will often be minors who are expected to become active in the business as adults. (See Chapter 13 for what to do if they don't go into the business.) Their interests will typically be held for them until maturity (age eighteen or twenty-one) in uniform gifts to minors accounts or uniform trusts for minors accounts.

To avoid having the account included in the donor entrepreneur's estate should he die before the recipient, the account custodian should be someone other than the donor.

Using other trust-type devices, the donor could arrange to postpone the minor's direct ownership of the transferred property beyond age eighteen or twenty-one. And even full ownership would be subject to valid limitations imposed on the interest transferred, for example, transferred stock could be non-voting.

Gifts to spouse

The entrepreneur may eventually want to bring his spouse into the business as owner or co-owner. It could be to give the spouse greater influence or control after the entrepreneur's death, maybe during a transition period until the children are fully capable. The entrepreneur's gifts of business interests to the spouse are exempt from gift tax (and income tax).

Give Equity Interests in Today's Business Entity

This can be simple. You give a part of the interest to the family member you want to carry on the business. Later you give more. And so on—until it has all passed to your successor.

Some entrepreneurs can easily pass on a portion of the equity in the existing business. It's easiest when the business is a corporation.

With a Corporation . . .

You simply give a portion of the stock you already own. Corporations are gift-friendly. It's easy to give amounts of stock that are calibrated to the dollar amount or percentage ownership you want to give.

Most entrepreneurs who make gifts, small or not so small, mean to keep control of their corporation. A common way is for the entrepreneur to hold most or all of the stock with voting rights. They will typically give nonvoting stock, though they usually hold most of that too, in the early years.

Many small business corporations have only voting stock. If that's your situation now and you want to have both voting and nonvoting stock for the future, you should arrange to recapitalize the corporation, calling in the voting stock and reissuing the new kinds.

If control is the first consideration, avoiding or minimizing gift tax comes next: You can make significant gifts while avoiding the gift tax, through use of valuation discounts. The depth of the discount will depend somewhat on the recipient's rights to influence operations, to cash out (liquidate) her stock interest, and other rights. These and other stockholder rights are determined under state law.

In statutory close corporation rules, an entrepreneur, even with little remaining stock, can maintain effective control, or require unanimous approval (giving the entrepreneur veto power) for specific actions or expenditures.

Gifts to the next generation transfer future earnings within the family. Earnings on shares transferred are taxable to the recipients when the earnings are distributed, if the corporation is a C (taxable) corporation. If it's an S corporation, the earnings are taxable to recipient stockholders in the year earned, whether or not distributed. The fact that minority stockholders can't force distribution of earnings diminishes the value of the stock and hence supports a valuation discount.

With other entities . . .

Giving is more complicated. With a sole proprietorship, the owner can simply transfer all his or her rights, in a single transaction, to the chosen successor. But we usually see shared ownership before the successor is to get it all. A sole proprietorship can share ownership only by creating a new and different entity, in which the entrepreneur and the family member become co-owners. The entity would be a partnership, limited liability company (LLC), or corporation. The entrepreneur gives the family member a portion of the entrepreneur's interest.

If the entity is a partnership of you and one or more others outside the family, you may not be able to give the family member a portion of *your* partnership interest. Partnership agreements typically give partners a right to veto the addition of another partner; LLC managing members typically have the same rights.

If the entity is a single member LLC, the entrepreneur adds a member by giving the successor a membership interest.

ACTION POINT ✓ Revise the LLC operating agreement to reflect the rights and status you want the new member to have. Typically, you would make it a manager-managed LLC, with the new member a non-manager, at least at first.

In any of these entities, the entrepreneur's gift of the equity interest triggers the gift tax and discount issues discussed under "Give Equity Interests in Today's Business Entity."

DISAPPEARING PARTNERSHIPS

In a two-person partnership, transfers of all one's remaining partnership interest to the other ends the partnership.

This change of entity, from partnership to sole proprietorship, is mainly the transferee's problem, though a seller partner often has a financial interest in the business's survival in some form. A limited partnership would lose its limitation of liability, and will often transform itself into an LLC, or maybe a C corporation. An LLC with a single member would be treated for tax purposes as a sole proprietorship unless tax status as a corporation is elected.

NO INCOME TAX

Generally there's no income tax on transfer or receipt of the interest. Later distribution of business earnings will be taxable to recipients, though owners of entities other than C corporations are taxed on firm earnings whether or not they're distributed. Distributions of business assets are generally taxable too, as explained in Chapter 10.

What happens when a family member employee becomes a co-owner?

Say it's a partnership and you give a partnership interest. If you want to restrict a family member's authority to make business decisions, you should take care to make him a limited partner in what is a limited partnership. And it would be good to make regular customers, creditors, and suppliers know the family member's limited authority.

Once an employee gets an equity interest—no matter how small—in an entity taxed as a partnership, he instantaneously stops being an employee of the entity and becomes a partner. That triggers these consequences, some beneficial, some not:

- No more income tax withholding on pay. Tax is now paid as estimated tax, and with the annual tax return.
- Some employee benefits change. Sometimes he can be included in the benefit plan, but will be denied the favorable tax treatment granted employees. And sometimes the new partner can still be treated as an employee with more or less full benefits (as with retirement plans, the most important benefit) or the particular benefit is allowed partners/LLC members. See chapters 4 and 5 for tax-favored benefits and perks allowed partners/LLC members.
- Employers and employees each pay FICA (Social Security and Medicare taxes) on employees' pay. Partners/LLC members have no "employer," so they pay self-employment tax, which combines the tax paid by employer and employee. The tax is on net earnings from self-employment, which of course may be more, or less, than what he was getting as an employee.

The rules for new partners also apply for new members of LLCs treated as partnerships, with this qualification: Some state laws treat LLC members as employees for certain purposes.

A C corporation employee who is awarded stock doesn't cease to be an employee, or lose rights to employee benefits. An S corporation employee awarded stock also doesn't cease to be an employee but can be disqualified for most employee benefits if his stock ownership is more than two percent of the total.

There's Giving and There's Keeping

Succession planning forces you to consider what's essential to the business and what's tangential. Maybe there's a building, or an investment asset acquired to establish or seal a relationship, or taken in exchange, or even unneeded cash. Consider whether that should come out to you personally, to become part of your individual investment wealth. However you get to deciding what to take out, it amounts to cashing in on your business success.

Generation Which?

Usually it's the entrepreneur's children who are to carry on the business. But of course it's often desirable to include other relationships: spouse, in-laws, step-children, siblings, and siblings' children. Include them, if you want them, in planning for "family." But be aware of these issues:

- We aren't planning here for nonfamily members—key employees—who may become co-owners as part of your business succession plan.
- Some of your gifts may be to family members who are minors, whom you expect to join the business later.

Succession Planning with a New Family Business Entity

Many entrepreneurs—especially sole proprietors—will need to create a new and different business entity to handle the transfer to the next generation. Leading candidates for this are family limited partnerships, family LLCs, and family corporations.

Family Limited Partnerships and Family LLCs

If you've looked at all into business succession planning, you'll have heard about family limited partnerships and, maybe, family LLCs. These are leading devices by which business owners pass interests in the business to the owner's family, especially the younger generation. And, almost always the equity interests pass by gift—though sometimes by "sales" that are at least partly gifts. In many cases, the transfers take place over several years, which is one way to pass ownership incrementally to the younger generation. Passing part ownership need not mean any surrender of control; the partnership agreement can specify where control lies.

In a typical partnership, each partner puts in something in exchange for a partnership interest. Often it's capital *and* services; sometimes it's one or the other. In a family partnership, the younger partners may not at first be able to contribute either. Parents in that case may give the child an asset to contribute. Of course, the entrepreneur parent usually contributes most of the business assets and at first takes back most of the partnership interests: usually this is the sole general partnership interest and many limited partnership interests. The other partners receive limited partnership interests in exchange for their much smaller contributions.

CASE STUDY

Dave has two college-age kids, Wendy and Chris. He puts assets from his business, Dave's Carpeting, into Dave's Carpeting L.P., the new family limited partnership. He takes back a general partnership interest and limited partnership interests totaling 96 percent of the business and the kids get two percent each. (In arrangements made for entrepreneurs in failing health, the younger generation might get general partnership interests.)

As sole general partner, Dave controls all partnership business decisions and all decisions on distributions of partnership profits and assets. As general partner, Dave is personally liable for partnership debts.

To avoid personal liability, Dave should transfer the general partnership interest to a limited liability entity—a corporation, say, which Dave controls as sole stockholder, or a single member LLC, which Dave controls as sole managing member. The *entity* is liable as general partner for family limited partnership debts. But generally only the *limited liability entity* assets (not Dave's own assets) can be reached by partnership creditors.

The *entity* would be taxable on the general partner's income, if it's a C corporation or the LLC elects C corporation tax status. *Dave* is taxed directly if the corporation elects S corporation taxation, or the LLC does not elect C corporation status.

Transfer Future Earnings, Within Limits

As I've shown, you can pass assets with no, or reduced, *transfer taxes* (gift and death taxes) on you. And the new owners get the future earnings from these assets, and must pay taxes on them, with no income tax on you or your estate. Shifting income to your family in this way reduces your income tax now and, potentially, estate tax later, since these earnings aren't in your estate. But for income tax purposes you can't shift more future income to family members than the interest you gave them really earns. Thus:

An entrepreneur who runs the business must draw reasonable pay for these services off the top. So, instead of, say, $100,000 of earnings divided among all partners in proportion to their interests, the managing partner is assumed to get and must pay tax on reasonable pay of, say,

$60,000. Partners are assumed to share the remaining $40,000 in proportion to their interests, and are taxed accordingly.

The return on capital for a recipient limited partner can't be greater than that for the entrepreneur donor. If the recipient's return on capital is eight percent, the donor can't get less. A greater return to the recipient would shift income and tax away from the donor. Tax law forbids that, and redirects income to the donor, for tax purposes.

When an entrepreneur transfers appreciated assets to the partnership, the entrepreneur's partnership interest generally must bear the tax on the appreciation, on any later sale of the asset, or of the entrepreneur's partnership interest.

There are additional rules that income and deductions allocated among partners must to some (flexible) degree reflect the value of their interests. Family LLCs work as well as family limited partnerships for family wealth transfers—in most cases. They work less well, reducing the donor's discount, where an LLC member can have greater rights than a limited partner under applicable state law.

Family Corporations

You can create a corporation, transferring assets from your sole proprietorship in exchange for the corporation's stock. The transfer escapes income tax if, as is normal, those who transfer wind up with at least 80 percent of the corporation's stock. You can thereafter give your stock to the next generation, passing on some and eventually all of the business, as covered in "Give Equity Interests in Today's Business Entity."

This can also work for entrepreneurs holding major interests in their partnerships and LLCs. Their transfers to a corporation are tax-free if those transferring own at least 80 percent of the stock after the transfer. They may transfer either their *interests* in the partnership or LLC, or *assets* of a partnership or LLC that were distributed to them, in liquidation of the partnership/LLC. Again, the entrepreneur receiving stock could give some, and eventually all, to family members.

Transfer Ownership Interests Through a Grantor-Retained Trust and Give While Keeping

This strategy is an indirect gift to the next generation, and is intended to reduce or avoid gift and estate taxes. It's a way the entrepreneur can receive a fixed income stream from the business, at least for a while, before the children take over.

Business, tax, and estate planners call the device a "grantor-retained annuity trust" (GRAT). The entrepreneur (the trust grantor) transfers some of his ownership interest to a trust. The trust is to pay the grantor a prescribed amount for a prescribed period of years, and after that to turn the ownership interests over to the next generation (who, in sexist trust-speak, are called "remainder men"). Grantor and trustee are often the same.

Since the grantor is keeping much of what goes into the trust for himself—the retained annuity—the gift that's subject to tax is only the present value of what's left after the annuity.

To oversimplify, if the business interest (say, stock in an S corporation) that the grantor puts in the trust is worth $1,250,000, and the annuity income stream the grantor retains out of this stock is worth $800,000, the gift (to the next generation) is $425,000—not enough (absent large previous gifts) to trigger a gift tax. In ideal circumstances, the stock is removed from the grantor's estate and the next generation gets it when the annuity ends, free of estate tax.

You can also use discounts in valuing your gift to the trust—the kind of minority and marketability discounts covered in Wealth Creation Strategy 60. The retained trust device can supplement the entrepreneur's program of making periodic gifts, to the next generation, of small interests in the business.

Estate Tax

If the business (with your other assets) is large enough to incur estate tax, funds in the GRAT may not escape estate tax. You have an annuity for a term of years, or for life. If you die before the term of years is up—or any time, if it's for life—the GRAT funds go into your taxable estate.

For example, suppose the annuity is to pay out over ten years. Your plan to pass what you've put in the trust to your successors free of estate tax fails, unless you live more than ten years.

A GRUT, the not-so-euphonious acronym for "grantor retained unitrust," is like a GRAT with a different way of calculating what the grantor receives.

Selling the Business to the Next Generation

Entrepreneurs can find several reasons to favor selling—making kids pay parents for the business—instead of giving away their ownership. Consider these:

- *Parental discipline.* "I earned what I have. My kids should do something to earn theirs." Andrew Carnegie thought that way. So does Warren Buffett.
- *Self-interest.* "I'll need money to pay for my retirement." Selling the business can provide the money—with varying degrees of certainty, depending on the sale deal the parties arrange.
- *To transfer future business growth out of the entrepreneur's estate.* This is Wealth Creation Strategy 65 (discussed later).

Here, as we consider selling your interest to the next generation, your first question may be: "How could my kids afford to buy me out?" There are several ways, with differing advantages and drawbacks.

- Give interests in early years and sell the rest
- Sell piecemeal
- Sell all at once, for installment payments
- Sell for a private annuity

- Make a bargain sale, combining sale and gift
- Do an insurance-funded buyout
- Arrange redemption by the business

Gifts, Then Sale

Sale to the next generation can be preceded by a program of modest, more-or-less periodic gifts of interests in the business. The gifts may start while the recipient family member is young—maybe even a minor. Over time you can assess the recipient's capacities in the business, and in investment management. Income the recipient receives from the business interests, and from working in the business, may make her a credible purchaser of your remaining interest or controlling interest, especially when the purchase price can be paid over time.

For the business interest you sell—the business interest you have left after previous gifts—you'll owe income tax on your selling price for that interest less your basis for that interest (after reductions for gifts you made previously).

63   Sell the Business Piecemeal

Say your son buys what he can afford each year—2 percent one year, 3 percent more the next. This is most convenient with a corporation or an LLC.

The son could get the money to buy by taking less in pay and applying the difference toward purchase of the equity interest. If the kid is an employee, this could even be done through payroll deductions. For kids short of money, you could help out with their living expenses by making gifts below the gift tax exemption ceiling or specially exempt gifts of payments of medical bills or tuition (see "Federal Gift Tax"), for the kid and his or her family.

I assume your sale price will reflect the true value (fair market value) of the interest sold. If so, you'll likely owe income tax (usually, capital gains tax, see "Capital Gains," later in this chapter) on each sale. The amount taxable is the price you charge for the interest sold, less your basis for the interest sold.

The kid's buy-in could instead be set up as a sale from the business (for example, buying stock from the corporation or an LLC member interest from an LLC). Normally entrepreneurs face no danger of income or gift tax on such a purchase (for fair market value), but it doesn't go far toward passing the entrepreneur's business wealth to the kid. The business is richer by what the kid puts in. The parent's business wealth stays about the same: a slightly smaller proportion of a slightly bigger pie.

The kids are taxable on the share of profits they're entitled to under the rules for the kind of business entity involved.

Capital Gains

Entrepreneurs selling interests in successful businesses almost always qualify for capital gains tax relief on their sales profits. This is true for sales of stock in C or S corporations. It's generally also true for sales of partnership interests. However, ordinary income treatment applies to that part of the profit attributable to a selling partner's share of partnership inventory (where substantially appreciated) and of partnership receivables (broadly defined to include receivables for goods and services, and recaptured depreciation). This rule also applies to LLC interests when (as is usual) the LLC is being taxed as a partnership.

Opportunities to minimize the tax in these ways are limited. Many owners and investors plan to avoid capital gains tax by holding on to assets until death, when the basis step-up effectively eliminates tax on unrealized capital gains (and some unrealized ordinary income).

The estate tax is something of a brake on holding until death, for the largest fortunes. Estates that escape tax on large unrealized capital gains may be subject to estate tax.

Warren Buffett, who didn't consult me in this matter, has nothing against taking capital gains *today*. Mr. Buffett, the second richest man in the world, said his total tax rate was 17.1 percent, which is less than what the ordinary U.S. citizen pays, because most of his income is taxed at capital gains rates.

Make Stock Interests Pay–Transfer Them as Compensation to Working Family Members

If your child works in the incorporated business, he or she can be awarded stock in the corporation, or additional interests, as compensation for services.

The child is taxable on the stock's value, while the corporation can deduct that value. Stock can be treasury stock, or stock newly issued for the purpose. This is essentially a deduction that's cost-free to the corporation. True, there's the cost of valuing the stock of a small business corporation, but that's also incurred for gifts to family members.

The child's compensation could be increased to cover her tax cost on the stock.

The stock interest the child receives effectively reduces what the entrepreneur owns, even though it's the corporation, and not the owner, doing the transfer.

Move Future Business Growth Out of the Entrepreneur's Estate

Maybe there's no big risk that the entrepreneur's business, plus his other holdings, could trigger estate tax today. But the business's value may rise, increasing estate tax risk for the future. More wealth is not a bad thing, but it spooks some entrepreneurs. One answer for them: Sell the business today, as an "estate freeze." Here's what I mean:

CASE STUDY

Suppose a business, worth $1,500,000 today, may grow at an average, say, 11 percent a year. In six years it would be worth $2,805,000—$1,305,000 more than today. If the owner, David, sells it to his children for $1,500,000 today (with, say, payment in installments), the $1,305,000 growth will belong to them. He has "frozen" the business portion of his estate, at the $1,500,000 he'll get on sale.

David will owe *income* (capital gains) tax on his sales proceeds minus his basis for the business interest he's selling. Payment of that tax can be deferred.

There's no *gift tax* if David sells at full value, and the growth won't be part of his estate where it could be subject to estate tax.

Yes, I know I'm making assumptions about what the kids could do as owners; you'll have to make your own. But remember that any significant growth under their ownership could easily outrun what you would be able to give them through exempt gifts—meaning that, on these assumptions, sale now could save estate tax.

Estate freezes of course also work to transfer future business growth to the kids even when you already expect to be subject to estate tax on sale proceeds and other assets.

Your assets after sale will include the proceeds from your sale (or the value of promised future payments) less income tax on the proceeds. Your estate will reflect what you do with these items and your other assets up to your death—but won't include *business* assets, which the kids now own.

Valuation disputes and earnouts

When buyer and seller can't agree on value, maybe they can agree on an appraiser to make the valuation, or on a method of valuation and an appraiser who must apply that method, or to arbitration.

Business sales often include an *earnout* feature: a contingent payment depending on future results. That is, the parties agree to a base price, plus an additional contingent amount, payable if specific financial results are achieved—usually, specified gross receipts or gross sales. Expected results could be refined to turn on specific factors attributable to the seller's achievement and legacy, such as amounts received from those who were customers of the business when the sale occurs. In earnout situations, the seller may stay on for a time as employee or consultant, to monitor business performance and financial reporting.

Sell All at Once, for Installment Payments

You could sell the whole business now, for periodic future installment payments. Or, if you've already passed some equity to the kids, sell what you have left, for future installments. There's no major current outlay from the kids, who will be paying, mostly in the future, out of what you and they expect to be future earnings.

Some entrepreneurs will worry that the kids may not honor their payment obligations. There are legal ways to compel return of the business if they renege, or money damages—if they have money.

Maybe more troubling is the risk that the business will fail in their hands, so they'll be unable to pay. There are legal ways to control some of their business decisions. This can be through provisions in the installment payment agreement, rather as some banks preclude certain actions by their borrowers. Or it can be by retaining a small share of the business entity, but one endowed with special powers, such as that of a managing member of an LLC, or under a statutory close corporation agreement.

It's preferable, though, to be satisfied that the kids know how to run the business before selling all or most of it for future payments.

Your profit on the installment sale, which for the business's fair market value, is normally subject to income tax (generally capital gains). But tax is normally paid in the future, over the period you receive installments. You figure your total profit (sales price less basis) and apply that profit percentage to each installment you collect. For example, with a selling price of $1,000,000 and a basis of $400,000, your profit percentage is 60 percent ($600,000/$1,000,000), so 60 percent of each installment is taxable (mostly at capital gains rates).

If you die before all installments have been paid, the profit element in unpaid installments is subject to income tax (generally, capital gains tax) at your death, and the value of promised future payments will be part of your estate.

ACTION POINT

Write the deal to charge interest on unpaid installments. You should get at least the Applicable Federal Rate. Interest received is taxable as ordinary income, and deductible by the payor debtor (who can't deduct other installment payments). A rate lower than the AFR empowers the IRS to effectively rewrite the deal for tax purposes. Such a rewrite reduces the selling price and capital gain, increasing the ordinary income interest element. With a reduced selling price, the sale may no longer be for fair market value. The difference between the fair market value and the reduced selling price could be a taxable gift. This IRS action doesn't affect the amounts that actually change hands between the parties, only how they are taxed.

Exception for receivables: When there's a sale of a partnership interest, profit attributable to the partner's share of partnership receivables is ordinary income (not capital gain) and is taxed immediately (not deferred). Remaining profit can be deferred, as capital gain. The same rule applies to a sale of an LLC interest.

When facing an immediate tax on receivables, make sure the installment in the first year is enough to cover the tax due that year on the receivables plus that due on that year's capital gain.

Bargain Sales

You may be tempted to sell your interest at a bargain price. This is perfectly legal (assuming your personal creditors won't be short-changed). But the amount of the bargain is a taxable gift, so you'll owe gift tax where your total lifetime gifts exceed $1 million; see "Federal Gift Tax." You'll also owe income tax on any excess of sale price over basis. A sale for less than basis is a loss, but the loss on a sale to a "related party," such as a close family member, isn't deductible.

If you're not closely monitoring what the interests you're selling are worth (after appropriate discounts), you may unintentionally sell at a bargain and incur unexpected gift tax.

A bargain sale can come after, and in addition to, current or past tax-exempt gifts of business interests. And it can come as part of an installment sale.

EXAMPLE

Dave today holds 40 percent of a family limited partnership, including the general partnership interest. The 40 percent interest is worth $1 million. His two children own 30 percent each of limited partnership interests, received as gifts over the past six years. Dave now wants to retire completely. He sells his 40 percent interest, half to each child (20 percent each), for $300,000 each, payable with interest at the commercial rate over the following five years. He's made a bargain installment sale. The amount of the bargain is taxable gifts of $200,000 to each child. Dave also has gain subject to income tax to the extent the $600,000 he receives exceeds his basis for the 40 percent interest.

If the general partnership interest had been held in a corporation or an LLC, as I advise, he could liquidate the corporation or LLC, take distribution of the interest, and sell it to the children. The corporation's liquidation, or Dave's sale of the interest received from the LLC, would be subject to income tax.

Sell to a "Defective" Trust

There are people who'd like to see a rational estate tax system. So you may understand their annoyance at the existence—and effectiveness—of the tax avoidance scheme called the "intentionally defective trust."

With this anomalous device, the grantor of the trust—the entrepreneur who sets it up—achieves his or her tax-saving goal by being treated as the owner of the trust for income tax purposes *but not* for estate tax purposes, or under state trust law.

Typically, the entrepreneur grantor sells her interest to the trust, for payment in installments. This freezes the business value in the entrepreneur's estate, passing future growth to the next generation—the strategy described in Wealth Creation Strategy 65.

Family members meant to be the next generation of owners are beneficiaries of the trust. The grantor is *not* the trust's trustee (the grantor's *spouse* could be trustee). The grantor retains some minor power over the trust that makes him or her taxable on trust income—that's the intentional "defect"—but the power doesn't make the trust property part of the grantor's estate.

When setting up the trust, it's common for the grantor to give the trust cash or assets which can be used for partial installment payments toward the trust's purchase of the grantor's interest. These amounts, often totaling ten percent or more of the purchase price, are exempt gifts to the beneficiaries (the next generation) if small enough to be exempt; otherwise they are taxable gifts to the extent they exceed the exempt amount.

Trust income—the earnings of the business—is paid to the *trust* but is taxable to the *grantor*. In the sometimes unreal world of estate tax avoidance, this is seen as a good thing, since the tax the grantor pays reduces the grantor's assets (and future estate) rather than the beneficiaries' assets. The trust then pays the grantor at least some of these business earnings, as trust payments on its installment note. The profit element in these installments is also taxable to the grantor. Yes, this is saying that what the trust gets is taxable to the entrepreneur, who is then also taxed on part of what the trust then pays him.

Use Insurance to Pay Estate Tax

This insurance strategy doesn't try to eliminate or sharply reduce estate tax, as gift and sale strategies can. It's a program to accept, and pay, estate tax out of insurance proceeds.

It has another special feature: Gift and sale programs pass ownership interests and often control of the business to the kids during the entrepreneur's lifetime. The entrepreneurs who choose this insurance program instead usually want to keep majority ownership and control to themselves for life. They accept that their continued ownership and control increases the likelihood that future business growth and accumulated earnings will wind up taxable in their estate. The insurance proceeds are to cover that. Using this strategy, the business can pass to the next generation as the entrepreneur's will dictates, usually not reduced by estate tax. To achieve this, the insurance proceeds must be:

Adequate to cover the tax. The amount of insurance coverage should be periodically adjusted to reflect the size of the taxable estate and the federal and state taxes due. Of course, the entrepreneur's personal wealth, aside from the business interest, figures in the calculation of the total taxes due.

Kept out of the entrepreneur's estate. To keep insurance out, the entrepreneur can't personally own it, and can pay the premiums only indirectly. The policy's beneficiary and owner could be an irrevocable life insurance trust.

The insurance, which the entrepreneur can't directly own or enjoy, has a cost, which diminishes the entrepreneur's assets and estate. That cost is incurred to pay a tax that would otherwise be borne by the entrepreneur's heirs. Is the insurance worth the cost? Who can say for sure? As always with insurance paid for over time, there's the depressing thought that the benefit is higher, and the cost lower, the sooner one dies.

Note that our planning here is for insurance to pay estate tax. Insurance used to buy interests in the business or to benefit heirs not in the business is covered in Chapter 13.

Transferring the Service Business

You may be passing on a business that doesn't have much in the way of capital assets.

I don't have a wealth creation strategy for the entrepreneur seller of a service business. I have instead an accept-the-world-as-it-is approach. I look at the transfer from the next generation new owner's point of view, and assume she is capable of performing the services the business exists to perform. That is, she already "owns" the essential skills, and has no need to pay the parent for them.

You created family wealth and family business continuity when you did your best to teach your children how to run the business. Now, the better they are at carrying on the business, the better equipped they'll be to meet their commitments to you. But don't expect these commitments to be great.

Sure, there's still the business goodwill, defined roughly as the characteristic or relationship that generates repeat business from past customers. That can be worth something. But it's not a lot when weighed against the son's or daughter's power to open a competing business nearby, using the same family name if not the business name.

Few entrepreneurs in service businesses should expect to collect much from "sale" of their interests to their children. Most or all of the "sale" proceeds will be retirement-type income for past services, or installments for a limited period. The keys issues:

- Who pays the entrepreneur—the business or the next-generation owner?
- How to secure the payment to the entrepreneur?

Who Pays?

The business can pay the entrepreneur severance pay/deferred compensation for past services. Or the business can pay for the entrepreneur's agreement (covenant) not to compete with the business the entrepreneur is leaving—assuming the entrepreneur might be reasonably capable of competing and the agreement is reasonably limited in time. The deal might provide for *both* deferred compensation and a non-compete. For qualified pension or profit-sharing plans in this setting, see below.

The family member buyer can pay. Here it's the purchase price for buying the entrepreneur's interest. The buyer can't deduct these payments (apart from interest on installments). The entrepreneur seller generally gets tax-favored capital gain, though installment interest is taxable ordinary income. When part of the sales proceeds is for the entrepreneur's share of receivables for services performed, that part is ordinary income and is effectively deductible by the buyer.

The tax rules are designed to benefit one party at the expense of the other. If the seller-entrepreneur gets the blessing of capital gains tax relief on a sale, the buyer, from the next generation, bears the pain of ordinary income taxation. The buyer is being taxed at ordinary rates on the business earnings, but has no offsetting deduction for amounts paid out as purchase price to the seller.

Make it win-win

A buyer who will finance the purchase out of future cash flow from a profitable business can pay a lot more if payments are deductible from business profits. This is because the buyer's deduction is worth more than the seller's capital gains relief (most *states* don't give capital gains relief anyway). Set what the business is to pay (say as deductible deferred compensation) so that the buyer's savings are shared between the parties.

Combined approach

The entrepreneur can sell an ownership interest to the family member, for what may be a modest price, and arrange further amounts in the form of a deferred compensation payout from the business.

Goodwill

This can be tricky. It may already belong to the business. If it belongs to the entrepreneur, she can sell it (usually for a modest amount), along with whatever else she is selling. Amounts allocated to goodwill are capital gain to the seller, and deductible over a fifteen-year period by the buyer.

Securing the Buyer's Payment

If severance pay/deferred compensation is secured by collateral or the like, future amounts due become taxable immediately. Bad news. Paying tax today on future dollars isn't my style. So where the entrepreneur seeks better security than the business's bare contractual promise to pay, structure the deal differently:

Make it a sale to the family member, taking back a promissory note for installments due, with a security interest in business or personal collateral to back the promise. Since the buyer can't deduct these payments (interest aside), the seller may need to cut the price. Or consider:

Qualified pension or profit-sharing plans

You should have one or more of these already. But plans not yet funded to the limit can be enriched, at the buyer's expense, if you start early enough.

For example, your defined benefit plan is set up to pay you, say, $100,000 each year after retirement at age sixty-five. You agree to transfer your interest if the pension amount is increased by $10,000 a year. The family member, if working in the business, could pay the extra cost by taking a smaller salary or, in a partnership or LLC, by bearing a larger allocation of firm expenses (where appropriately arranged).

This greatly relieves the security problem. Funds to support the pension are set aside in a trust, effectively guaranteeing payment to the retiree.

Strategy Review

Your goal in this chapter is the effective transfer of your business to the next generation, with maximum protection for family wealth and your individual ownership. These are the leading strategies:

1. Gift programs during your lifetime maximize the share of your business you can pass to the next generation. You may be able to do this through tax-exempt gifts:

- In many cases this can be done with your current business entity.
- When the current business entity is unsuitable, as with sole proprietorships, it can be done through creation of a new business entity designed for maximum tax avoidance with maximum business control.
- Giving business interests to a "grantor-retained trust" can effectively transfer those interests in the future, sometimes at little or no tax cost, while generating an income stream for you in the interim.

2. Sale programs are alternatives to, or supplements to, gift programs. Consider:
   - Piecemeal sales, which transfer small pieces of ownership, at minimum risk to entrepreneurial control and at modest tax cost.
   - Sales of the business can transfer future growth from the entrepreneur's estate to the buyer, with long-term postponement of estate tax on that growth, a transaction often called an "estate freeze."
   - Sale to the next generation can be an installment sale. It achieves an "estate freeze," pays the purchase price out of future earnings, and defers the seller's income tax.
   - Sale to a "defective" grantor trust is another estate freeze device that is effective only if the seller survives a predetermined period after sale.

3. Entrepreneurs in corporations can arrange transfer of stock in a tax-favored way—from the corporation, as compensation for services, to working members of the next generation.

4. Entrepreneurs intending to keep ownership and control for life can effectively excuse the business from estate tax on the interests passing at death. This is done through purchase of insurance owned in trust to pay estate tax.

Providing for Heirs Who Don't Join the Business

Chapter

13

WEALTH CREATION STRATEGIES 69–75

Forget the estate tax for the moment. A bigger cause for liquidating a business when the entrepreneur dies is lack of enough assets to pay the entrepreneur's bequests to family members who *don't* join the business. Of course, even businesses that survive may make headlines when family "outs" squabble over inheritances with family "ins."

CASE STUDY

The Connally family's business was sold when its founder, Frank Connally, died. The family couldn't afford to keep it going, because of Frank's misguided estate plan.

Frank left his life insurance, pension assets, and family home to his wife, Mary. And he left the business in equal shares to his three children: Kevin, who was active and effective in the business, and Janet and Dan, who wanted nothing to do with it.

With all Frank's liquid assets going to pay Frank's bills, debts, and death taxes, Kevin couldn't afford to buy his siblings out. So the three sold the business and divided the proceeds.

It's not the end of the world if your kids sell the business after you're gone. But if you *want* the business to go on, and at least one capable family member wants the same thing, you probably can swing it through one or more of the following wealth creation strategies. And, no, you won't have to stiff the other family members. You can provide liberally, within your means, for nonworking members and still continue the business, your family's wealth machine, through its active family members.

Allocate Nonbusiness Wealth to the Nonworking Heirs

You might have investments—stock and so on—that could be allocated, all or mostly, to the nonworking heirs. Of course, liquid assets are often needed for debts and expenses at death, sometimes including estate taxes. Take these needs into account in your planning.

Maybe these assets won't be enough in themselves to fulfill the dollar value of what you intend for the nonworking heirs. You might therefore rearrange what your spouse is to receive. (Maybe your spouse will be active in the continuing business. In that case your planning for him or her should be consistent with what's recommended in this chapter for those who will carry on the business.)

Remember that what your surviving spouse receives generally reduces the amount subject to estate tax. So, depending on circumstances, some bequests to the spouse may be enough to remove an estate tax problem.

Your retirement plan assets could go entirely to your spouse, which excuses those assets from estate tax in your estate. And you can arrange to make life insurance proceeds free of estate tax (and income tax) regardless of which family member gets them. So you might direct all of it to the nonworking heirs, or share some of it with the spouse.

When estate tax is not a concern, some of your bequests to your spouse could be interests for life, with remainders to the nonworking children. The family home is an example of that.

<table>
<tr><td>WEALTH
CREATION
STRATEGY
70</td><td># Give or Bequeath
"Inessential" Business Assets
to Nonworking Heirs</td></tr>
</table>

Many a business owns assets held and even used in the business that don't have to be *owned* by the business. I've already offered wealth creation strategies for holding this type of asset outside the business—Chapters 8 and 10. Such assets, under suitable controls, could properly go to nonworking family members, as their share, or a big part of their share, of the entrepreneur's estate.

Like real estate. It's very common to split the real estate the business owns and occupies off into other hands; the real estate can then be leased back to the business. In this case, the real estate now owned by or for the nonworking heirs can yield them a steady stream of income from the business. To avoid intrafamily disputes, a long-term lease could be required, with rent increases (or decreases) based on objective factors like cost of living, or fixed by outside arbitration.

Similar arrangements could be made for other business property, such as equipment, or a patent, split off and leased back to the business.

Consider having the lease arrangement allow for substitution, replacement, or sale of property that becomes obsolete or unsuitable as the business changes. Business management—family members who run the business—should decide business needs, but fair terms should be provided to the property owners.

Some businesses own securities or other investments taken to secure a business relationship with the issuer, or in connection with a sideline activity. Such assets could be transferred to or cashed in for the nonworking heirs.

Okay so far, but how to get "inessential" assets to the nonworking heirs.

You as entrepreneur can just give or bequeath the assets, as you choose. Well, maybe it's not quite that easy. Your gift of property exceeding in value the gift tax–exempt amount (see Chapter 12, "Federal Gift Tax") is a taxable gift, which can lead to gift tax on you. And there may be estate tax consequences on such gifts, or for property bequeathed at your death. That can be okay, if your estate (what passes to beneficiaries other than your spouse and charity) will be less than $3.5 million and your taxable gifts total less than $1 million.

But if gift or estate tax is reasonably likely, make a program of annual gifts in the value of the exempt amount, or less, until the whole asset is transferred. In theory this can be done by giving a fractional or percentage interest in the property. But this isn't practical: You and the nonworking heirs will then each own a share—and nonworking heirs will eventually own a majority share—as tenants in common, of property needed for your business.

Better that you transfer the property to an LLC in which you are managing member, taking back all the interests. Then you can give percentage interests each year, within the gift tax exemption ceiling, until all of it passes to the nonworking heirs. (Corporations or limited partnerships are alternatives.)

A single member LLC is effectively a sole proprietorship (unless status as a corporation was elected, which rarely happens). Even here, you should create a separate LLC to hold the property, and then distribute interests as just described.

Whatever new LLC you create is a new business, needing the formalities you went through forming your main business. Property ownership registrations must be changed, with appropriate arrangements where the property is subject to debt.

Steps for other business entities

What about when your business entity is a corporation, a partnership, or an LLC with two or more members? You need to get the property out of the business that now holds it. I cover that process in Wealth Creation Strategy 49.

Then you must get it into the hands of the nonworking heirs, or of an entity that holds the property on their behalf. Here you would follow the gift program described above for sole proprietors. In many cases you could have the business transfer the asset, or a part interest in the asset, directly to the nonworking heirs (or their holding company). But such a transfer will still be treated first as a distribution *to* you, then as gifts *by* you.

Or, you (or more likely your entity) could buy the asset from the business and distribute entity interests as exempt gifts. The business would have a sales profit. Your share of that profit is taxable to you in the year of sale, if you're in a business entity other than a C corporation. In a C corporation you'd be taxable on earnings distributed to you,

Give Nonworking Heirs Limited-Control Interests

It may be that our entrepreneur's other assets are insufficient, and non-working heirs—if they are to share in the entrepreneur's wealth—must get an interest in the business. If so, that should be interests with little or no power to influence the business operations or force a liquidation of the business.

If it's a C corporation, nonvoting stock is such a limited interest; voting stock would be held by the active members. Nonvoting stock in C corporations could be preferred stock, with a fixed dividend rate (maybe subject to conditions), and usually an accumulation feature that will make up in good times for previously skipped dividends. S corporation stock could also be nonvoting, but without a "preferred" feature. Corporations could instead operate as statutory close corporations (see Chapter 8) under an agreement giving control to designated active members.

With family limited partnerships, the nonworking heirs would be limited partners; the general partner would be a limited liability entity controlled by one or more persons active in the business. In an LLC, active members would be manager members; nonworking heirs would be non-manager members.

Safety net for nonworking heirs

You may want the governing business document to prevent active members from unfairly treating nonworking heirs:

Have the document:

- Require distribution of enough funds to cover owners' taxes on earnings, for entities whose owners are taxed directly on business earnings (meaning entities other than C corporations).
- Encourage distribution of a specified minimum percentage of earnings.
- Forbid distribution to active members at a higher rate of return on equity than to nonworking heirs.
- Limit compensation and other benefits of active members.
- Allow nonworking heirs to "put" their interests to the business—giving them an option to redeem or liquidate their interests at a predetermined or arbitrated price, in specific circumstances (say, distributions averaging less than 50 percent of earnings over a five-year period). Specifics on redemptions and liquidations will be covered shortly.

Put Limits on What Nonworking Family Members Already Own

Family members who won't be active in the business may already own "unlimited" interests—such as voting stock. They might have received such interests as children, usually in custodianship or trust.

Now, knowing they don't plan to be active, or that you don't want them active, it would be good to transform those interests into the kind of limited interests described in Wealth Creation Strategy 71. This can be done via a recapitalization if it's a corporation. Recapitalization of a family limited partnership or LLC is also possible, but less likely to be necessary at this stage, since the family members' interests in these entities were probably limited from the start.

In a corporate recapitalization, the nonworking heir's voting stock would be exchanged for nonvoting stock (and, in the case of C corporations, often for nonvoting preferred stock subject to special benefits and limitations). In theory, holders of stock, facing loss of voting rights, have recourse under state law. In purely family settings, minority owners will go along with a recap deal offered by the majority owner who is the source of their share of present and future family wealth.

The IRS challenges valuation discounts coming out of recapitalizations that are done to load artificial limitations on stock that will be the subject of future gifts. I don't recommend such artificial limitations.

Have the Business
Buy You Out

Redemptions and liquidations are ways the business buys you out—the *business*, rather than another family member. They are also ways to buy out nonworking heirs. Redemptions are the way with corporations; liquidations are the way with partnerships and LLCs.

In a redemption or liquidation, it's usual that every remaining owner in effect pays for the buyout, and every such owner's proportionate interest is increased. This differs from a sale by the entrepreneur to an individual purchaser whose interest goes up while others' proportional interests go down. The entrepreneur may care whose share of the business goes up how much in the transaction. The entrepreneur will surely care about the security for future payments due, when payment is to be deferred or in installments.

Nonworking heirs are usually willing to be bought out by the business—once they realize their situation:

- There's virtually no market for interests in small family businesses. Few outsiders want to buy into a minority position, especially a limited one. Sales to outsiders are often effectively precluded anyway by the governing business document (for example, by requiring unanimous consent to the sale).
- The nonworking heir has no influence of business policy or operations.
- The nonworking heir has little right and little opportunity to earn substantial sums or benefits as an employee of the business.

- The nonworking heir has no right to force a liquidation of the business to get at his share of assets and accumulated profits.
- Business earnings may be retained, or largely retained, and not distributed.

Redemptions—Corporate Owners

I'm talking here about complete redemptions, in which the corporation buys all your stock, or all your remaining stock. In a redemption, you give up your stock and receive a distribution of cash or property, or both, in exchange.

Complete redemptions of C corporation stock qualify for capital gains treatment, which carries a reduced tax rate. Gain is redemption proceeds minus the basis for your stock, which comes back to you tax-free. Redemptions can also be done in installments over time, which defers tax until payments are received.

It's a complete redemption only if thereafter (for at least ten years) you are not an officer, employee, or director of the corporation and have no personal financial interest in the corporation (except by inheritance). Also, you can't own interests in the corporation through other entities—for example, it's not a complete redemption if you're a partner in a partnership that owns stock in that corporation. If you flunk these requirements, your redemption is a dividend with, usually, a higher tax cost.

Liquidation—for Partnerships and Most LLCs

This is when all of a partner's interest (or all the partner's remaining interest) is bought by the partnership. The entrepreneur partner surrenders his interest and receives one or more liquidating "distributions." A distribution of *property* is generally tax-free. (There are exceptions— for example, where a partner contributed the property now being distributed, see Wealth Creation Strategy 49.) Distributions of *money* in addition to or instead of property usually result in tax. "Money" is expansively defined. Marketable securities are "money." And relief from one's share of a partnership liability is also treated as money, to the extent of that relief. Such relief is common when a partnership interest is liquidated.

Taxable distributions are often capital gains, but there are major exceptions. The total distribution is allocated proportionately to the entrepreneur's share of partnership "ordinary income items" (the receivables and inventory described in Chapter 12, Wealth Creation Strategy 63) and to other items. The allocation to such items (reduced by the entrepreneur's basis in those items) is fully taxable ordinary income. Allocations to the balance of the entrepreneur's partnership interest, minus allocable basis, are capital gains (or, for qualifying property distributions, untaxed).

Compared to sales

Redemptions and liquidation, like sales, can be done in installments over time, deferring tax until payments are received. The entrepreneur sometimes has a greater need to make sure future payments are adequately secured when it's a sale (to an individual) rather than when it's a redemption or liquidation of an interest (to the business).

The entrepreneur's income tax treatment on redemption or liquidation is generally the same as with a sale of his or her interest. However, in a service partnership liquidation, a special step is needed to get capital gain treatment for liquidation payments for goodwill: The partnership agreement must provide for reasonable payment for goodwill.

ACTION POINT ✓

If your partnership agreement currently lacks provision for goodwill, have it amended to provide for reasonable payment for goodwill, and have this done before you start to work out your departure from the firm.

We've been assuming that redemption, liquidation, or sale is for the full fair market value of the interest involved. A sale at a bargain price is a gift, generally a taxable gift, in the amount of the bargain. A redemption or liquidation at a bargain to a family business is a gift, made proportionately to the owners of the business who benefit from the gift.

Redemption or liquidation at your death

Planning for redemption or liquidation at death means that the entrepreneur intends to remain active and, usually, in control, for the rest of his or her life. So be it.

The business will be a big asset in your estate. You can strongly influence just how big an asset by action now, during your lifetime, to set the price your business successors must pay for it (that is, pay your estate or heirs).

For redemption or liquidation taking place at the entrepreneur's death, you need a mechanism to set the redemption price, since the entrepreneur won't be around to negotiate one. That mechanism is a *buy-sell agreement*. And you may need a way for the business to pay that price. That will usually be with life insurance. Both these strategies are covered later.

There's little or no income tax on a redemption or liquidation at death. This is because the entrepreneur's estate gets a "basis step-up," a tax basis equal to the fair market value of the entrepreneur's interest—generally a basis that effectively eliminates taxable gain. Exception: The entrepreneur's share of accounts receivable, in a *liquidation*, doesn't get a basis step-up and is taxed as ordinary income.

Redemption or liquidation now, rather than at death, shifts future growth away from you and your estate and into the hands of the next generation—as I describe in Wealth Creation Strategy 73. Maybe you want that. If not, basis step-up, a buy-sell agreement to fix the estate tax value, and life insurance funding, can resolve some of the issues that arise when you hold on to ownership and control until death.

Redemption or liquidation of nonworking heirs' interests may also be arranged to coincide with the entrepreneur's death, and may be funded by life insurance. The income tax rules I've described for redemptions or liquidations during life, of a retiring entrepreneur, would also apply to such a redemption or liquidation of a nonworking heir.

LLCs

Rules and strategies for liquidation of partnership interests apply equally to liquidation of interests in an LLC taxed as a partnership.

S Corporations

Distributions in complete redemption of a stockholder's stock in an S corporation are treated as for liquidations of a partnership interest, except that distributions traceable to earnings when the S corporation was a C corporation are generally taxable dividends.

Use Buy-Sell Agreements to Fix Buyout Terms

Buy-sell agreements have their place in single-family businesses, though they're more often used—and are more elaborate and complex—in businesses with two or more *unrelated* owners or families.

The planning here is for single-family businesses. The buy-sell sets the terms by which the principal owner's (the entrepreneur's) interest in the business is sold (sometimes also the nonworking heirs' interests)—the most important term being the price. The buy-sell transaction is usually triggered by the death of the principal owner, though it could also be triggered by his or her disability or retirement (rarely, in single family businesses).

These agreements are good for the business, supporting its continuation by fixing the mechanism for change of ownership and control. They define, to some degree, who can acquire and control. They can prevent transfer to outsiders who would be unable or unsuitable to continue the current business entity. Family members in the entrepreneur's estate benefit by having price and terms negotiated, in effect, by the entrepreneur during life, from a position of strength. And the agreement may identify and to some degree arrange the source of buy-out funds—usually, insurance on the entrepreneur's life.

The agreement will indicate or specify who buys out the entrepreneur's interest—that is, whether the buyer is the business or a co-owner. The owner (seller) must be obligated to sell but the agreement can give the prospective buyer an option to buy or—to put the entrepreneur's estate in a stronger position—impose an obligation to buy. It can be written to allow the business to assign its right to buy to a co-owner, when such acquisition is preferable to the parties—for example, to give a particular family member a controlling interest.

Warning: The reverse, assigning *from* co-owner *to* business, is a tax trap when the business is a C corporation. A C corporation's payment of a stockholder's obligation is a taxable dividend to the stockholder.

Buying is of course greatly aided when insurance proceeds are provided the prospective purchaser, as will be covered in Wealth Creation Strategy 75.

Setting the price

Valuation, or valuation methods, are negotiated at arm's length in nonfamily settings. In family settings, it's different, but you'll need a fair and reasonable method if you want the value you use to be accepted for estate tax purposes. If the entrepreneur's business interest passes to the next generation for less than it's worth, the difference is a bequest that could be subject to estate tax. This is true whether the interest passes directly (in a purchase by the next generation of owners) or indirectly (in a purchase by the business that benefits the next generation of owners).

In getting to the price, you should have the business valued, and a valuation of your own interest if there are co-owners. This interest could include a control premium, an extra percentage of value, for your control of the business—which would not preclude a partially offsetting discount for lack of marketability. The valuation method should be retained for use in future valuations. If the business radically changes, or is converted into investment holdings instead of an active business, the valuation method should be changed.

If the business is buying, business owners-to-be may need a long-term payout, to avoid immediate heavy drain on business assets. One approach is to limit payments to a specified percentage of business gross receipts—which may stretch out the payment period.

Buy-sell to buy out nonworking heirs

Buy-sell agreements can be a mechanism for when nonworking heirs, and active members, don't get along. The agreement can fix a price, generally below fair market value, at which a nonworking heir can "put" his or her interest and get bought out, where necessary. And the agreement can set a different and higher price, usually above fair market value, for a "call," in which the active member (or maybe the business) has a right to buy out the nonworking heir. The entrepreneur can decide, say, the percentage below fair market value (for the put) or above fair market value (for the call), but the actual fair market value may need to be determined at the time of the transaction.

Fund the Buyout with Life Insurance

Funding the entrepreneur's buyout with insurance can be a family wealth builder which, like much in life, comes at a cost and, in this case, a fairly high cost. First, let's consider who owns the insurance:

Insurance Owned by the Business

Throughout this strategy I use insurance on the entrepreneur's life that escapes estate tax. For how to arrange this, see Wealth Creation Strategy 57. The insurance will be used, with the entrepreneur's consent, given in advance, to buy the entrepreneur's interest.

The business's premium payments on the insurance aren't deductible. This is true for C corporations and S corporations insuring the life of a stockholder, and for partnerships (including LLCs) insuring a partner (or member). If the entrepreneur is the business's major owner, she is bearing the largest part of the cost of his or her own future buyout—through reduction of her share of business profits. This amounts to an indirect gift to co-owners whose interests will increase when the entrepreneur is bought out—but it's one not subject to gift tax.

ACTION POINT ✓

In setting the value of the interest to be bought out, be careful to exclude the interest's share of future life insurance proceeds to be used for the buyout.

Insurance proceeds received by the business in this setting are exempt from federal income tax. (However, C corporations may be subject to federal alternative minimum tax on insurance proceeds in excess of basis, and on increases in cash surrender value.)

Insurance Owned by Business Co-owner

In this strategy the co-owner as an individual owns insurance on the entrepreneur's life—so that it escapes estate tax in the entrepreneur's estate. The insurance will be used to buy the entrepreneur's interest. We are not dealing with insurance owned by a partnership, or where several partners individually insure each other.

Premiums paid by the co-owner aren't deductible. Premiums paid by a C corporation on behalf of a stockholder (in this case, the purchasing co-owner) are dividends or compensation to the stockholder, and deductible by the corporation where paid as compensation. An entrepreneur owner of the corporation might choose to have the corporation increase the co-owner's pay to, in effect, subsidize the co-owner's premium payment. Insurance proceeds paid to the co-owner are exempt from income tax.

The Buyout Transaction

When the business owns the insurance

The business uses its insurance proceeds to buy the entrepreneur's interest, in a redemption (if a corporation) or a liquidation (if a partnership or LLC). The business gets the money income-tax-free (possible exception for C corporation alternative minimum tax) and estate-tax-free. The entrepreneur's estate generally avoids income tax on its redemption/liquidation receipts (because of the basis step-up in the entrepreneur's interest at death).

When the co-owner owns the insurance

The individual co-owner gets the insurance proceeds free of income tax and free of estate tax, and uses them to buy the entrepreneur's interest. The entrepreneur's estate gets the proceeds in exchange for the entrepreneur's ownership interest (stock, partnership interest, or LLC membership interest). The entrepreneur's estate generally avoids income tax on its sale because of the basis step-up in the entrepreneur's interest at death.

What's Happened, Why, and Its Cost

A tax-free sale of the business, so that the full value of the business can pass to your heirs, is a great outcome. But *we* had nothing to do with *that*. The heirs could have sold the business, free of income tax, with no help from us, thanks to the basis step-up.

What's happened here is more than that: Your heirs got full value for the business and those active in the business now own it. That's thanks to the insurance.

It wasn't free. Insurance has a cost, often a major cost, and one that can't be fully predicted, depending as it does on the entrepreneur's actual longevity. The costs—the premiums, and what it costs to set up and operate the insurance trust (where the business buys), must be balanced against what the costs produced—the insurance proceeds. You, as principal owner of the business, usually help subsidize the buyout through your reduced profits to pay the premiums.

The insurance costs reduce your assets and estate so your heirs can acquire an asset that's free of estate tax. The insurance has shifted money from your estate to the next generation.

Insurance proceeds may be more or less than the agreed purchase price. If more, the proceeds belong to the insurance owner (still free of income tax). If less, the insurance owner must raise the needed funds to fulfill the purchase obligation. Because of the high insurance costs, the buyout may be arranged so that the insurance is intended to provide only part of the price, with the balance to be paid over time in installments.

When Insurance Goes to Nonworking Heirs

Buyout of the nonworking heir may be funded out of insurance payable at the entrepreneur's death. The insurance owner is taxed as described above. The nonworking heir's gain is taxable (capital gain). He or she gets no tax exemption for amounts received from the insurance owner, and no basis step-up.

Strategy Review

Your goal in this chapter is to keep your business thriving after you're gone, while providing fairly for family members who won't be part of the business.

Your leading strategies:

1. Planning allocation of your *nonbusiness* assets can leave the *business* in the hands of family members able to continue its success.
2. Examine the business for "inessential" assets that nonworking heirs can hold and lease to the business under careful terms, and for inessential assets they can inherit outright.
3. Nonworking heirs' limited participation in business profits may sometimes serve as their proper share of family wealth, while active family members control operations.
4. To make sure business success can't be put at risk by nonworking heirs not active in the business, adjust—maybe recapitalize—the business to give control to those working members you want to have control.
5. An economically effective way to pass control to chosen successors who are business co-owners is to arrange to be bought out by the business and, if nonworking heirs are co-owners, to have them bought out too.
6. A buy-sell agreement can arrange buyouts by the business, or by an individual co-owner, as you choose, and can determine price and terms.
7. Buyouts funded by life insurance in effect allow tax-free sale of the business to active family members who will carry it on, with sales proceeds going to, or shared by, nonworking heirs you want to provide for.

Index